IRISH
KNITTING

To Irish craft workers,
past and present

IRISH KNITTING

Patterns inspired by Ireland

Rohana Darlington

A & C Black • London

ACKNOWLEDGEMENTS AND CREDITS

I would like to thank the following organisations and people for their patient and helpful advice, support, information and hospitality:

Winston Churchill Memorial Trust; Crafts Council of Ireland; National Museum of Ireland; National Library of Ireland; Trinity College Library; Kerry Folk-life Centre at Muckross House; National Parks and Monuments Service: (Commissioners of Public Works, Ireland); Irish Tourist Board; Kennedy's of Ardara; Subud International Cultural Association at Subud groups in Cork and Chester; Poynton Library; Mary D Dirrane and Mrs O'Flaherty of Inishmore; Muriel Gahan and Anna Higginbotham; Pádraig and Philomena O'Cuimin; Salamah Subiotto of Obair Gréis; Richard Rutt, Bishop of Leicester; Sue Leighton-White; Linda Babb; Margaret Lewis and Mrs Georgina Boyd.

Tesni Hollands and Anne Watts at A & C Black (Publishers) Ltd for their help and encouragement.

Rowan Yarns for the generous donation of their beautiful yarns.

John Simmons for his excellent studio photography.

May I also thank the following for their kind permission to reproduce their photographs:
Irish Tourist Board (Newgrange passage grave, Co. Meath)
National Museum of Ireland (gold gorget from Glenisheen; bronze trumpet from Loughnashade; Tara brooch from Drogheda; early Aran sweaters)
Trinity College Library, Dublin (page from the Book of Kells)
Muckross House, Killarney (hand embroidered sampler, Kilmoyly Female School)
National Library of Ireland (carding and spinning fleece and fishing fleet in Ardglass harbour; both part of the Lawrence Collection)

My husband Mashud for his humour and practical help; daughters Juwariah, Hanafiah and Irmani for their help as models and advisers; my son Afandi for his lovely photographs; Zoë and Sara Le Brow for modelling the children's wear.

Designed by Janet Watson

First published 1991
A & C Black (Publishers) Limited
35 Bedford Row, London WC1R 4JH

© A & C Black (Publishers) Limited

ISBN-0-7136-3339-5

A CIP catalogue record for this book is available from the British Library

Typeset by August Filmsetting, Haydock, St Helens
Printed and bound by
Wing King Tong Co Ltd, Hong Kong

CONTENTS

INTRODUCTION 7

HISTORIC 9

NEWGRANGE 9
INISHMORE 13
CRIOS 17
TORC 21
LA TÈNE 23
TARA 29
KELLS MOSAIC 35
DUBLIN SILVER 41
HERALD 47

YEARS OF OPPRESSION 53

CARRICKMACROSS 55
SHAMROCK LACE LAYETTE 59
PRIMROSE PETALS 65
KERRY BEDSPREAD 69
SAMPLER 75
FISHER GANSEY 83

ARANS 86

THE AMERICAN CONNECTION 86
HOW ARAN PATTERNS 88
DEVELOPED
DIAMOND AND CABLE ARAN 91
CARRAGEEN 97
HONEYCOMB CABLE ARAN 101
BETROTHAL ARAN 105
ROPE PLAIT ARAN 111

COUNTRY LIFE 114

SAILBOATS 115
GALWAY RACER 121
SEABIRDS 125
WILD FUCHSIAS 131

TECHNICAL INFORMATION

ABBREVIATIONS 135
CABLE ABBREVIATIONS 135
LACE ABBREVIATIONS 136
BOBBLE ABBREVIATIONS 136
KNITTING TERMS OCCASIONALLY
  USED IN THE PATTERNS 137
KNITTING AND FINISHING
  TECHNIQUES 137
COMPARATIVE TERMS 138
YARN EQUIVALENTS 138
CONVERSION CHART FOR YARN
  WEIGHTS AND MEASUREMENTS 139
CONVERSION CHART FOR NEEDLE
  SIZES 139
YARN SUPPLIERS 140

SELECTED BIBLIOGRAPHY 141

INDEX 143

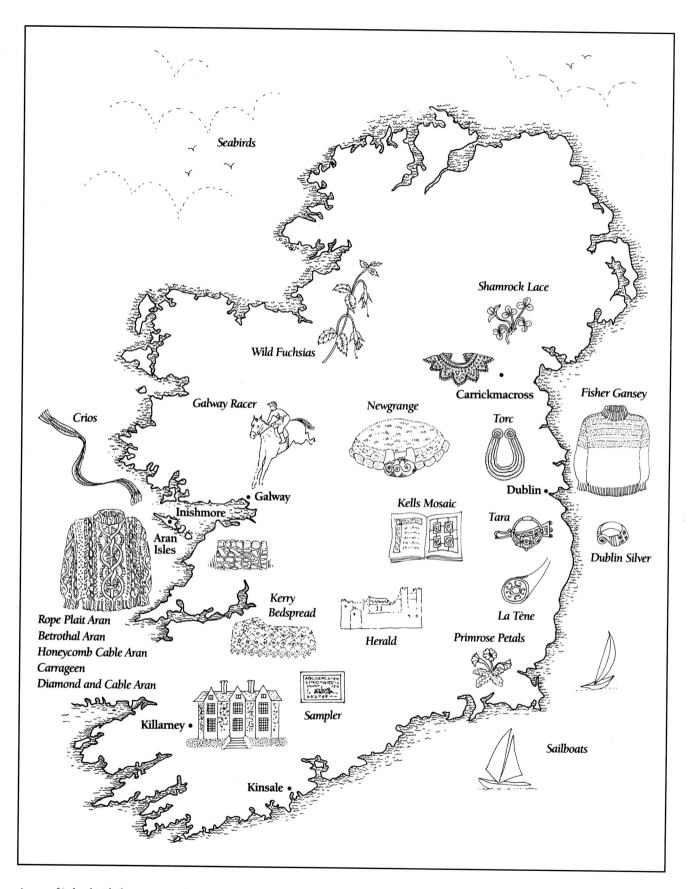

Seabirds

Shamrock Lace

Wild Fuchsias

Carrickmacross

Crios

Galway Racer

Newgrange

Torc

Fisher Gansey

Galway

Inishmore

Aran Isles

Kells Mosaic

Dublin

Tara

Dublin Silver

La Tène

Rope Plait Aran
Betrothal Aran
Honeycomb Cable Aran
Carrageen
Diamond and Cable Aran

Kerry Bedspread

Herald

Primrose Petals

Killarney

Sampler

Kinsale

Sailboats

A map of Ireland with the inspirational source of each garment illustrated

INTRODUCTION

This is the story of a search which developed into a journey of exploration and discovery.
As a textile designer, I'd always loved the complex sculptured beauty of the world famous Aran knitting and longed to learn more about its rather obscure origins.

When lecturing, I'd often been asked if I believed the romantic tales which maintained Bronze Age Phoenician sailors introduced intricate knitting techniques to the remote and windswept Irish Aran Isles. Inhabited since Neolithic times, the islands theoretically could have been visited by Mediterranean merchants skilled in textile arts, trading wine for copper from the Waterford coast and gold from the Wicklow mountains.

Others wondered whether the stitches had perhaps been evolved later, by ninth century Aran islanders inspired by the interlace designs that decorate the early Christian illuminated manuscripts and High Crosses.

Inishmore, the largest of the three Aran Isles, thirty miles out from Galway, was certainly once an important centre of Christian learning. As one of the earliest sancturies of the pioneers of the monastic movement, since the sixth century it had connections with monasteries all over Europe and beyond, including Iona, off the west coast of Scotland.

It was on Iona in AD 820 that the exquisitely illustrated Book of Kells was begun, which contains a picture of the prophet Daniel wearing what appears to be an Aran sweater and matching leggings. Yet the intertwining patterns that embellish it have sources as diverse as pagan Germanic and fifth century Coptic Christian. Aran knitting books declared it was impossible to discover the real source of its origins, as these were supposedly lost in the mists of time.

Skeptical about the various conflicting explanations, I wanted to try to get closer to the truth, and in 1984 at last my chance came. My journey made possible by the Winston Churchill Travelling Fellowship I'd been awarded, I set off on a fascinating exploration of Ireland, eventually arriving at Inishmore. Armed with a copy of J.M. Synge's book *The Aran Islands* which describes life there between 1898 and 1902, I felt like a knitting sleuth about to become involved in a textile who-dunnit.

My travels became an odyssey through time as well as place as I delved into Ireland's cultural heritage, and I found myself compelled to create a collection of knitwear inspired by the lovely things I saw as a tribute to those early craftspeople.

The stunning visual impact of the Irish art treasures, monuments and landscape evoked powerful images of innumerable garments. Inevitably, I had to distil my selection of exciting source material to the items featured here. I would have had to emigrate to Ireland permanently to develop everything that stimulated me creatively.

I've arranged the designs here in a historically chronological order so the progression of Irish culture can be clearly followed. They range from easy to knit to the more challenging, and I've included garments for every member of the family, as well as a traditional bedspread.

easy   intermediate   experienced

I hope my collection will convey some of the pleasure I felt when working on it. And that, unlike most detective stories, you'll enjoy discovering the outcome of my Aran knitting investigations half way through the book instead of having to wait till you get to the end!

NEWGRANGE

(3000 BC – 2500 BC)

My search for the source of Ireland's earliest patterns began at Newgrange, Co. Meath.

These eerie passage graves, dating from 3200 BC, are decorated with mysterious carved designs which are particularly intriguing. The tombs can be traced back to historic Mediterranean traditions, but there are no exact parallels for the origin of the strange geometric shapes and whorls. Spiral designs are universal, but the unusual markings of three interlinked spirals incised in one of the inner chambers is unique to Newgrange and unknown anywhere else.

Carved entrance stone with spiral decoration from the Newgrange passage graves

The patterns are thought by some to represent the soul leaving the body at death, and re-birth. Others consider they depict an astronomical map of the heavens. The entire structure reveals a sophisticated knowledge of astronomy. The tomb is designed to allow a direct beam of sunlight to shine through a specially constructed narrow slit in the roof at sunrise each winter solstice, illuminating the whole normally dark interior for precisely seventeen minutes.

It would be easy to imagine that these swirling sculptured patterns could in some way be reflected in Aran knitting, especially the rectangular shapes, but as I was to discover later, this was not the case. Nevertheless, although knitting would have been unknown in Ireland at this time, it was interesting to speculate on the textile skills the builders of Newgrange may have used.

Remains of knotless knitting (nalbinding) have been discovered preserved in the ice bound peat bogs of Denmark, dating from 1400 BC. Nalbinding is made with a darning needle, but looks remarkably like true hand-knitting made with two knitting needles. And at Star Carr in Yorkshire, England, fine bone needles used for making fishing nets from twisted bark fibre were found, dating from 7000 BC, made by a people who lived near the sea like the Newgrange settlers of the Boyne valley. The sea routes between Ireland and Britain and Scandinavia were well established when the Newgrange graves were constructed.

It seems possible that nalbinding, netting and weaving were all practised at Newgrange, but unfortunately no remains of textile fragments have been found at the site.

I found the place incredibly awe-inspiring in spite of its many visitors. The soft colours of the surrounding fields and trees and the dramatic patterns on the ancient stones compelled me to create this country jacket. I used subtly flecked silks and wools to convey their weathered texture.

This jacket combines yarns in a variety of weights and colours, with plenty of scope for individual choice by the knitter. The materials specified below are therefore to be used as a guide rather than as exact amounts. I mixed silks and chenilles with chunky tweed and lightweight wools for a rich but not too heavy fabric.

MATERIALS
YARN

Rowan Chunky Tweed (bulky) for Borders in
A Green Waters (707) – 3 × 100g/10¾oz

Rowan Botany (sport) for Edging in
B Turquoise (90) – 1 × 25g/1oz

Rowan Silkstones (sport) for Welt and Cuffs in
C Blue Mist (832) – 2 × 50g/3¾oz

Patterned area (Back, Fronts and Sleeves)

575g/20½oz of a variety of yarns divided up as folls:

Rowan Cotton Chenille (same weight as Chunky Tweed)
Light colours only for swirls, using chunky (bulky) yarns.
In Grey/Green (361) – 2 × 100g/7½oz; and in same chenille in Cloud Blue (360) – 1 × 100g/3¾oz. Also, 1 × 25g/1oz in a variety of toning light coloured yarns. I used oddments of fawns and pale blues, and a little of the *Chunky* A that is used in the borders.

Rowan Silkstones
Darker colours only for background, using a mixture of lighter weight (4 ply) (sport) yarns.
In D Eau de Nil (835) – 4 × 50g/7¼oz as main colour. Also, 1 × 50g/2oz in a variety of oddments of browns, turquoises and stone mixes, remembering to include some of the Botany (90) that appears in the edging, and some of the *Silkstones* Blue Mist (832) used in the Welts to bring everything together.

NOTES ON MATERIALS

After knitting the patterned area, around 175g/6½oz of yarns in various colours will be left over, due to the motifs needing small extra quantities to complete the jacket, in colours only available in 100g/3¾oz hanks. These will however add to your collection of useful materials to inspire your next multi-coloured creation and should not be considered as wasteful. Yarns can be collected quite cheaply at sale time and in this way a good stock of colours and textures can be built up for future garments of this kind.

You could reverse the colours, and have darker swirls on a lighter ground, but I preferred to use heavier weight yarns for the shapes to create a subtle embossed effect reminiscent of the carved surface of the Newgrange stones.

NEEDLES

1 pair 3¾mm (US 5) 100cm (39″) circular needles
1 pair 5mm (US 8) 100cm (39″) circular needles
2 stitch holders

SIZE AND MEASUREMENTS

One size only to fit up to 107cm (42″) bust
Actual width across back at underarm 58cm (23″)
Length from centre back neck to hip 65cm (25½″)
Sleeve seam from underarm 45cm (18″)

TENSION (GAUGE)

21 sts and 20 rows to 10cm (4″) over patterned area on 5mm (US 8) needles or size needed to obtain this tension (gauge).

NOTES ON TECHNIQUES

Although it looks complicated, this jacket is made using only two simple techniques – 2 × 2 rib and fairisle.

When working the patterned area in fairisle, carry colour not in use *very* loosely across back of work, weaving it around working yarn every 3rd st to avoid long floats and puckering. Choose as many colour changes as you like but only use two colours at a time in any one row.

JACKET BORDER AT LOWER EDGE OF PATTERNED AREA (Make 1)

Using 5mm (US 8) circular needles as straight and A, cast on 14 sts.
Row 1: (RS) (K2, P2) rep to last 2 sts, end in K2.
Row 2: (P2, K2) rep to last 2 sts, end in P2.
Cont in 2 × 2 rib until strip measures 96cm (38″). Cast (bind) off ribwise.

CUFF BORDERS (Make 2)

Using 5mm (US 8) circular needles as straight and A, cast on 14 sts. Work in same 2 × 2 rib as for Border until strip measures 25cm (10″). Cast (bind) off ribwise.

JACKET PANELS TO TRIM FRONT EDGES

(Make 2)

Using 5mm (US 8) circular needles as straight and A, cast on 14 sts. Work in 2 × 2 rib as above until strip measures 45cm (18″). Do not cast (bind) off, but transfer to stitch holders until later.

PATTERNED AREA (BACK, FRONTS AND SLEEVES)

This is made with the Back, 2 Front panels and Sleeves all in one piece. Work in Rows, not rounds.

Using 5mm (US 8) circular needles as straight and D, cast on 124 sts. Foll chart, beg at RH side **Row 1**, reading from right to left for RS (K) rows and from left to right for WS (P) rows, work in fairisle throughout.

Begin at Back (page 11) and end at Front edges (page 12). Work Sleeve and neck inc and dec simultaneously, using separate balls of yarn. Introduce colour changes as desired at beg or end of rows only, but use no more than two colours in each row. Work in patt until 185 rows have been completed. Cast (bind) off.

MAKING UP

Darn in any loose ends, then block patterned piece to eliminate any puckering. Press well with warm iron over damp cloth on RS. Do not block or press ribbed borders.

Using invisible seaming, join edges of Sleeves at wrist to Cuff Borders from underneath, making sure the 4 ribs rem intact. Using invisible seaming, join ribbed Border along entire lower edge of Back and to both lower edges of Fronts, matching ends carefully.

Take ribbed Front panels and leaving 9cm (3½″) at cast on edge to protrude *below* jacket Border to allow for Welt to be attached later, using invisible seaming join to Front edges. Leave the ends on the stitch holders parallel to neck edge shaping row until later.

NECKBAND

Sl the 14 sts from the stitch holder on the LH ribbed Front panel onto a 5mm (US 8) circular needle. RS facing, using **A** pick up evenly and K94 sts from the neck edge of the patterned piece, ending by ribbing the 14 sts from the stitch holder on the RH Front panel. Turn and rib back along these 122 sts, setting 2 × 2 ribs along the Back neck and shoulder edges. Cont in rib until 11 rows have been completed. Break off yarn.

Change to 3¾mm (US 5) circular needles used as straight and in **B**, rib 2 rows. Change to **C**, rib 2 more rows, then cast (bind) off ribwise.

BORDER EDGES (Make 2)

Using 3¾ (US 5) circular needles as straight, RS facing and **B**, pick up evenly and K130 sts, beg at top neck edge of ribbed Front panel. Turn, WS facing, and beg at lower edge, P2, K2 until last 2 sts at neck edge rem, end in P2. Work 1 more row in rib in **B**, then change to **C**, rib 2 rows, then in **C** cast (bind) off loosely ribwise. Work other side similarly.

CUFFS (Make 2)

Using 3¾mm (US 5) circular needles as straight and **B**, RS facing, from Cuff borders pick up evenly and K56 sts.
Next Row: In **B**, K2, P2 to end of row. Change to **C**, and work in rib until Cuff measures 9cm (3½"). Cast (bind) off ribwise.

WELT (Make 1)

Using 3¾mm (US 5) circular needles as straight and **B**, RS facing, pick up evenly and K218 sts from along inside of lower edge of jacket Border, taking care to keep the ribs intact. Turn and set in P2, K2 rib, ending in P2. Rib 1 more row, then change to **C**. Cont in rib until Welt measures 9cm (3½"). Cast (bind) off ribwise.

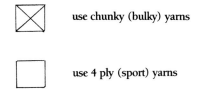

 use chunky (bulky) yarns

 use 4 ply (sport) yarns

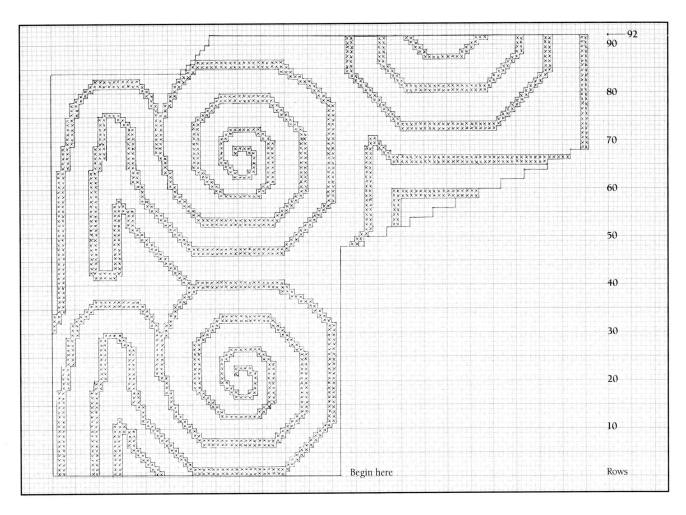

Begin here

Rows

Right Back and Left Sleeve

Left Front and Left Sleeve

FINISHING

Using backstitch, attach Welt edges to sides of each of the ribbed Front panels. Darn in any loose ends at neckline to form a continuous border, then complete neatening of jacket.

Fold Sleeves over and using backstitch for st st and invisible seaming for ribbing, join side and Sleeve seams.

Press seams lightly on WS with warm iron over damp cloth, omitting ribbing.

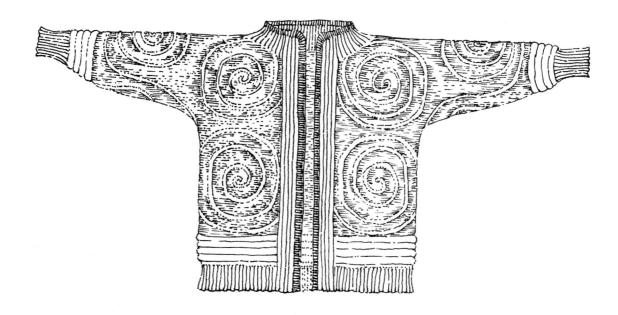

INISHMORE

(2500 BC)

Continuing my exploration of Irish pattern, I travelled next to Inishmore, largest of the three Aran Isles, off the west coast of Ireland beyond Galway. Exposed to the Atlantic Ocean, the dramatic limestone islands have attracted successive waves of settlers since Neolithic times.

All over the wild storm lashed land, dry stone walls said to have been begun by late Stone Age farmers to enclose tiny fields still stand intact today. They owe their survival over so many centuries to their ingenious lace-like construction which allows the full force of gales to blow through gaps between their interlocking stones. I found their bold but intricate patterns irresistible, and tried to capture them in the texture of this sleeveless pullover.

Dry stone wall on Inishmore. Gaps in the interlocking construction allow the wind to blow through safely.

Although the first builders of these walls were skilled in many textile crafts – spinning, dyeing, plaiting and braiding, and weaving to name a few – it is unlikely that they knew how to knit. The earliest examples of true knitting rather than similar looking nalbinding cannot be traced until centuries later in Egypt, and so the Phoenician theory unfortunately must be discounted.

Yet the legacy of pattern that their walls bequeath to today's islanders remains. It is reflected, as I was to find out later, in the traditional diamond motifs of Aran knitting, said to represent the fields with their protective boundaries still being built and re-built on Inishmore.

I used a chunky slubbed Irish produced wool for my interpretation of the walls to create an easy to knit pullover that, unlike the walls, can be made in only three days.

MATERIALS

YARN

Kilcarra 'Cottage' Chunky (bulky) Knit Wool in Donegal (4718)
9 (9:10) × 50g/16oz (16:17¾)

NEEDLES

1 pair 4mm (US 6) 60cm (24″) circular needles
1 pair 5mm (US 8) 35cm (14″) straight needles
1 cable needle
1 spare needle

SIZES AND MEASUREMENTS

In 3 sizes to fit:
Chest size 94cm (37″): 99cm (39″): 104cm (41″)

Actual width across back at underarm
49cm (19½″): 52cm (20½″): 54cm (21½″)

Length from centre back neck to hip, all sizes 66cm (26″)

Armhole base to hip 42cm (16½″)

TENSION (GAUGE)

14 sts and 24 rows to 10cm (4″) over pattern on 5mm (US 8) needles or size needed to obtain this tension (gauge).

SPECIAL ABBREVIATIONS

C2F   Sl 1 st onto cable needle, hold at front, K1, then K1 from cable needle.

C2B   Sl 1 st onto cable needle, hold at back, K1, then K1 from cable needle.

SFC   Sl 1 st onto cable needle, hold at front, P1, then K1 from cable needle.

SBC   Sl 1 st onto cable needle, hold at back, K1, then P1 from cable needle.

BACK

Using 4mm (US 6) circular needles as straight and Kilcarra Chunky (bulky) Knit wool, cast on 66 (72:78) sts. Work in K1, P1 single rib until Welt measures 9cm (3½″). Change to 5mm (US 8) straight needles and work in patt as folls:

Row 1: (WS) P.
Rows 2 & 3: P.
Rows 4, 5 & 6: (K3, P3), rep to end.
Rows 7, 8 & 9: P.
Row 10: K.
Row 11: (K4, SBC), rep to end.
Row 12: (K5, C2B), rep to last 5 sts, K5.
Row 13: (SBC, K4), rep to end.

Row 14: K.
Rows 15, 16 & 17: P.
Rows 18, 19 & 20: (P3, K3), rep to end.
Rows 21, 22 & 23: P.
Row 24: K.
Row 25: (SFC, K4), rep to end.
Row 26: K5, (C2F, K4) rep to last 5 sts, K5.
Row 27: (K4, SFC), rep to end.
Row 28: K.

These 28 rows form the patt repeat. Cont in patt as set until work measures 41cm (16″) from beg of Welt, and **Row 22** of third patt rep has been completed.**

SHAPE ARMHOLES

At beg of **Row 23** of third patt rep, cast (bind) off 6 sts and work to end of row in patt as set. At beg of **Row 24** of third patt rep cast (bind) off a further 6 sts. Foll patt, dec a further 1 st at beg of next 4 rows. (50:56:62) sts. Cont to work in patt with no further dec until **Row 22** of fifth patt rep has been completed.

SHAPE SHOULDERS

Cast (bind) off 4 (5:6) sts at beg of **Rows 23, 24, 25 and 26**. 34 (36:38) sts.
Cast (bind) off 2 (3:4) sts at beg of **Rows 27 and 28**. 30 (30:30) sts.
Cast (bind) off purlwise.

FRONT

Work as for Back until armhole shaping.**

SHAPE ARMHOLE AND DIVIDE FOR NECK

At beg of **Row 23** of third patt rep, cast (bind) off 6 sts. Purl across next 27 (30:33) sts in patt specification, then sl rem 33 (36:39) sts on a spare needle and leave. Turn and beg V neck shaping, and cont armhole shaping as folls:

Row 24: Cast (bind) off 1 st at beg of row for neck shaping, work in patt to end of row.
Row 25: Cast (bind) off 1 st at beg of row for armhole shaping, cont in patt.
Row 26: Work in patt with no dec.
Row 27: Cast (bind) off 1 st at beg of row to complete armhole shaping, cont in patt.
Row 28: Cast (bind) off 1 st at beg of row for neck shaping, cont in patt. Cont in patt as set but dec 1 st at beg of foll rows to cont neck shaping (all sizes). On fourth patt rep *Rows 4, 8, 12, 16, 20, 24 and 28*. Commence fifth patt rep and cont neck shaping as folls: dec 1 st at beg of *Rows 4, 8, 12, 16 & 20*.
This completes neck shaping, all sizes. Cont in patt until **Row 22** is completed.

SHOULDER SHAPING

Row 23: Cast (bind) off 4 (5:6) sts, patt to end.
Row 24: No dec, patt across.
Row 25: Cast (bind) off 4 (5:6) sts, patt to end.
Row 26: Work in patt, then cast (bind) off on *Row 27*.

Complete other shoulder, reversing shapings.

Using backstitch, join both shoulder seams at Front and Back, then make armhole bands as folls:

ARMHOLE BANDS

RS facing, using 4mm (US 6) circular needles as straight, pick up and K100 sts evenly, beg at armhole edge. Work 5 rows in K1, P1 rib, then cast (bind) off . Work both armholes, then using backstitch for patt area and invisible seaming for ribbing, join side seams.

NECKBAND

Using 4mm (US 6) circular needles, RS facing, beg at left shoulder seam, pick up evenly and K45 sts down LH side of neck. Pick up 1 st at centre front, then a further 45 sts up the RH side of neck and 31 sts across Back neck. (122 sts). Now work in K1, P1 rib as folls:

Round 1: K1, P1 rib until within 2 sts of centre front st. P2tog, K the centre st, then P2tog TBL, rib to end.
Round 2: Cont in this way, keeping centre front st a 'knit' rib on RS, and gradually dec 1 st on each side of centre st as shown in *Round 1*.
Cont to dec sts as shown, but retaining centre st until 5 rounds of rib have been worked. Cast (bind) off knitwise.

MAKING UP AND FINISHING

Darn in any loose ends. Press seams on WS with warm iron over damp cloth, omitting ribbing and patt areas.

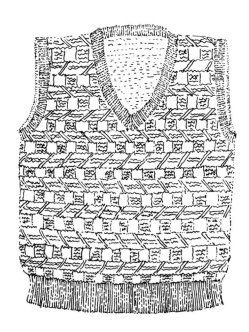

CRIOS

(2500 BC – 800 BC)

My search for further clues to the history of Aran knitting led me to the tiny Kilronan Folk Museum on Inishmore. Its modest two rooms annexed to a guest house were crammed with fascinating objects showing the traditional way of life of the islanders.

Here I found unspun fleece, carding combs, and a large ball of handspun wool, the original undyed bainin yarn that was used to make the first Aran sweaters. There were examples of these sweaters on display, but the earliest only dated back to the 1930s.

However, equally interesting were the brightly coloured hand-woven belts – Crios – which were worn by the islander's currach fishermen with their plainer tweed trousers and jackets, knitted sweaters and crocheted caps.

Made on portable foot-tensioned back-strap looms, they were woven in wool in narrow strips, and then plaited at each end leaving long fringes. This technique is very ancient and is found all over the world. It could even have been practised by the pre-Celtic Bronze Age farmers who succeeded the earliest wall-builders of Inishmore.

Similar belts were made by monks in monasteries, and were much sought after as they were often accredited with healing properties. They could have been made in Inishmore in the sixth century foundation of St Enda.

Perhaps, more mundanely, they evolved naturally as the islanders experimented with their own home spun wool. Originally, the belts were made using vibrant reds, blues and yellows with imported madder, indigo and home made vegetable dyes. Later, green was introduced. Nowadays, sadly they are only obtainable on the island as machine made tourist souvenirs.

I designed this vividly coloured child's sweater to commemorate this lovely old island craft.

MATERIALS

YARN

Rowan DK (Lightweight) (Knitting Worsted) in foll colours and quantities

A	Red (115)	8 (8:10:12) × 25g/7¼oz (7¼:9:10¾)
B	Green (124)	1 (1:1:1) × 25g/1oz (1:1:1)
C	Blue (108)	2 (3:3:3) × 25g/2oz (3:3:3)
D	Yellow (12)	1 (1:1:1) × 25g/1oz (1:1:1)

NEEDLES

1 pair 3¼mm (US 3) 60cm (24″) circular needles
1 pair 4mm (US 6) 60cm (24″) circular needles
2 stitch holders
1 spare needle

SIZES AND MEASUREMENTS

In 4 sizes to fit: Chest size 72cm (28½″): 79cm (31½″): 86cm (34″): 94cm (37″)

Actual width across back at underarm
38cm (15¼″): 42cm (16¾″): 45cm (17¾″): 49cm (19½″)

Length from centre back neck to hip
47cm (18½″): 49cm (19½″): 52cm (20½″): 54cm (21½″)

Sleeve seam from armhole inset
40cm (16½″): 43cm (17″): 44cm (17½″): 46cm (18″)

TENSION (GAUGE)

23 sts and 29 rows to 10cm (4″) over st st on 4mm (US 6) needles or size needed to obtain this tension (gauge).

NOTES ON TECHNIQUES

Patterned areas in this design are worked in the fairisle method. When working be careful to carry colour not in use *very* loosely across back of work to avoid puckering. Twist yarns together at colour joins in row to avoid holes.

BACK

Using 3¼mm (US 3) circular needles as straight and A, cast on 88 (96:104:112) sts then cont in patt as folls, introducing and breaking off yarn at beg and end of rows as required, to make Welt.

Row 1: (WS) (In A, K2, P2), rep to end.
Row 2: (In B, K2, in C, K2), rep to end.
Row 3: (In C, K2, in B, P2), rep to end.
Row 4: (In B, K2, in C, P2), rep to end.
Row 5: (In A, P2, in C, P2), rep to end.
Row 6: (In C, K2, in A, P2), rep to end.

Row 7: (In A, K2, in C, P2), rep to end.
Row 8: In C, K.
Row 9: (In C, K2, P2), rep to end.
Row 10: (In B, K2, in C, P2), rep to end.
Row 11: (In C, K2, in B, P2), rep to end.
Row 12: (In B, K2, in C, P2), rep to end.
Row 13: (In C, K2, in B, P2), rep to end.
Row 14: (In C, K2, P2), rep to end.
Row 15: (In C, K2, P2), rep to end.
Row 16: (In C, K2, in A, K2), rep to end.
Row 17: (In A, K2, in C, P2), rep to end.
Row 18: (In C, K2, in A, P2), rep to end.
Row 19: (In C, P2, in B, P2), rep to end.
Row 20: (In B, K2, in C, P2), rep to end.
Row 21: (In C, K2, in B, P2), rep to end.
Row 22: In A, K.
Row 23: (In A, K2, P2), rep to end.

Change to 4mm (US 6) circular needles used as straight and work in st st, using fairisle where necessary, as folls:

Row 24: (RS) In D, K.
Row 25: In D, P.
Row 26: In A, K.
Row 27: In A, P.
Row 28: (In A, K1, in C, K1), rep to end.
Row 29: (In C, P1, in A, P1), rep to end.
Row 30: (In C, K1, in A, K1), rep to end.
Row 31: (In A, P1, in C, P1), rep to end.
Row 32: In C, K.
Row 33: In C, P.
Row 34: In D, K.
Row 35: (In B, P1, in A, P1), rep to end.
Row 36: (In C, K1, in D, K1), rep to end.
Row 37: (In B, P1, in A, P1), rep to end.
Row 38: In D, K.
Row 39: In C, P.
Row 40: In C, K.
Row 41: (In A, P1, in C, P1), rep to end.
Row 42: (In C, K1, in A, K1), rep to end.
Row 43: (In C, P1, in A, P1), rep to end.
Row 44: (In A, K1, in C, K1), rep to end.
Row 45: In A, P.
Row 46: In A, K.
Row 47: In D, P.
Row 48: In D, K.
Row 49: In A, P.
Row 50: In A, K.

Cont in A in st st until work measures 28cm (11"): 30cm (12"): 33cm (13"): 35cm (14"), from beg of Welt.

ARMHOLE SHAPING

Cast (bind) off 8 sts at beg of next 2 rows. (72:80:88:96) sts.**

Cont in st st until Back measures 44cm (17½"): 47cm (18½"): 49cm (19½"): 52cm (20½"), ending with a purl row.

DIVIDE FOR NECK

RS facing, K27 (30:33:36) sts. Sl rem 45 (50:55:60) sts onto spare needle.
Next Row: Turn and P2tog, then P to end.
Next Row: K to last 2 sts, K2tog.
Rep last 2 rows once more. Purl one more row, then cast (bind) off. RS facing, rejoin yarn and transfer 18 (20:22:24) sts for Back neck onto a stitch holder, knit to end of row, then turn.
Next Row: P to last 2 sts, P2tog.
Next Row: K2tog, K to end.
Rep last 2 rows once more. Purl one more row, then cast (bind) off.

FRONT

Work as for Back until **. After armhole shaping is complete, cont in st st in A until work measures 39cm (15½"): 42cm (16½"): 44cm (17½"): 47cm (18½"), ending with a purl row.

DIVIDE FOR NECK

RS facing, K29 (32:35:38) sts, then transfer rem 43 (48:53:58) sts onto spare needle.
Next Row: P2tog, then P to end.
Next Row: K to last 2 sts, K2tog.
Rep last 2 rows twice more. Cont in st st with no further dec until work measures 44cm (17½"): 47cm (18½"): 49cm (19½"): 52cm (20½"). Cast (bind) off.
Next Row: Rejoin yarn, RS facing, transfer 14 (16:18:20) sts for centre Front neck from spare needle onto stitch holder. Cont to K across rem 29 (32:35:38) sts. Work other shoulder similarly, reversing shapings. Cast (bind) off.

Using backstitch, join shoulders, then work Neckband.

NECKBAND

Using 3¼mm (US 3) circular needles, RS facing, beg at left shoulder seam, pick up evenly and knit in B, K2, in C, K2, 20 sts from left Front (all sizes), 14 (16:18:20) sts across centre Front sts from stitch holder, 20 sts from right Front (all sizes), 8 from right Back (all sizes), 18 (20:22:24) sts across centre Back from stitch holder, and 8 from left Back (all sizes). (88:92:96:100) sts.

Working in rounds, introducing and breaking off yarn as required, set 2 × 2 rib as folls:

Round 1: (In B, K2, in C, P2), rep to end.
Round 2: (In B, K2, in C, P2), rep to end.
Round 3: (In C, K2, in A, K2), rep to end.
Round 4: (In C, K2, in A, P2), rep to end.
Round 5: (In C, K2, in A, P2), rep to end.
Round 6: (In B, K2, in C, K2), rep to end.
Round 7: (In B, K2, in C, P2), rep to end.
Round 8: (In B, K2, in C, P2), rep to end.
Round 9: In A, K.
In A, cast (bind) off ribwise.

SLEEVES

Using 4mm (US 6) circular needles as straight and **D**, RS facing, beg at armhole lower edge pick up evenly and K80 (84:88:92) sts from Back and Front yoke shoulders along armhole edge. Do not pick up the 2 groups of 8 cast (bound) off sts. Cont in patt as folls:

Row 1: (WS) In **D**, P.
Row 2: In **A**, K.
Row 3: In **A**, P.
Row 4: (In **C**, K1, in **A**, K1), rep to end.
Row 5: (In **A**, P1, in **C**, P1), rep to end.
Row 6: (In **A**, K1, in **C**, K1), rep to end.
Row 7: (In **C**, P1, in **A**, P1), rep to end.
Row 8: In **C**, K.
Row 9: In **C**, P.
Row 10: In **D**, K.
Row 11: (In **B**, P1, in **A**, P1), rep to end.
Row 12: (In **C**, K1, in **D**, K1), rep to end.
Row 13: (In **B**, P1, in **A**, P1), rep to end.
Row 14: In **D**, K.
Row 15: In **C**, P.
Row 16: In **C**, K.
Row 17: (In **C**, P1, in **A**, P1), rep to end.
Row 18: (In **A**, K1, in **C**, K1), rep to end.
Row 19: (In **A**, P1, in **C**, P1), rep to end.
Row 20: (In **C**, K1, in **A**, K1), rep to end.
Row 21: In **A**, P.
Row 22: In **A**, K.
Row 23: In **D**, P.
Row 24: In **D**, K.
Row 25: In **A**, P.
Row 26: In **A**, K.

Cont in **A** in st st, dec Sleeve by 1 st at beg and end of rows as folls:

SLEEVE SHAPING

Sizes 1 (2:3): Dec 1 st at beg and end of every 5th row until 40 (44:48) sts rem, cont in st st with no further dec until Sleeve measures 35cm (14"): 37cm (14½"): 38cm (15").

Size 4: Dec 1 st at beg and end of every 6th row until 52 sts rem and Sleeve measures 39cm (15½").

Change to 3¼mm (US 3) circular needles used as straight and work Cuffs.

Row 1: (In **C**, K2, in **B**, K2), rep to end.
Row 2: (In **B**, P2, in **C**, K2), rep to end.
Row 3: (In **C**, P2, in **B**, K2), rep to end.
Row 4: (In **C**, P2, in **A**, P2), rep to end.
Row 5: (In **A**, P2, in **C**, K2), rep to end.
Row 6: (In **C**, P2, in **A**, K2), rep to end.
Row 7: In **C**, K.
Row 8: (In **C**, P2, K2), rep to end.
Row 9: (In **C**, P2, in **B**, K2), rep to end.
Row 10: (In **B**, P2, in **C**, K2), rep to end.
Row 11: (In **C**, P2, in **B**, K2), rep to end.
Row 12: (In **B**, P2, in **C**, K2), rep to end.
Rows 13 and 14: (In **C**, P2, K2), rep to end.
Row 15: (In **A**, K2, in **C**, K2), rep to end.
Row 16: (In **C**, P2, in **A**, K2), rep to end.
Row 17: (In **A**, P2, in **C**, K2), rep to end.
Row 18: (In **B**, P2, in **C**, P2), rep to end.
Row 19: (In **C**, P2, in **B**, K2), rep to end.
Row 20: (In **B**, P2, in **C**, K2), rep to end.
Row 21: In **A**, K.

In **A**, cast (bind) off ribwise.

MAKING UP AND FINISHING

Darn in all loose ends neatly. Using backstitch for st st areas and invisible seaming for ribbing, join side seams and attach Sleeve edges to cast (bound) off armhole edges. Using backstitch, join Sleeve seams in st st areas, and using invisible seaming, join ribbed Cuffs. Press seams on WS with warm iron over damp cloth, then press RS similarly, omitting ribbing.

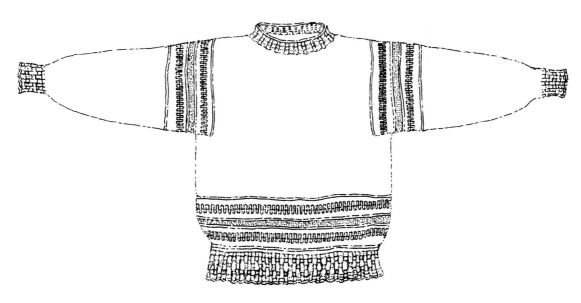

TORC

(800 BC – 200 BC)

The original builders of the stone walls of Inishmore were only one of a succession of invading tribes to settle in Ireland.

As the Stone Age gave way to the Bronze Age and knowledge of metallurgy came in with each new wave of immigrants from Europe, native Irish gold began to be shaped into personal ornaments of a breathtaking barbaric elegance.

Most magnificent of these are the ceremonial torcs. Worn by chieftains as symbols of wealth and rank, they may also have been used as a talisman, believed to bestow magical power on the wearer.

Made with increasing artistry, by 800 BC they were traded throughout western Europe. Eventually siezed as booty by Imperial armies, they came to be highly prized by the sophisticated wives of Roman patricians.

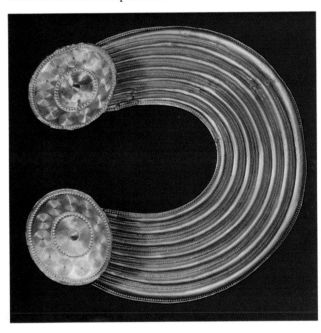

Gold gorget from Glenisheen

Although at this time knitting would still have been unknown in Ireland, many of the patterns that decorate these torcs translate easily into knitting designs. A gold gorget dating from 700 BC from the National Museum in Dublin inspired this summer top in silk. The embossed repoussé dots, ribbed edges and cabled guilloche plaits typical of the gold work of the period are used extensively in Aran knitting, as if echoes of this Bronze Age Celtic heritage still reverberate in Ireland's crafts.

MATERIALS

YARN

Naturally Beautiful Aura 8/2 Silk in Gold (P36)
250g (300:350:400)/9oz (10¾:12½:14¼)

NEEDLES

1 pair 2¾mm (US 2) 60cm (24″) circular needles
1 pair 2¾mm (US 2) 60cm (24″) spare circular needles
Stitch holder

SIZES AND MEASUREMENTS

In 4 sizes to fit: Bust size 81cm (32″): 86cm (34″): 91cm (36″): 96cm (38″)

Actual width across back at underarm
44cm (17½″): 46cm (18½″): 49cm (19½″): 52cm (20½″)

Length from shoulder seam to hip
66cm (26″): 67cm (26½″): 68cm (27″): 69cm (27½″)

TENSION (GAUGE)

27 sts and 30 rows to 10cm (4″) over st st on 2¾mm (US 2) needles or size needed to obtain this tension (gauge).

SPECIAL ABBREVIATIONS

MB4   (K into front and back of next st) twice, making 4 sts out of 1, (turn and K4 sts, turn and P4 sts) twice, then using LH needle, lift 2nd, 3rd, 4th sts over 1 st and off needle.

BACK AND FRONT THE SAME

Using 2¾mm (US 2) circular needles as straight and silk, cast on 115 (123:131:139) sts.

Row 1: (WS) K.
Row 2: P.
Rows 3, 4 & 5: K.
Row 6: P.
Row 7: K.
Row 8: Make hem as folls: sl the spare circular needle into the loops formed by the cast on 115 (123:131:139) sts. Then, holding the LH needle and the spare needle parallel with each other, knit the sts together with the RH needle to form the hem.
Rows 9 & 10: K.
Row 11: P.
Row 12: (P1, MB4) rep to last st, P1.
Rows 13–19: P.
Row 20: As *Row 12*.
Row 21: P.

Row 22: K.

Rows 23–26: Rep *Rows 21 & 22* twice more.

Row 27: P.

Row 28: Make a tuck as folls: Sl the spare needle into the backs of the loops at the WS of *Row 21*, picking up 115 (123:131:139) sts. With RH needle, K the st from the spare needle tog with the st on the parallel LH needle, to form a tuck in the fabric, making 1 st from the 2. (115:123:131:139) sts.

Row 29: P.

Rows 30–47: As *Rows 12–29*.

Row 48: As *Row 12*.

Rows 49–51: P.

Row 52: K.

Cont in st st until work measures 44cm (17½"): 45cm (18"): 46 cm (18½"): 47cm (19") from hem edge, ending with a purl row.

ARMHOLE SHAPING

All sizes RS facing, cast (bind) off 4 sts at beg of next 2 rows. (107:115:123:131) sts.

Sizes 2, 3 & 4 only Cast (bind) off 4 sts at beg of next 2 (4:6) rows.

All sizes Cast (bind) off 4 sts at beg of next 2 rows, then cast (bind) off 1 st at beg of next 4 rows. (95 sts)

DIVIDE FOR NECK

All sizes RS facing, K48 sts, sl rem 47 sts onto a stitch holder.

RH shoulder Turn and cont in st st, dec 4 sts at beg of next 4 alt (every other) rows. (32 sts) Work 1 row, then dec 3 sts at beg of next row at neck edge. (29 sts) Work 1 row, then dec 2 sts at beg of next 6 alt (every other) rows at neck edge. (17 sts) Work 1 row, then dec 1 st at neck edge of foll 14 alt (every other) rows. (3 sts) Work 6 (8:10:12) more rows in st st, on rem sts, then cast (bind) off.

LH shoulder Transfer the 47 sts on the stitch holder onto the 2¾mm (US 2) needle. Rejoin yarn at inside neck edge, RS facing. Dec 3 sts at beg of row, K this row, then P next row. Dec 4 sts at beg of next 3 alt (every other) rows to match RH shoulder. Cont to work as opposite shoulder, reversing shapings, but ending with 5 (7:9:11) rows of st st on 3 sts. Cast (bind) off.

YOKE

Align Back and Front, WS facing each other, then using backstitch, sew the 3 st shoulder straps together. Turn garment inside out again so RS faces, and beg at RH shoulder seam, using 2¾mm (US 2) circular needles pick up evenly and knit 200 (210:220:230) sts from Front and Back neck edge.

Taking care not to twist the yoke, work continuously in rounds as folls:

Round 1: (P1, MB4), rep to end of round.

Rounds 2–8: K.

Round 9: Make a tuck, using the spare circular needle to pick

up the loops from the back of the sts of *Round 2* in the method described in *Row 28*.

Round 10: K.

Round 11: As *Round 1*.

Round 12: K.

Round 13: P.

Round 14: K.

Round 15: (K8, K2tog), rep. to end. (180:189:198:207) sts. Cast (bind) off.

ARMHOLE EDGES

Starting at lower edge of Front, using 2¾mm (US 2) circular needles as straight, RS facing, pick up evenly and knit 100 (112:124:136) sts, working up Front, across shoulders and down Back. Then work as folls:

Row 1: (WS) P.

Row 2: K.

Rows 3–5: P.

Row 6: K.

Row 7: P.

Cast (bind) off loosely.

MAKING UP AND FINISHING

Using slip st, sew down cast (bound) off edge of armholes to inside edge to form a hem identical to hem made at lower edge of body. Turn inside out and using backstitch, join side seams. Darn in any loose ends neatly. Press gently on RS, with warm iron over damp cloth, omitting bobbles and textured areas.

LA TÈNE

(200 BC–AD 500)

Continuing my visit to the National Museum, I was drawn to the fine examples of Irish metalwork which are decorated in the distinctive La Tène style.

This vigorous but graceful art form with its flamboyant curvilinear pattern is considered to be the first truly indigenous art of temperate Europe. It was however influenced by three separate sources: geometric and stylized animal patterns from the central European Hallstatt culture, Greco-Etruscan foliage and zoomorphic designs, and red coral and enamel embellishment from southern Europe and Persia.

The Iron Age people who produced this metalwork were descended from the Keltoi/Celtae – the first Celts – a slave owning, cattle-raiding warlike race from central Europe who were themselves displaced westwards, and settled in Ireland. As Ireland was never occupied by the Romans and so remained uninfluenced by classic representational art forms, it developed its own particular La Tène style to perfection. This later contributed significantly to the evolution of Irish Christian art.

Some time afterwards, a separate group of Iron Age La Tène metalworkers, the Fir Bolg, refugees from north-eastern Gaul, invaded the Aran Isles. In spite of their skill as weavers, they would not have been able to lay down the foundations of Aran knitting, for this craft was probably still unknown in the west at this time. Instead, these early Aran islanders dressed in kilt length woven woollen or linen tunics for both sexes, with long cloaks. Humbler members of the tribe wore tight trousers in brilliant colours that scandalised the classic writers of the day.

There are a rich variety of examples of Irish La Tène metalwork at the National Museum, and perhaps the finest of these is the pure gold Broighter torc. But I chose the Loughnashade bronze trumpet as my chief design source, because the decoration can be seen so clearly.

It also has a fascinating history. Dating from AD 100, it was discovered in the last century in a small lake in Co. Armagh near the ancient royal seat of the Ulster Kings at Emain Macha. Translated from the Irish, the name means 'The Lake of the Treasures', and was a votive site into which offerings to Celtic deities were cast.

Trumpets of this type were used in war, and the terrifying effect they had on the enemy when blown before a battle began is described by classic writers.

This sweater can be made with as many different yarns and colours as you like. Or, for a simpler effect, try knitting it using only two different coloured random-dyed yarns, one in dark shades and the other in light.

I used a variety of lightweight flecked wools and silk/wool mixes for my main texture, adding small quantities of mohair, chenille, silk, mercerised cotton and random-dyed irregularly spun wool. It would be particularly lovely in hand-dyed and hand-spun yarns.

I chose colours to reflect the subtle gleam of the La Tène metalwork I saw in the National Museum. I used soft mulberries, charcoals, blue-greys and silvers, enlivened with streaks of turquoise, purple, peat browns and deep greeny-blacks.

MATERIALS

YARNS
Approximately 200g/7¼oz of dark shades, and 400g/14¼oz of light shades of a variety of different yarns of similar weight. Very small amounts of heavier weight yarns can be incorporated to add texture but be careful not to overdo it.

I selected from the following yarns:

ROWAN
Cabled Mercerised Cotton
A Mulberry (310)

Fine Cotton Chenille
   Black (377)

DK (Lightweight) Wool (Knitting Worsted)
   Pale Blues (47 & 48)
   Dark Blues (53 & 54)

Grainy Silks (52% Silk, 48% Wool)
   Twie (809)
   Flint (801)

Bronze trumpet from Loughnashade

Silkstones (52% Silk, 48% Wool)
- Blue Mist (832)
- Marble (833)
- Woad (829)
- Beetle (834)

JAMIESON & SMITH
2 Ply Jumper Weight Wool in the following colours
- B Blue Fleck (1291)
- C Medium Blue (33)
- Turquoise (FC 34)
- Peat Brown (FC 13)
- Grey Fleck (203)
- Amethyst (124)

COLINETTE YARNS
Mezzotint Wool, Aran (Fisherman) weight, slubbed and loosely spun
Charcoal (25)

KILCARRA YARNS

Mohair
- D Pale Grey (98)
- Pale Blue (18)
- Purple (12)

NEEDLES
1 pair 2¾mm (US 2) 60cm (24") circular needles
1 pair 3¾mm (US 5) 100cm (39") circular needles

SIZE AND MEASUREMENTS
One size only to fit up to 106cm (42") bust

Actual width across back at underarm   58cm (23")

Length from centre back neck to hip   63cm (25")

Sleeve seam from underarm   47cm (19")

TENSION (GAUGE)
20 sts and 32 rows to 10cm (4") over patterned area on 3¾mm (US 5) or size needed to obtain this tension (gauge).

BACK, FRONT AND SLEEVES

NOTES ON TECHNIQUES
These are worked in one piece, beg at lower Front edge. Work using the intarsia technique, using a separate length of yarn for each area shown in chart. As many different colours and yarns as you like can be used in each row, but remember to work dark and light tones as shown for motifs.

Twist yarns together at each join, then leave in position to be worked in next row. Keep lengths fairly short, around 152cm (60") to avoid tangles when working. Knit the ends in as you work, by wrapping the ends around the new colour thread for two or three sts beyond where they were last used to minimise later darning in.

Working from chart, reading from right to left for RS (K) rows and from left to right for WS (P) rows, beg at Row 1.

Using 3¾mm (US 5) circular needles as straight, and a light shade of yarn, cast on 121 sts. Work from Row 1 until Row 112 has been completed.

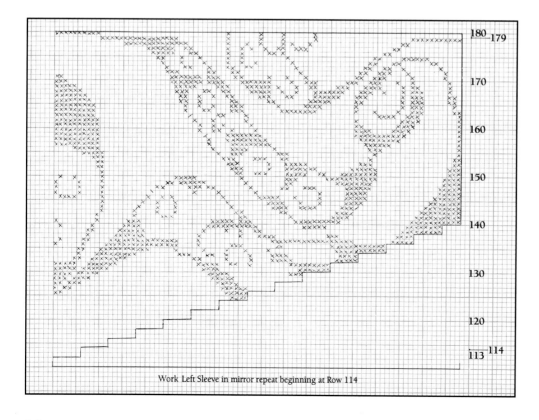

Work Left Sleeve in mirror repeat beginning at Row 114

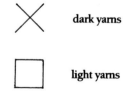

dark yarns

light yarns

Right Sleeve

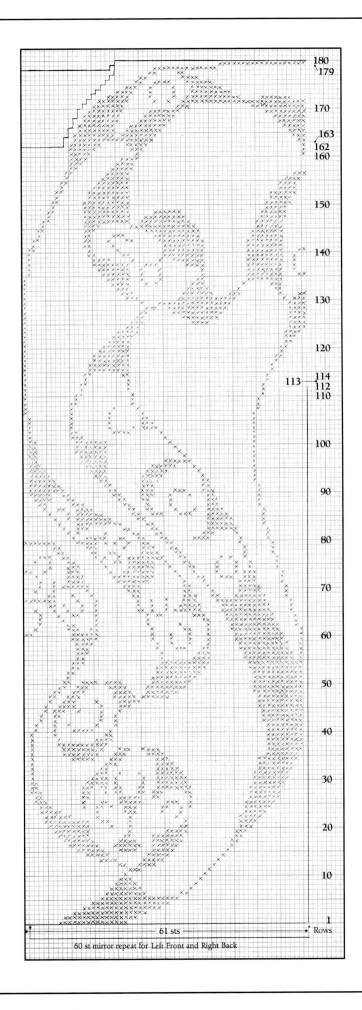

Right Front

SLEEVE SHAPING

Cast on 6 sts, work as shown in chart, then work across Front on **Row 113**. Turn, cast on 6 sts of other Sleeve, work as shown in chart in purl, then purl across **Row 114**.

Cont to inc in this way until Sleeve shaping has been completed. Cont to work as shown in chart until **Row 162** is finished.

NECK SHAPING

Work across **Row 163**, then cast (bind) off 17 sts for neck when shown in chart. Work across rem sts, then cont to shape for neck as shown, working both sides simultaneously, with separate lengths of yarn, until **Row 180** has been completed.

Turn pattern, and beg to work Back, reading chart downwards. Work **Row 180** once only, beg patt rep at **Row 179** again.

Cast on 37 sts at **Row 179** as shown in chart to end Back neck shaping, then cont to foll patt as shown, working across Sleeves and Back until Sleeve dec begins. Dec these similarly to match Sleeve fronts. Cont until **Row 1** is reached again. Cast (bind) off.

NECKBAND

Using 2¾mm (US 2) circular needles, RS facing, beg at Back neck at LH corner in appropriate yarn of your choice. (I used **A**). Pick up evenly and K56 sts along Back neck, 18 sts along right Front neck, 19 sts from across Front neck and 18 sts from left Front neck. (111 sts). Work 10 rounds in st st, then cast (bind) off very loosely in 3¾mm (US 5) needles.

CUFFS

Using 2¾mm (US 2) circular needles as straight, pick up evenly from wrist and K56 sts in appropriate yarn of your choice. (I used **A**). Working in rows, not rounds, set 1 × 1 rib (K1, P1) and rib 2 rows. Change to a second colour of your choice (I chose **B**), and rib 11 rows. Change to third colour (I chose **C**) and rib 1 row. Change to fourth colour (I chose **D**) and rib 1 row. Change back to **C**, rib 1 row, then change to **B**, rib 11 rows, change to **A**, rib 2 rows to rep colour sequence. Cast (bind) off ribwise.

WELTS

Using 2¾mm (US 2) circular needles as straight and **A**, RS facing, pick up evenly and K112 sts from Back lower edge. Set same rib patt and using same colour changes, work as for Cuffs, casting (binding) off ribwise in same way. Work other Welt for Front similarly.

MAKING UP AND FINISHING

Darn in any loose ends, then block, taking care not to stretch ribbing. Turn Neckband over towards inside neck to form a piped edge, then catch down neatly using slip stitch. Using backstitch for st st and invisible seaming for ribbing, join Sleeve and Front and Back seams.

Lightly press seams on WS with warm iron over a damp cloth.

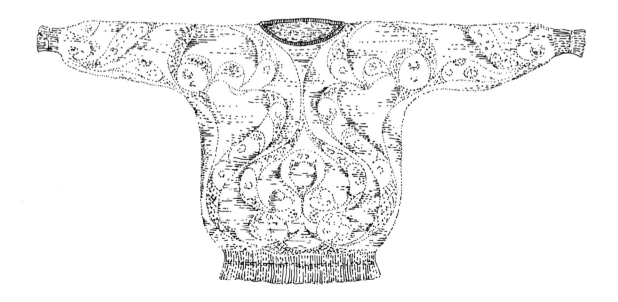

TARA

(*AD 500 – AD 600*)

Moving on through the National Museum, I was thrilled to actually see the famous Tara Brooch for myself at last.

This beautiful piece of jewellery, intricately worked in gilded silver with gold filigree interlacing and decorated with amber and amethyst glass, dates from the eighth century. It has no known connection with Tara, the Royal seat of the High Kings of Ireland. Instead, it was found in a box washed up on the seashore near Drogheda, Co. Louth.

Tara brooch found at Drogheda

Nevertheless, it has become a symbol for all that is exquisite in Irish craftwork and immediately I saw it I envisaged creating a very special garment inspired by it.

I chose to emphasise the original shape and colours in the yoke, and to decorate the front and back centre panel with the trellis work that embellishes the centre of the brooch. This trellis work also appears as one of the most popular stitches in Aran knitting, but it is very unlikely that knitted trellis work was being developed on the islands at this time.

Although during this period a form of knitting existed in Egypt, it is unclear whether the two needle method had been developed by then. Theoretically, it could have been brought to the Aran Isles, to the ecclesiastical centres founded by St Enda and St Brecan and modelled on the Coptic Church, by middle eastern monks travelling from these monasteries. But unfortunately there are no surviving textile examples to support this idea.

Looking at the Irish Gaelic word for knitting: 'Kniótail', which derives from the Old English (Anglo Saxon) word 'cynttan' or 'knotten', meaning to 'Tie, or with a knot', it is tempting to imagine knitting was commonly practised in Ireland at this time. But it seems it is not until the fifteenth century that the source word can be found to apply specifically to textiles, and then in connection with cap-making.

Descriptions of clothing during the ninth century in Ireland make no mention of knitting, although they clearly describe other textile techniques. In the following account of Étain, future wife of Eochad Airen, ancestor of King Conaire we read of her being luxuriously dressed wearing jewellery similar to the Tara brooch.

'She wore a purple cloak of good fleece, held with silver brooches dressed with gold, and a smock of green silk with gold embroidery.'

(Description taken from ninth century story, 'Togail Bruidne Da-Derga' mentioned in *The Celts*, Pelican, 1970)

MATERIALS

YARN

Rowan Sea Breeze Soft Cotton in the following colours and quantities

A	Wheat (523)	8 × 50g/14¼oz
B	Sienna (535)	1 × 50g/2oz
C	Caramel (524)	1 × 50g/2oz
D	Burnt Orange (550)	1 × 50g/2oz
E	Purple (543)	1 × 50g/2oz
F	Polka (530)	1 × 50g/2oz
G	Rain Cloud (528)	1 × 50g/2oz
H	Lilac (544)	1 × 50g/2oz
I	Terracotta (525)	1 × 50g/2oz

NOTES ON MATERIALS

Colours **B – I** are used in small quantities, and as the yarn is only available in 50g balls, there will be quite a bit over. Some of this could be used for other garments in this book (Seabirds, Sailboats and Galway Racer) or can be kept to add to your collection of yarns for future knitting projects.

NEEDLES

1 pair 2¾mm (US 2) 35cm (14″) straight needles
1 pair 3¼mm (US 3) 40cm (15½″) circular needles
1 cable needle
1 stitch holder

SIZE AND MEASUREMENTS

One size only to fit up to 96cm (38″) bust

Actual width across back at underarm   53cm (21″)
Length from centre back neck to hip   60cm (24″)
Sleeve seam   46cm (18″)

TENSION (GAUGE)

26 sts and 35 rows to 10cm (4″) over moss st on 3¼mm (US 3) needles or size needed to obtain this tension (gauge).

NOTES ON TECHNIQUES

This sweater uses a variety of techniques, sometimes combining them in one part of the garment. The techniques used are: *intarsia, fairisle, cabling,* with moss st and ribbing.

Intarsia   Use this technique on the yoke, working from the chart, and combining with cabling and fairisle sections as indicated. Use only short lengths of yarn to avoid tangling, with separate lengths of yarn for each colour shown in the chart. Twist yarns together at each join to avoid holes, then leave in position to be worked in next row. Knit the ends in as you work by wrapping them around the new colour thread for two or three sts beyond where they were last used, to minimise later darning in.

Fairisle   Use this technique to break up areas of solid colour as shown on chart to convey delicacy of Tara metalwork. Carry colour not in use very loosely across back of work to avoid long floats and puckering.

Cabling   Use cable needle and refer to instructions in chart, and written instructions in Special Abbreviations below. To make Yoke use separate colours as specified, combining with intarsia method.

SPECIAL ABBREVIATIONS

C2F   Sl 1 st onto cable needle, hold at front, K1, then K1 from cable needle.
C2B   Sl 1 st onto cable needle, hold at back, K1, then K1 from cable needle.
C4F   Sl 2 sts onto cable needle, hold at front, K2, then K2 from cable needle.
C4B   Sl 2 sts onto cable needle, hold at back, K2, then K2 from cable needle.
C6F   Sl 3 sts onto cable needle, hold at front, K3, then K3 from cable needle.
C6B   Sl 3 sts onto cable needle, hold at back, K3, then K3 from cable needle.
FC   Sl 2 sts onto cable needle, hold at front, P1, then K2 from cable needle.
BC   Sl 1 st onto cable needle, hold at back, K2, then P1 from cable needle.
SFC   Sl 1 st onto cable needle, hold at front, P1, then K1 from cable needle.

SBC   Sl 1 st onto cable needle, hold at back, K1, then P1 from cable needle.
M1   Make 1 st by picking up loop between sts from row below and knit it TBL.
Bobble   With first colour, K2tog. With second colour, make 3 sts, by K1, P1, K1 into the same st. Turn, K3 in second colour, turn, K3 in second colour, sl st over next st, rep until 1 st remains. With first colour, make 1 new st by picking up loop between sts from row below and knitting it TBL.

BACK

Using 2¾mm (US 2) straight needles and A, cast on 122 sts. Set patt for Welt as folls:

Row 1: (K2, P2), rep to last 2 sts, K2.
Row 2: (P2, K2), rep to last 2 sts, P2.
Rows 3 & 4: *Rep Rows 1 & 2.*
Row 5: (K2, P2, FC, BC, P2), rep to last 2 sts, K2.
Row 6: (P2, K3, P4, K3), rep to last 2 sts, P2.
Row 7: (K2, P3, C4F, P3), rep to last 2 sts, K2.
Row 8: As *Row 6*.
Row 9: (K2, P2, BC, FC, P2), rep to last 2 sts, K2.
Row 10: As *Row 2*.
Rep from *Rows 1–10* once more, then rep *Rows 1–9* again.

INCREASE ROW

WS facing, K10, (M1, K6) 17 times, end in M1, K10. (140 sts).

Change to 3¼mm (US 3) circular needles used as straight and set patt for Back.

NOTES ON BACK AND FRONT PATTERNING

The Back and Front are both patterned in the same way. They each have 2 Side Panels (*Pattern A*) and a Central Trellis Panel (*Pattern B*). Begin by working first Side Panel in *Pattern A* over 59 sts, then work Central Trellis Panel in *Pattern B*, over 22 sts, and end in second Side Panel in *Pattern A*, over 59 sts.

PATTERN A – MOSS ST (59 sts)
Pattern Row: K1, (P1, K1) rep to end, and rep each row.

PATTERN B – CENTRAL TRELLIS PANEL (22 sts)
Row 1: P1, K2, P2, K1, P4, C2F, P4, K1, P2, K2, P1.
Row 2 and all subsequent even rows in Patt B: K the P sts of previous row and P the K sts.
Row 3: P1, K2, P2, SFC, P2, SBC, SFC, P2, SBC, P2, K2, P1.
Row 5: P1, K2, P3, SFC, SBC, P2, SFC, SBC, P3, K2, P1.
Row 7: P1, K2, P4, C2F, P4, C2B, P4, K2, P1.
Row 9: P1, K2, P3, SBC, SFC, P2, SBC, SFC, P3, K2, P1.
Row 11: P1, K2, P2, SBC, P2, SFC, SBC, P2, SFC, P2, K2, P1.
Row 13: P1, K2, P2, K1, P4, C2B, P4, K1, P2, K2, P1.
Row 15: P1, K2, P2, SFC, P2, SBC, SFC, P2, SBC, P2, K2, P1.
Row 17: As *Row 5*.
Row 19: P1, K2, P4, C2B, P4, C2F, P4, K2, P1.
Row 21: As *Row 9*.

Row 23: As *Row 11*.
Row 24: As *Row 2*.

These 24 rows form the pattern repeat. Cont to work them with the Moss St Side Panels until work measures 40cm (15½″) from beg of Welt hem.

ARMHOLE SHAPING

Cont in patt, cast (bind) off 3 sts at beg of next 2 rows, 2 sts at beg of foll 2 rows, and 1 st at beg of foll 6 rows. (124 sts).**

Cont to work Back first as folls: cont in patt with no further dec until work measures 53cm (21″) from beg of Welt and 64 further rows have been completed. RS facing, beg to shape for Yoke.

YOKE SHAPING

In Moss St, work across 12 sts, then cast (bind) off 100 sts, then work in Moss St across rem 12 sts. Transfer the first 12 sts to a stitch holder and in Moss St work back across second group of 12 sts. Dec 4 sts at beg of next row, working in Moss St along next 8 sts, then dec 2 sts at beg of next 3 alt (every other) rows. Cast (bind) off rem sts. Return to first group of 12 sts, transfer these to the needle again, and complete Yoke, reversing shaping, working similarly.

FRONT

Work as for Back, until**is completed.

Referring to chart of Front Yoke, introduce inset intarsia patterning and Yoke shaping as shown. Read from right to left for RS (K) rows and from left to right for WS (P) rows in sequence, joining in colours as indicated and breaking off yarns not required.

PATTERNED YOKES

Foll charts carefully, make Front and Back Yokes separately. Cast on 8 sts for Front Yoke, cont to work from left to right, then from right to left across chart, matching increases. Cast on 100 sts for Back Yoke, working similarly and matching increases. Darn in all loose ends when completed, then with invisible seaming join together at shoulders so a circle is created. Press on WS with warm iron over damp cloth.

LOWER YOKE PIPING

Using 3¼mm (US 3) circular needles and **B**, beg at LH shoulder, RS facing, pick up evenly and K170 sts from along lower edge of Front Yoke, then cont along lower edge of Back Yoke in similar way making a further 144 sts. (314 sts). Working in rounds in st st, work 5 rounds then cast (bind) off. Turn this back and using slipstitch sew into place to form piped edge.

UPPER YOKE PIPING

Using 3¼mm (US 3) circular needles and **B**, beg with Front Yoke, RS facing, at LH side of central raised point as shown in chart. Pick up evenly and K39 sts along Front Yoke centre to shoulder, 110 sts along Back upper Yoke and 39 sts along upper Front Yoke. (188 sts).

Work 5 more rounds as before, then cast (bind) off. Turn back and make piped edge as shown earlier.

SLEEVES

Using 2¾mm (US 2) needles and **A**, cast on 50 sts. Set Cuff patt as shown for Welts. Rep the patt from **Rows 1–10** once more, then rep **Rows 1–9** again.

INCREASE ROW

WS facing, work inc row as folls:
(K2, M1), rep to last 2 sts, K2. (74 sts).

Change to 3¼mm (US 3) circular needles used as straight, and set Moss St Panels and Central Trellis Panel as folls:

Following **Pattern A** and **Pattern B**, set out Moss St over 26 sts, Trellis over 22 sts, Moss St over 26 sts. Cont in patt as set, but inc 1 st at beg and end of every 5th row, until 130 sts exist, and work measures 42cm (17″) from beg of Cuff.

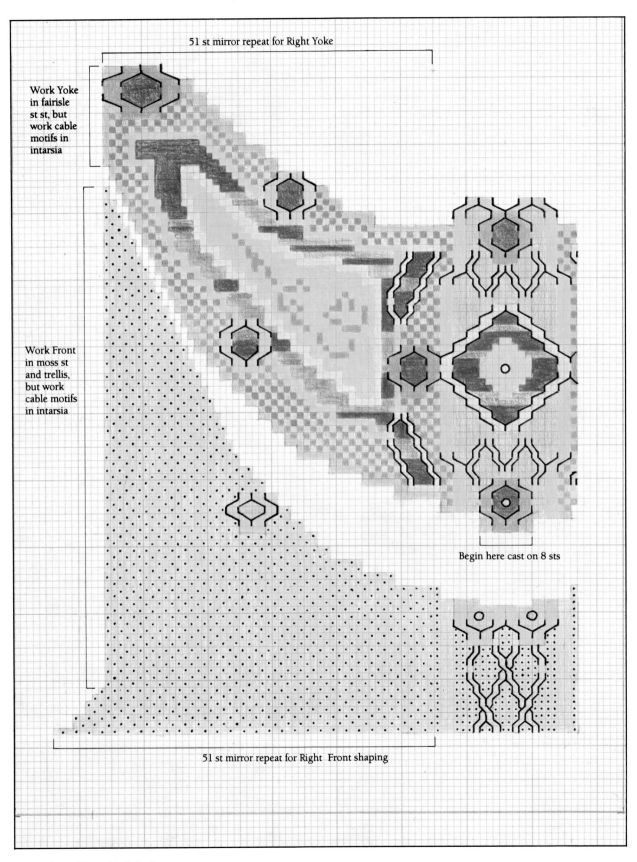

Work Yoke in fairisle st st, but work cable motifs in intarsia

51 st mirror repeat for Right Yoke

Work Front in moss st and trellis, but work cable motifs in intarsia

Begin here cast on 8 sts

51 st mirror repeat for Right Front shaping

Front Yoke and Front Neck shaping

SHAPE SLEEVE HEAD

Cast (bind) off 3 sts at beg of next 2 rows, 2 sts at beg of foll 2 rows, then 1 st at beg of each foll row until 68 sts rem. Cast (bind) off.

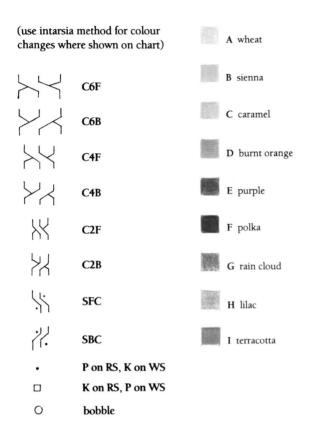

(use intarsia method for colour changes where shown on chart)

	C6F
	C6B
	C4F
	C4B
	C2F
	C2B
	SFC
	SBC
•	P on RS, K on WS
□	K on RS, P on WS
O	bobble

A	wheat
B	sienna
C	caramel
D	burnt orange
E	purple
F	polka
G	rain cloud
H	lilac
I	terracotta

MAKING UP AND FINISHING

Darn in all loose ends then press pieces on WS with warm iron over damp cloth, omitting ribbing. Using invisible seaming, join Yokes to Front and Back, aligning centres. Pin Sleeves into position, aligning centre of Trellis Panel to shoulder seams, matching armhole edges carefully and arranging Sleeve head gathers to form even folds at top of armhole and Yoke edge. Using backstitch sew firmly into place. Using backstitch for Moss and invisible seaming for rib, join Sleeve seams and side seams, then press all seams on WS with warm iron over damp cloth.

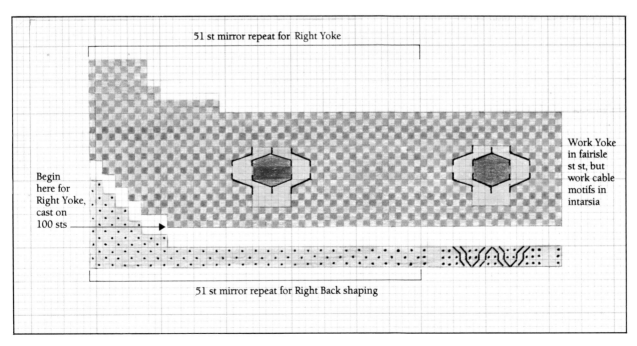

Back Yoke and Back Neck shaping

KELLS MOSAIC

(AD 600 – AD 800)

The claim that the Book of Kells contains proof that Aran knitting was well established by the ninth century led me next to the Library of Trinity College in Dublin.

This sumptuously decorated group of manuscripts, the culmination of the golden age of Christian culture in Ireland between the seventh and tenth centuries overflows with a wealth of richly coloured intricate patterns and ornamental texts. These patterns developed from the fusing of the curvilinear La Tène style with Saxon and Coptic art forms.

Ornamental text from the Book of Kells (folio 8R)

Fascinating as it was to discover the illustration of a figure wearing leggings and tunic decorated with a lattice work design, the assertion that this depicts Aran knitting can't really be taken seriously. Similar elaborate patterns embellish almost every motif in the manuscripts, including the animals, and don't necessarily reveal knitting expertise.

In fact, the earliest actual surviving example of true knitting on two needles rather than nalbinding, comes from Islamic Egypt and is dated as late as the twelfth century.

Although an earlier specimen, a tiny doll's hat only 5cm long dating from 1000 BC was found at al-Bahnasā in Egypt, this appears to have been made on a circular peg frame, rather than on knitting needles. These early knitting frames were made from wood and bone pegs, and produced a tubular fabric like the cotton reel 'French' knitting bobbins children use today. This method was continued by nomadic Arabs as they tended their flocks in the deserts.

Whether the Arabs developed the two needle method from the circular frames, or whether this technique was evolved by Coptic Christians from nalbinding at a much earlier date than medieval times is unclear, and can only be determined when relevant textiles are discovered.

Nevertheless, the Book of Kells remains a rich source of information on the costume of the period. As the Christian culture took root and flourished in Ireland, an increasingly complex structure of society had developed. An elaborate hierarchy had already evolved which established the Costume Laws requiring specific clothing to be worn to distinguish the aristocracy from the lower orders, a concept far removed from the austere simplicity of the earlier Christian hermits of the Aran Isles.

By this time, textiles were being produced and imported in such diversity of colours and patterns that the upper classes tried to impose a caste system of easily identifiable uniforms. Only kings and princes were permitted to wear seven colours simultaneously, and the number of colours allowed decreased according to rank. The peasants were only supposed to wear one colour, usually a drab brown or green.

Fortunately the illustrators of the Book of Kells didn't seem to feel it necessary to restrain their use of colour so strictly. Returning to the extraordinary subtlety and delicacy of their work, I couldn't resist trying to capture the mosaic of their soft glowing colours in this sweater in wools and silk.

MATERIALS

YARN

Jamieson & Smith 2 ply Jumper Weight Shetland Wool in the following colours and quantities

A	Jade Green (1293)	50g/2oz
B	Cream (FC43)	200g/7½oz
C	Burnt Orange (FC8)	50g/2oz
D	Gold (28)	100g/3¾oz
E	Burgundy (FC10)	50g/2oz
F	Pale Yellow (66)	150g/5½oz
G	Apricot (1281)	150g/5½oz
H	Brown (143)	50g/2oz
I	Pink (FC6)	25g/1oz
J	Emerald Green (FC11)	50g/2oz
K	Aquamarine Blue (FC39)	25g/1oz
L	Smoke Blue (FC52)	50g/2oz

Naturally Beautiful Aura 8/2 Silk

M	Gold (36)	50g/2oz

NEEDLES

1 pair 2¾mm (US 2) 100cm (39") circular needles
1 pair 3¼mm (US 3) 40cm (15½") circular needles
1 pair 3¼mm (US 3) 25cm (10") straight needles
2 pairs 3¼mm (US 3) spare circular needles
1 set of double pointed spare needles
2 stitch holders.

SIZE AND MEASUREMENTS

One size only to fit up to 101cm (40") bust

Actual width across back at underarm   56cm (22")

Length from centre back neck to hip   63cm (25")

Sleeve seam   50cm (20")

TENSION (GAUGE)

28 sts and 35 rows to 10cm (4") over st st on 3¼mm (US 3) needles or size needed to obtain this tension (gauge).

NOTES ON TECHNIQUES

In this sweater, the elaborately coloured bands of pattern are treated as 'knitted tapestry', while the interconnecting bands of plain knitting give the fabric structural strength and the knitter a rest from complex work. The techniques used are fairisle stranding, and intarsia with fairisle details.

When working the patterned areas in fairisle, carry colour not in use *very* loosely across the back of the work, weaving around the working yarn every 3rd st to avoid long floats and puckering.

When working the intarsia areas, use short lengths of yarn around 60cm (24") to avoid tangles, with separate lengths of yarn for each colour as shown on the chart. Twist yarn together at each join to avoid holes, then leave in position to be worked in next row. Knit in the ends as you work by wrapping them around the new colour thread for two or three sts

beyond where they were last used to minimise later darning in.

Where intarsia and fairisle methods are used in different areas of the same pattern band be extra careful not to pull work too tight.

WELT

Using 2¾mm (US 2) circular needles and A, cast on 312 sts, then work 1 round in K1, P1 rib. Change to B, then work in rib as set until Welt measures 9cm (3½"). Change to 3¼mm (US 3) circular needles and in C, work 2 rounds in st st.

BACK

Divide sts as folls: place 5 sts onto first stitch holder and leave. Transfer next 145 sts onto circular spare needle and leave. Place next 11 sts onto second stitch holder and leave. Transfer next 145 sts onto second spare needle to make Front later, then place rem 6 sts onto first stitch holder (11 sts). The 11 sts on each stitch holder will later form decorative side panels.

Now work Back as folls: using 3¼mm (US 3) circular needles as straight, work from charts from right to left for RS (K) rows and from left to right for WS (P) rows in sequence, joining in and breaking off different coloured yarns as indicated.

Begin with Chart 1. Work across the 145 sts for Back, working the 32 st rep 4 times, and across the 17 sts of 5th rep. Use fairisle, complete by finishing **Row 15** on a K row, RS of work, then work 'ridged band' as folls:

Keeping to colour and yarn sequence as shown in Chart 2, work:

Row 16: (WS) In **M**, P.
Rows 17 & 18: In **D**, K.
Row 19: In **F**, K.
Row 20: In **F**, P.
Rows 21 & 22: In **D**, K.
Row 23: In **M**, K.

Next, work Chart 3 patt with **F** and **G**, beg at 10th st of 42 st rep, using fairisle, work across the 145 sts of Back, repeating patt.

Next, work 2nd 'ridged band' from Chart 2, keeping same colour sequence, but altering stitch sequence as folls:

Row 31: (RS) In **M**, K.
Rows 32 & 33: In **D**, P.
Row 34: In **F**, P.
Row 35: In **F**, K.
Rows 36 & 37: In **D**, P.
Row 38: In **M**, P, end on WS.

Next, work 'ornamental text' patt band from Chart 4.
Beg on RS with a K row, work in intarsia generally, but where areas of same 2 or 3 colours are used in some quantity, work in fairisle.

Work 'ridged band' again, rep *Rows 16–23*, using colours and yarns as in Chart 2.

Next, work Chart 5 patt, using **F** & **G**, rep the 4 st patt in fairisle 36 times and first st of 37th rep across the 145 sts of Back over the 7 rows.

Next, work 'ridged band' again, using colours and yarns as in Chart 2 again, but stitch sequence from *Rows 31–38* again.

Next, work from Chart 6, beg with 2 rows in **C**, then working next 11 rows of 48 st rep 3 times, and first st of 4th rep in combination of fairisle and intarsia methods, as explained for Chart 4. Use **B** as background yarn to work in fairisle, introducing small lengths of yarn in new colours as required, working these in intarsia. End with 2 rows in **C**, on RS.

Next, rep *Rows 16–38* as before, for 'ridged band', fairisle patt, and 'ridged band' again.

ARMHOLE SHAPING

Cast (bind) off 1 st at beg and end of next row, leaving 143 sts, and working across 1st row of patt in Chart 7. Work Chart 7 in intarsia.

Next, rep *Rows 16–23* of 'ridged band'.
Next, rep Chart 5 fairisle patt again.
Next, rep *Rows 31–38* again for 'ridged band'.
Next, work from Chart 8, using intarsia generally, but fairisle for centres of diamonds.
Next, rep *Rows 16–23* of 'ridged band', then rep Chart 3 patt in fairisle.

DIVIDE FOR NECK

Knit 1 row in **M**, break of yarn, then turn work so RS faces and in **D**, K52 sts. Leave rem 91 sts on spare double pointed needle. Turn, WS facing, and in **D**, K2, K2tog, then K to end.

Next Row: In **F**, K to last 4 sts, K2tog, K2.
Next Row: In **F**, P2, P2tog, P to end.
Next Row: In **D**, K to last 4 sts, K2tog, K2.
Next Row: In **D**, K to end.
Cast (bind) off in **D**.
RS facing, slip 39 sts onto spare double pointed needle for Back neck.
In **D**, K rem 52 sts on first double-pointed needle with circular needle again.

Next Row: In **D**, K to last 4 sts, K2tog, K2.
Next Row: In **F**, K2, K2tog, K to end.
Next Row: In **F**, P to last 4 sts, P2tog, P2.
Next Row: In **D**, K2, K2tog, K to end.
Next Row: In **D**, K to end.
Cast (bind) off in **D**.

FRONT

Using 3¼mm (US 3) circular needles as straight, work as for Back until 13th row of Chart 8 has been worked.

DIVIDE FOR NECK

RS facing, in **C**, K56 sts. Slip next 87 sts onto spare double pointed needle and leave. Turn, and work the 56 sts as folls:
Next Row: In **C**, P2, P2tog, P to end.
Next Row: In **M**, K to last 4 sts, K2tog, K2.

Next Row: In **D**, P2, P2tog, P to end.
Next Row: In **D**, P to last 4 sts, P2tog, P2.
Next Row: In **F**, P2, P2tog, P to end.
Next Row: In **F**, K to last 4 sts, K2tog, K2.
Next Row: In **D**, P2, P2tog, P to end.
Next Row: In **D**, P to last 4 sts, P2 tog, P2.
Cont with no further dec, in patt to match Back, i.e. work Chart 3, then as *Rows 31–38*. In **D**, cast (bind) off.

Turn work and cont neck shaping as folls:

Beg at armhole edge, WS facing, in **C**, P56 sts. Leave rem 31 sts on spare double pointed needle for Front neck, turn, then cont as folls:

Next Row: RS facing, in **C**, K2, K2tog, K to end.
Next Row: In **M**, P to last 4 sts, P2tog, P2.
Next Row: In **D**, K2, K2tog, K to end.
Next Row: In **D**, K to last 4 sts, K2tog, K2.
Next Row: In **F**, K2, K2tog, K to end.
Next Row: In **F**, P to last 4 sts, P2tog, P2.
Next Row: In **D**, K2, K2tog, K to end.
Next Row: In **D**, K to last 4 sts, K2tog, K2.
Cont in patt to match other side with no further dec. In **D**, cast (bind) off.

A jade green

B cream

C burnt orange

D gold

E burgundy

F pale yellow

G apricot

H brown

I pink

J emerald green

K aquamarine blue

L smoke blue

M gold

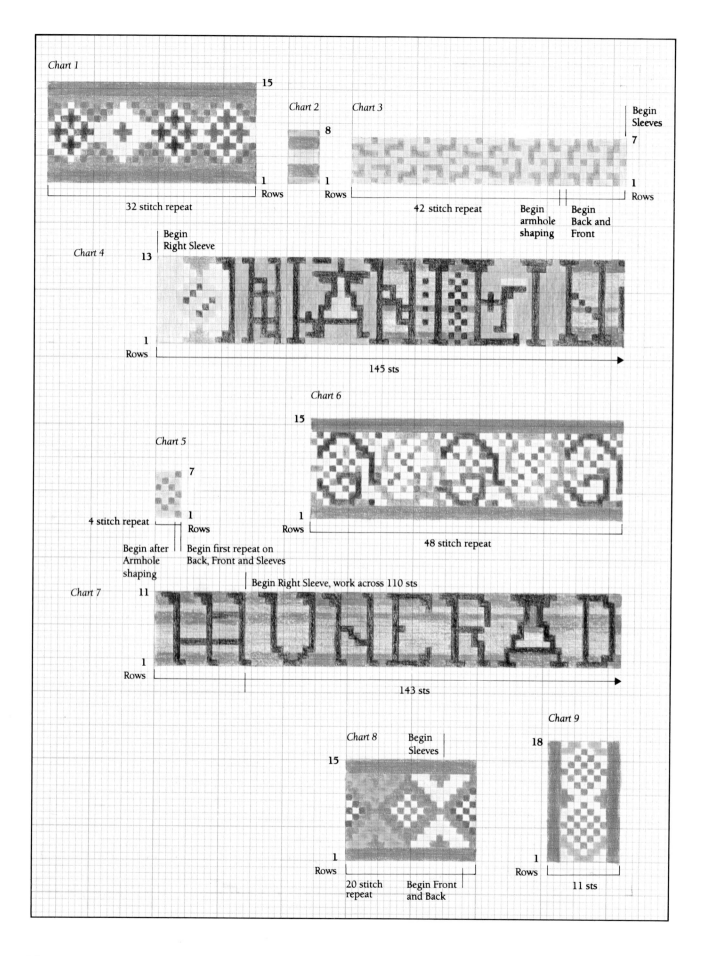

Chart 1

15

1

32 stitch repeat

Rows

Chart 2

8

1

Rows

Chart 3

Begin
Sleeves

7

1

Rows

42 stitch repeat

Begin
armhole
shaping

Begin
Back and
Front

Chart 4

Begin
Right Sleeve

13

1

Rows

145 sts

Chart 6

15

1

Rows

48 stitch repeat

Chart 5

7

1

Rows

4 stitch repeat

Begin after
Armhole
shaping

Begin first repeat on
Back, Front and Sleeves

Chart 7

Begin Right Sleeve, work across 110 sts

11

1

Rows

143 sts

Chart 8

Begin
Sleeves

15

1

Rows

20 stitch
repeat

Begin Front
and Back

Chart 9

18

1

Rows

11 sts

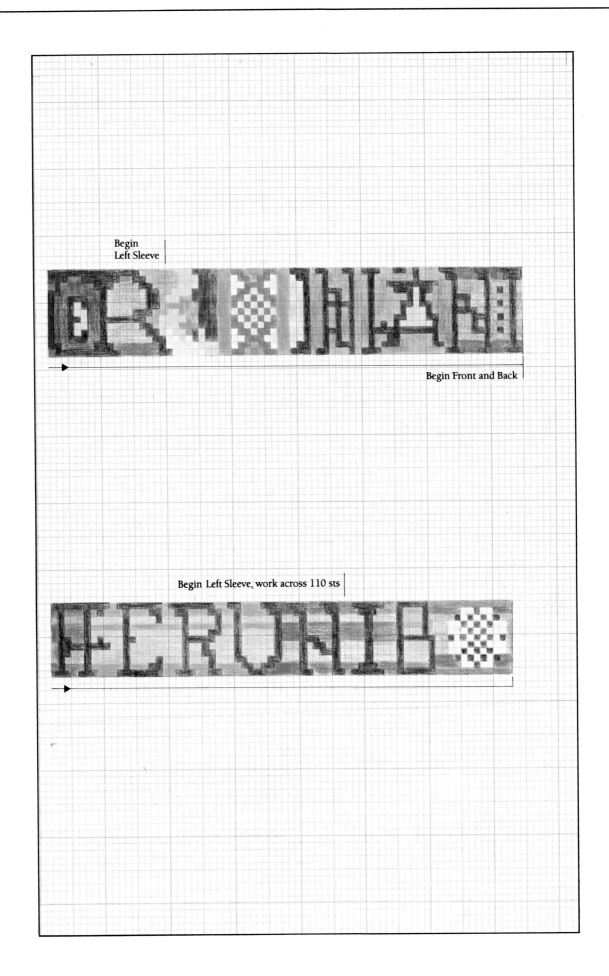

Begin
Left Sleeve

Begin Front and Back

Begin Left Sleeve, work across 110 sts

NECKBAND

Using backstitch, join shoulder seams. Using 2¾mm (US 2) circular needles and **C**, RS facing, K across the 39 sts from spare needle to make Back neck. Pick up evenly and K26 sts from right Front neck, 31 sts from spare needle for Front neck, and 26 sts from left Front neck. (122 sts). In **C**, K second round. Change to **B**, then in K1, P1 single rib, work a further 7 rounds. Change to **A**, rib 1 round, then cast (bind) off in **A** ribwise.

SIDE PANELS (Make 2)

Using 3¼mm (US 3) straight needles, work the 11 st patt from Chart 9 from the 11 sts on the stitch holders. Work in fairisle until 6 reps of patt have been completed. Leave sts on stitch holders again, then using invisible seaming attach Side panels to Front and Back sides to form body of garment.

SLEEVES

Using 3¼mm (US 3) circular needles as straight and **C**, pick up evenly and K130 sts, beg at centre of sts on stitch holder

(i.e. after 5 sts), working up armhole and down Back armhole edge, incorporating last 6 sts from the stitch holder. Work 2 rows in **C**, then cont in patt from Chart 8 at starting point indicated, but every 5th row, dec 1 st at beg and end of row until 90 sts exist. Cont to work in patt, but work 'upside down' as shown, so designs match main body. Cont in this way until Chart 4 has been completed. Work 1 more 'ridged band' patt, then 2 rows of st st in **C**. In **B**, work 1 row in st st, then in **B**, dec sts as folls:

WS facing, P1, P2tog to end. Change to 2¾mm (US 2) circular needles used as straight and work in **B** in K1, P1 single rib. In **B**, cont in single rib until Cuff measures 9cm (3½"). Change to **A**, work 1 row in single rib, then cast (bind) off in **A**, ribwise.

MAKING UP AND FINISHING

Darn in any loose ends. Using backstitch for st st and invisible seaming for ribbing, join Sleeve seams. Press all seams on WS with warm iron over damp cloth, then turn to RS and press similarly, omitting ribbing.

DUBLIN SILVER

(AD 800–AD 1171)

In 795, the peaceful flowering of Christian culture in Ireland was shattered by the invasion of the Vikings. Raiders from western Norway attacked the monasteries and established a chain of bases along the Irish coast. These were to develop into wealthy trading centres ideally placed in the extensive network of trade routes which stretched from Scandinavia and northern Europe, along the Atlantic seaboards and into the Middle East.

Dublin was founded in this way in the ninth century, and became a major centre for the silver trade. Here, Scandinavian craftsmen transformed imported Moorish silver coins into the stylish jewellery that can now be seen in the National Museum in Dublin. The 104 separate hoards and 150 single finds of Irish silver demonstrate the wealth that this trade created.

The Viking metalworkers brought with them their own styles which inevitably influenced Irish art forms. The first of these, the Jellinge style, appears on bossed silver brooches of the late tenth century and favours animals and entwining disjointed ribbons. The Ringervike style followed in the late eleventh century featuring interlacing plant motifs with free ending lobed tendrils. Finally, the Urns style of writhing intertwining serpents followed, and was perfected in a more disciplined form in such treasures as the Cross of Cong.

The Viking settlement towns were frequently raided by the Irish, and the following contemporary description of the booty they carried off from Limerick reveals their wealth, and the diversity of textiles available at this time. They took:

> 'their jewels, their saddles beautiful and foreign, their gold and silver, their beautifully woven cloth of all colours and kinds, their satins and silken cloths pleasing and variegated both scarlet and green.'

This cloth had been disseminated from the orient with the spread of Islam during the seventh century, and by the time of the first Viking invasions of Ireland, textiles from the ancient silk centres of the east had reached Europe.

It is possible that towards the end of this period of Viking invasion and settlement, among their imports knitted goods from Egypt or Arabia could have arrived in Ireland. But the earliest surviving examples of Egyptian knitting are all in stranded coloured patterns, and totally different from the raised relief Aran designs I'd come to investigate. Instead, clues to the development of this knitting style seemed to lie more clearly in the elaborately carved High Crosses which developed at this time.

During this period, stone had become the focus of artistic expression. The Church began to build the conspicuous Round Towers as look-out posts and places of refuge, and the High Crosses became symbols of a threatened religion they were determined would not easily be destroyed by the invading barbarians. The interlace patterns which decorated many of them continued the ancient design forms which by now had become architypical of Irish art, and which were to reappear later in Aran knitting.

By 1014, the Vikings were finally defeated at the Battle of Clontarf by Brian Bóroimhe (Boru), High King of Ireland. Intermarrying and converting to Christianity, they began to integrate more fully into Irish society, and their vigorous art became another strand in the pattern of Irish culture.

Although during the next 150 years the perpetual dynastic power struggles among the Irish Kings continued, the country was at least free from foreign invasion.

I was inspired by the impressive collection of Viking silver jewellery in the National Museum, and made this luxurious jacket in mohair, wool and silk to try to capture its textures.

MATERIALS

YARN

Kilcarra Mohair in the following colours and quantities

A	Pale Grey (98)	5 × 50g/9oz
B	Dark Grey (99)	5 × 50g/9oz
C	White (20)	1 × 50g/2oz

Jamieson & Smith 2 Ply Jumper Weight Wool

D	Natural Grey	4 × 50g/7¼oz

Naturally Beautiful Aura 8/2 silk

E	Silver (P72)	150g/5½oz

NEEDLES

1 pair 4mm (US 6) 100cm (39") circular needles
1 pair 4mm (US 6) 100cm (39") spare circular needles
1 cable needle

TRIMMINGS (NOTIONS)

4 × 3cm (1½") mother of pearl buttons in dark smoke grey

SIZE AND MEASUREMENTS

One size only to fit up to 96cm (38") bust

Actual width across back at underarm   51cm (20")

Length from centre back neck to hip   60cm (24")

Sleeve seam   43cm (17")

TENSION (GAUGE)

30 sts and 30 rows to 10cm (4") over pattern on 4mm (US 6) needles or size needed to obtain this tension.

NOTES ON TECHNIQUE

This jacket uses a variety of techniques and stitches as indicated in chart. Cabling, garter stitch, bobbles and intarsia motifs all combine to create a richly textured fabric.

When joining in contrast yarns as indicated, use short lengths (60cm, 24") to avoid tangling, but leave long enough ends to darn in neatly later, after using a colour not required for some time. Work can be neatened by darning in ends after every 10cm (4") or so, and ends can be wrapped around the new colour thread for two or three sts beyond where they were last used, to minimise later darning in, but *not* over cabled areas. Twist yarns together at each join to avoid holes, then leave in position to be worked in next row.

Back, Sleeves and 2 halves of Front are all made in one piece, with Welt, Cuffs and Collar added later.

SPECIAL ABBREVIATIONS

C6F   Sl 3 sts onto cable needle, hold at front, K3, then K3 from cable needle.

MB4   (K1 into front and back of next st) twice, making 4 sts from 1, (turn and K4 sts, turn and P4 sts) twice, then using LH needle, lift 2nd, 3rd and 4th sts over 1 st st and off needle. When working MB4, push completed bobble through to RS if worked on a WS row, and when darning in later, sew firmly into position, securing it invisibly onto RS.

BACK, SLEEVES AND FRONT

Begin at base of Back. Using 4mm (US 6) circular needles as straight and **D**, cast on 155 sts. Work from chart reading from right to left for RS (K) rows and from left to right for WS (P) rows where applicable. Work across **Row 1** of 42 st patt rep 3 times, then across first 29 sts of patt rep again. Rep 80 rows of patt in this way, then recommence patt at **Row 1** again, work in patt as set until **Row 10** of second patt rep has been worked and **Row 90** has been completed.

SLEEVE SHAPING

Row 91: In **D**, cast on 12 sts. Working to patt to set, incorporate new sts into patt and work across **Row 91** to end.

Cont to inc 12 sts at beg of each row in this way to form Sleeves until 8 inc each side have been worked and 347 sts exist.

Rows 107 & 108: Inc 9 sts at beg of each row, (365 sts), then cont working in patt until second rep has been completed with no further inc.

DIVIDE FOR NECK

Beg at **Row 1** of third patt rep, work across 155 sts, then transfer these sts onto spare needle. Cast (bind) off next 55 sts, then work in patt across rem 155 sts. Cont to work on these 155 sts in third patt rep until **Row 53** of patt (actual **Row 213**) has been completed.

RIGHT SLEEVE SHAPING

Next Row: Dec 9 sts at beg of row, work in patt to end.

New Row: Work in patt with no dec.

Cont dec 12 sts at beg of foll 8 alt (every other) rows until 50 sts remain.

RIGHT FRONT

Work rem rows of third patt rep with no further dec, then complete 80 rows of last (fourth) patt rep. Cast (bind) off.

LEFT SLEEVE AND LEFT FRONT

Using 4mm (US 6) needles as straight, work across 155 sts from spare needle. Join in new yarns as needed, then work in patt beg at **Row 2** of third patt rep (actual **Row 162**) until actual **Row 212** has been completed.

LEFT SLEEVE SHAPING

Beg Sleeve shaping on next row as shown for first Sleeve, dec at outer edge on alt (every other) rows until 50 sts remain. Work left Front on 50 sts as for right Front, cast (bind) off.

CUFFS

Using 4mm (US 6) circular needles as straight and **A**, RS facing, pick up evenly and K36 sts from Sleeve edge at wrist. Set next row in K1, P1 single rib, rib 21 rows then cast (bind) off.

WELT

Using backstitch, join underarm Sleeve seams down to waist edge. Using 4mm (US 6) circular needles as straight and **A**, RS facing, pick up evenly and K127 sts from along right Front, Back and left Front edges. Set K1, P1 single rib, rib 21 rows, then cast (bind) off.

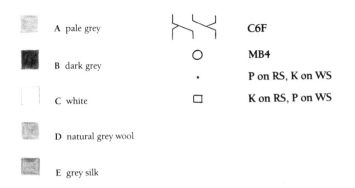

A pale grey

B dark grey

C white

D natural grey wool

E grey silk

C6F

MB4

. P on RS, K on WS

□ K on RS, P on WS

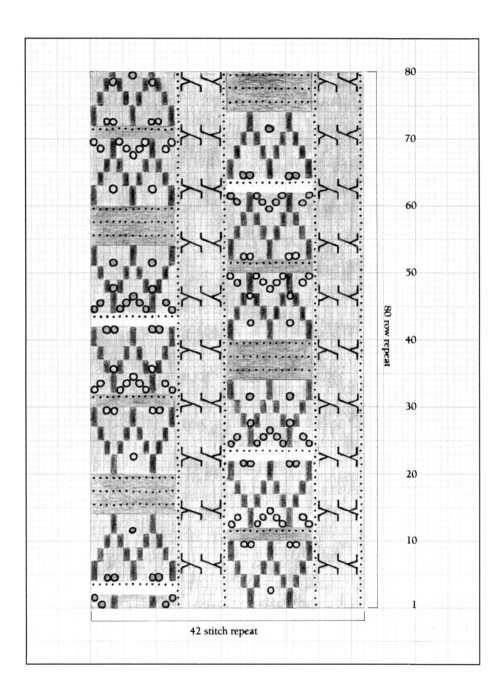

42 stitch repeat

80 row repeat

COLLAR

Using 4mm (US 6) circular needles as straight and A, RS facing, beg at lower edge of Welt, pick up evenly and K156 sts from left Front side (including Welt) until neck is reached. Cont to pick up and K55 sts from across Back neck, and 156 sts from right Front and Welt side. (367 sts.) Work in same K1, P1 rib for 14 rows, then work buttonholes as folls:

Row 15: (Left Front adjoining) RS facing, rib 6, rib 2 tog, rib 28, rib 2 tog, rib to end.
Row 16: Rib across all sts to buttonholes, leave yarn aside. Join in new small ball of A, work across next 28 sts in this rib, leave yarn aside again, join in new small ball of A, rib across last rem sts in this.
Rows 17–19: Work across sections in rib with separate balls of A to make buttonholes, leaving gaps where buttons come through.

Row 20: Close buttonholes as folls: Using original ball of A again, rib 7, inc 1 st across first buttonhole, rib 28, inc 1 st across second buttonhole, rib across rem sts to end.
Rows 21–34: Rib.
Rows 35–40: As *Rows 15–20*.
Rows 41–53: Rib.
Cast (bind) off ribwise.

MAKING UP AND FINISHING

Darn in all loose ends and press seams lightly on WS with warm iron over damp cloth. Sew on 4 buttons at appropriate positions. Fold over collar, but do not press.

HERALD

(1171–1500)

The power struggles between the rulers of the various kingdoms within Ireland continued until 1171 when Rory O'Connor, the last High King, was deposed. In a plot by Dermot Macmurragh, another contender to the Irish throne, in alliance with Henry II of Norman England and ambitious Welsh barons, the country was once again invaded.

All over the land, castles sprang up to defend the invaders against the continual attacks from clansmen of the dispossessed former Irish chieftains. But during the next three centuries, Irish resistance against the Anglo-Normans persisted.

Dunguaire Castle, Kinvarra

Typical of the continuing opposition was the recruitment of the 'galloglass' – Gaelic mercenaries from Scotland who were settled in Ireland to attack the colonised towns, already weakened by the Black Death's toll on their Norman inhabitants. But in the end, it was the ability of the Irish to absorb the invading foreigners into their own way of life as they had done with the Vikings earlier, by intermarriage and by encouraging them to adopt Irish dress and customs, that ensured the continuing development of the indigenous culture.

Inevitably, the Anglo-Norman rule brought its own changes, and it was during this period that sheep-rearing became a major activity, replacing cattle-raising and flax growing in importance, until wool production became one of Ireland's main exports. Although clothing at this time was still made from woven linen and wool, with small amounts of imported silk for the wealthy, it was during the thirteenth and fourteenth centuries that hand-knitting began to develop more widely in Europe, and so eventually became established in Ireland.

Evidence of hand-knitting on two, four or more needles as we know it today, in many different colours and showing knowledge of plain, and perhaps purl stitches began to emerge not only in Egypt, but also in Europe. Purses, stockings, cushions, caps and Bishop's liturgical gloves decorated in knitted lace all show how far the technique had evolved by this time. Particularly interesting are the knitted cushions from Burgos in northern Spain, which are decorated in a variety of heraldic designs and Arabic inscriptions. They may indicate the route knitting took in its spreading out into Europe from Egypt and Arabia with the expansion of Islam.

As there are no surviving examples of knitting in Ireland from this period, it is unclear whether the technique had yet reached the country. In many places the new skills were to become closely guarded secrets, and although knitted goods were traded, their method of construction remained a mystery to the uninitiated outside the newly forming knitting guilds. It seems most unlikely that Aran knitting had yet begun. However, knitted items may have reached Ireland with returning English knights from the Crusades.

I designed this lively patterned sweater to recall this age of knights and battles in Irish history. Each motif represents emblems of Ireland's heritage – crosses for Christianity, fish, shells and waves for the surrounding sea, armorial devices, and castles which still dominate the landscape today.

MATERIALS

Rowan DK (Lightweight) (Knitting Worsted) Wool

A	Navy (54)	4 × 25g/7¼oz
C	Royal Blue (56)	2 × 25g/2oz
	Bright Orange (17)	1 × 25g/1oz
	Lemon Yellow (12)	1 × 25g/1oz
	Apricot (14)	1 × 25g/1oz
D	Scarlet (42)	1 × 25g/1oz
	Turquoise (55)	1 × 25g/1oz
	Violet Blue (501)	1 × 25g/1oz
	Pale Blue (48)	1 × 25g/1oz
	Burgundy (70)	1 × 25g/1oz
	Burnt Orange (403)	1 × 25g/1oz
	Coral (25)	1 × 25g/1oz
	Petrol Blue (108)	1 × 25g/1oz
	Silver Grey (47)	1 × 25g/1oz
	Golden Yellow (13)	1 × 25g/1oz
	Light Blue (51)	1 × 25g/1oz
	Peach (22)	1 × 25g/1oz
	Pale Apricot (402)	1 × 25g/1oz

Rowan Fleck DK (Knitting Worsted) Wool

B	Blue Mix (56F)	8 × 50g/14½oz

NEEDLES

1 pair 3¼mm (US 3) 40cm (15½") circular needles
1 pair 4mm (US 6) 60cm (24") circular needles
1 set of double pointed spare needles
2 stitch holders
Cable needle

SIZE AND MEASUREMENTS

One size only to fit up to 112cm (44") bust

Actual width across back at underarm   61cm (24")

Length from centre back neck to hip   67cm (26½")

Sleeve seam   46cm (18")

TENSION (GAUGE)

18 sts and 28 rows to 10cm (4") over Moss St on 4mm (US 6) needles or size needed to obtain this tension (gauge).

NOTES ON TECHNIQUES

This sweater is made in a variety of techniques – moss stitch cabling, bobbles, intarsia and fairisle to create an interesting texture.

Intarsia: Use this for all the motifs except the Heraldic Waves design. Work from chart, introducing new colours as specified. Use only short lengths of yarn for each colour to avoid tangling. Twist yarns together at each join to avoid holes, then leave in position to be worked in next row. Knit the ends in as you work by wrapping them around the new colour thread for two or three sts beyond where they were last used to minimise later darning in.

When working intarsia motifs, read from right to left for RS (knit) rows and from left to right for WS (purl) rows in sequence.

Fairisle: Use this for Heraldic Waves design. Read chart from right to left for RS (knit) rows and from left to right for WS (purl) rows, introducing new colours as specified, again using only short lengths of yarn. Carry colours not in use *very* loosely across back of work to avoid long floats and puckering.

Moss St: Work background in Moss St as shown in chart, but remembering to work areas immediately next to coloured motifs in st st to avoid ugly 2-colour joins where indicated in chart.

SPECIAL ABBREVIATIONS

C4F Sl 2 sts onto cable needle, hold at front, K2, then K2 from cable needle. In this sweater, work these cables using intarsia, *not* fairisle, or the Welt will be too rigid in texture.

MB3 These decorative bobbles are easier to knit separately and sew into position to obtain perfect placing in the garment. Make as folls: Using colour required and 4mm (US 6) needles, cast on 3 sts. **Row 1** K1, P1, K1. **Row 2** P3. **Row 3** P2, then sl first st on RH needle over centre st on LH needle, P1, then sl first st on RH needle over remaining st. Sl yarn through last st leaving enough to sew bobble onto garment.

BACK

In this sweater, no armhole shaping is necessary, as shaping is provided by adding cabled side panels.

Begin with Border. Using 4mm (US 6) circular needles as straight and A, cast on 100 sts. Work from chart, using intarsia where necessary, working in st st until *Row 19* has been completed. Do not change needles, but make *Body area* next. Change to B, WS facing, P1 row.

Row 21: Set patt of Moss St as shown, working P and K sts as indicated in chart. Cont to work Moss St background in B, and motifs in st st in colours as shown, until *Row 171* has been completed. Do not work bobbles at this stage, work in Moss St where they will later be sewn on.

DIVIDE FOR NECK

Row 172: Work 36 sts in Moss St, then transfer rem 64 sts onto spare double pointed needle. Turn and dec 1 st at inside neck edge, Moss St to end of row.

Next Row: Moss St to neck edge, dec 1 st. Cast (bind) off. Leave 28 sts at centre Back neck as shown in chart on spare double pointed needle. Work other shoulder similarly. Cast (bind) off.

FRONT

Work as for Back until **Row 145** has been completed.

DIVIDE FOR NECK

Row 146: Work across 41 sts, transfer rem 59 sts to spare double pointed needle. Turn and work 2 rows as shown in chart.
Row 149: Cast (bind) off 2 sts at beg of row, Moss St to end.
Rows 150–152: Moss St.
Row 153: Cast (bind) off 2 sts at beg of row, Moss St to end.
Row 154–156: Work in patt.
Row 157: Cast (bind) off 2 sts at beg of row, work in patt.
Rows 158–160: Work in patt.
Row 161: Dec 1 st at neck edge, work in patt.
Rows 162–164: Work in patt.
Row 165: Dec 1 st at neck edge, work in patt. Cont in **B** in Moss St until 175 rows have been completed as shown in chart. Leave 18 sts on spare needle for Front neck, then work other shoulder similarly. Cast (bind) off.

SLEEVES

Using 4mm (US 6) circular needles as straight and **A**, cast on 58 sts. Work Border as shown in chart, then work main area of Sleeve, inc 1 st at beg and end of each 9th row as shown until 82 sts exist and **Row 111** has been completed. Cast (bind) off along **Row 112**.

NECKBAND

Using backstitch, join shoulder seams, then work as folls:

Using 3¼mm (US 3) circular needles as straight and **A**, RS facing, K 28 sts from needle at Back neck, pick up and K4 sts from left Back neck, 23 sts from right Front neck, 18 sts from needle at Front neck, 23 sts from left Front neck, and 4 sts from right Back neck. (100 sts.) P 1 row in **A**, then K 1 row in **D**, then P 1 row in **A**. RS facing, work cable patt as folls: using intarsia with separate balls of contrast yarn, *not* fairisle.

Row 1: (In **A**, P2, K2, P2; in **C**, K4), rep 9 more times.
Row 2: (In **A**, P4; in **C**, K2, P2, K2), rep 9 more times.
Rows 3 & 4: As *Rows 1 & 2*.
Row 5: (In **A**, P2, K2, P2; in **C**, C4F), rep 9 more times.
Row 6: As *Row 2*.
Rep *Rows 3–6* once more, then cast (bind) off.

SIDE PANELS (Make 2)

Using 3¼mm (US 3) circular needles as straight and **A**, cast on 14 sts. Work patt using separate balls of yarn and intarsia as folls:

Row 1: In **A**, P1, K2, P2, in **C**, K4; in **A**, P2, K2, P1.
Row 2: In **A**, K1, P2, K2; in **C**, P4; in **A**, K2, P2, K1.
Rows 3 & 4: As *Rows 1 & 2*.
Row 5: In **A**, P1, K2, P2; in **C**, C4F; in **A**, P2, K2, P1.
Rep *Rows 2–5* 33 more times. Cast (bind) off.

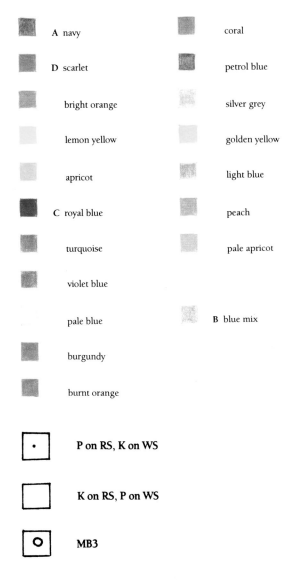

A navy	coral
D scarlet	petrol blue
bright orange	silver grey
lemon yellow	golden yellow
apricot	light blue
C royal blue	peach
turquoise	pale apricot
violet blue	
pale blue	**B** blue mix
burgundy	
burnt orange	

- ▫ with dot: **P on RS, K on WS**
- ▫ blank: **K on RS, P on WS**
- ▫ with o: **MB3**

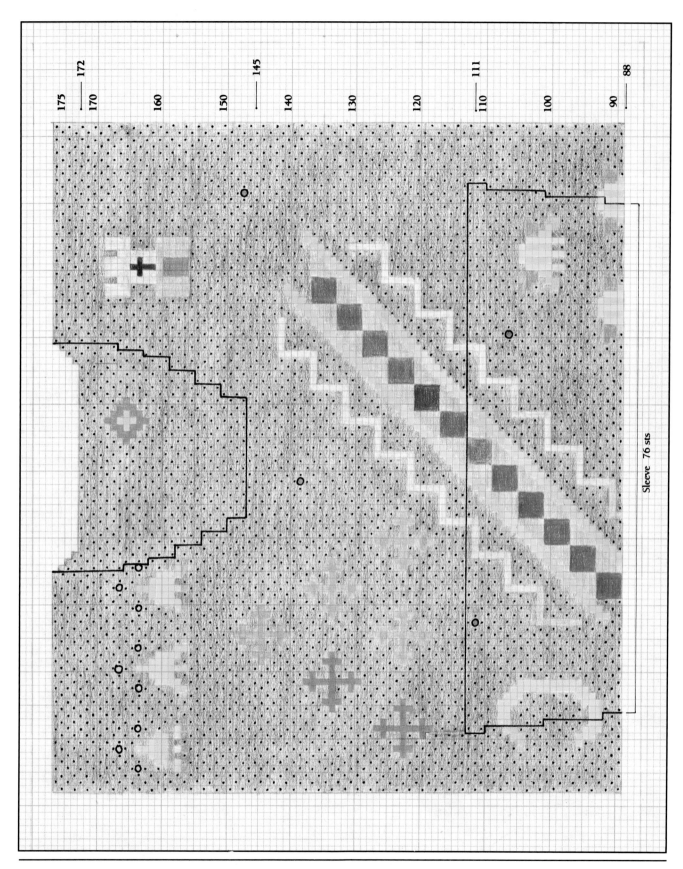

Upper half of Front, Back and Sleeve

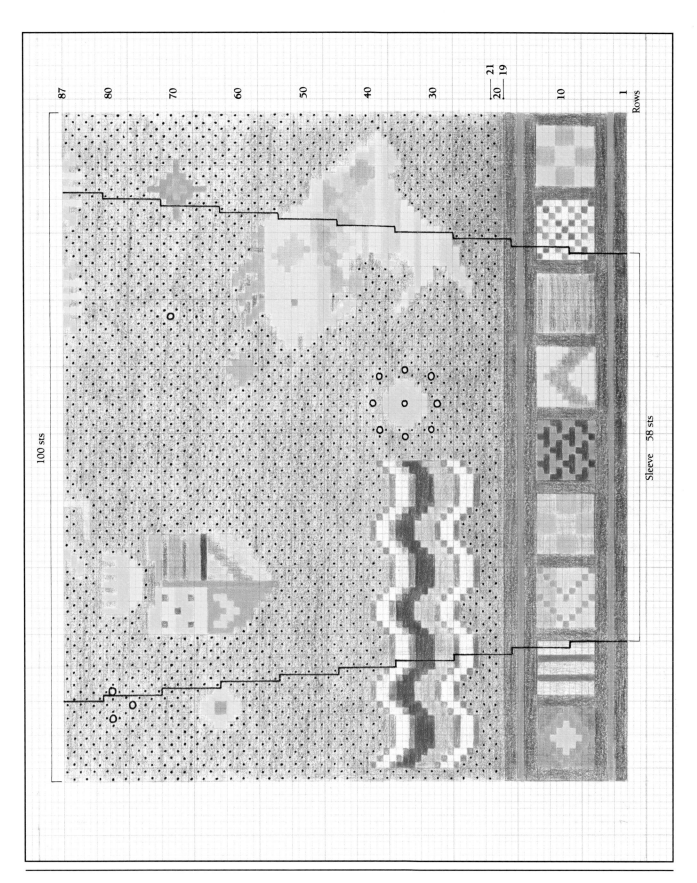

Lower half of Front, Back and Sleeve

WELTS

Using 3¼mm (US 3) circular needles as straight and A, RS facing, pick up evenly and K98 sts from lower edge of Back Border. Set cable patt as folls, using intarsia, not fairisle, with separate balls of yarn for each colour.

Row 1: In A, P2, (In C, K4; in A, P2, K2, P2), rep 8 more times, then in C, K4; in A, P2.
Row 2: In A, K2. (In C, P4; in A, K2, P2, K2), rep 8 more times, then in C, P4; in A, K2.
Rows 3 & 4: As *Rows 1 & 2*.
Row 5: In A, P2. (In C, C4F; in A, P2, K2, P2), rep 8 more times, then in C, C4F; in A, P2.
Rep *Rows 2–5* five more times, then cast (bind) off in patt. Work Front Welt similarly.

CUFFS

Using 3¼mm (US 3) circular needles as straight and A, pick up evenly and K60 sts from Sleeve Border edge at wrist. Work cable patt next as folls:
Break off yarn, turn, rejoin yarn RS facing.

Row 1: (In A, P2, K2, P2; in C, K4), rep 5 more times.
Row 2: (In C, P4; in A, K2, P2, K2), rep 5 more times.
Rows 3 & 4: As Rows 1 & 2.
Row 5: (In A, P2, K2, P2; in C, C4F), rep 5 more times.
Rep *Rows 2–5* five more times. Cast (bind) off.

MAKING UP AND FINISHING

Darn in all loose ends. Using invisible seaming, join Side Panels to edges of Back and Front to form armhole recesses. Using backstitch, join Sleeves to body, then using backstitch for Moss St and invisible seaming for ribbing, join Sleeve seams and Neckband seam.

Press seams on WS with warm iron over damp cloth, but do not press rest of sweater.

YEARS OF OPPRESSION
(1500–1850)

I found the following 350 years of Irish history with its seemingly endless succession of tragic events too heart-breaking to inspire any garments for my collection. Foreign occupation by the English and the consequent political oppression, religious fanaticism and punitive massacres culminating in the horrific years of famines and mass emigration of the 1840s were not conducive to creative design.

These events delayed the development of hand-knitting in Ireland, and its progress there was much slower than in England and the rest of western Europe. Irish crafts did not really begin to flower again until their re-emergence in parallel with the growth of Irish political freedom in the nineteenth century.

Although as early as 1576 English hand-knitted stockings were being imported to Dublin, it was not until 1620 that descriptions of Irish made hand-knitted stockings appear. And the Irish were understandably reluctant to adopt new English fashions such as the knitted caps introduced by the hated Protestant settlers.

Further development of Irish hand-knitting on an industrial scale was crushed by the English with the 1699 protectionist Woollen Export Act. This prohibited the export of Irish woollen goods to anywhere other than England, causing Irish manufacturers to emigrate to America, taking with them their skills and capital.

However, with the repeal of the act in 1780, by the late eighteenth century communal hand-knitting sessions where the knitters sang as they worked together in the open air had become part of Irish rural life. The items made on these occasions were usually hosiery, and the curious 'soleless stockings' – 'máirtíní' – worn by country girls working on waterlogged peat can be traced to these origins.

By the nineteenth century, hosiery knitting as a cottage industry had become established in rural and coastal areas such as Glenties and Ardara in Co. Donegal, Portlaw in Co. Waterford, Ballina in Co. Mayo, Birr in Co. Offaly and the Aran Isles.

During the 1830s the first knitting pattern books were published and these contributed greatly to the spread of hand-knitting techniques. These skills were also beginning to be taught at convents, along with sewing, crochet, lace-making, embroidery and weaving, to school children. By 1835 it had become socially acceptable for the middle classes to knit for pleasure, as well as a moral virtue, as opposed to the supplementing of meagre subsistence incomes by poor country people. After the famine of the 1840s, it was increasingly the contribution of the Church, and later, in 1891 that of the government-established philanthropic Congested Districts Boards which played such a vital part of the renaissance of Irish crafts, and so prepared the way for Aran knitting as an industry.

CARRICKMACROSS
(1820–1897)

During the nineteenth century, many altruistic schemes were initiated by the famine relief committees to try to create paid work that poor women could do at home while caring for their children. Lace-making, previously an occupation of wealthy artistic ladies of leisure, was considered ideal for this purpose. Bobbin lace, crochet lace and appliqué lace were all developed, with lace knitting from Scotland eventually reaching Ireland and influencing Aran knitting.

The earliest of all the many lace-making schools in Ireland was founded in 1820 by Mrs Grey Porter, wife of the Rector of Donaghmoyne. She developed the Italian craft of appliqueing net with cambric motifs – not really a true lace, but a very attractive type of delicate embroidery – and began to teach the skill in her neighbourhood. The cambric was easily obtainable from the linen centre of the north, and the skill of 'sprigging' – a dainty embroidery on linen – was already established in the area. Before long, the sale of the lace products began to prevent the emigration of the pupils, and so the school grew rapidly, moving to new premises and in time adding Guipure lace-making to the curriculum. In 1897 it was taken over by the nuns at the Convent of St Louis at Carrickmacross, who today still continue to teach the craft and export lace all over the world.

Sister Cronin, from the convent of St Louis, showing a hand-appliquéd lace wedding veil made by the nuns

Convents such as this did much to revise and develop needlecrafts in Ireland, and at the Carrickmacross convent, hand knitting was among other crafts taught to the school children, often using the newly published pattern books.

When I visited the convent searching for the beginnings of Aran knitting, I noticed a nun diligently crocheting in a quiet corner. Her work inspired this lady-like design with a knitted lace collar similar to the crochet she was making.

MATERIALS

YARN

Twilleys 'Bubbly' Cotton in Ecru (21)
8 × 50g/14¼oz

Anchor Pearl Cotton No 5 in White
1 × 10g/½oz

NEEDLES

1 pair 2mm (US 0) 25cm (10″) straight needles
1 pair 2¾mm (US 2) 60cm (24″) circular needles
1 pair 3¼mm (US 3) 35cm (14″) straight needles
1 set of double pointed spare needles
1 cable needle

SIZE AND MEASUREMENTS

In one size only to fit up to 112cm (44″)

Actual width across back at underarm   58cm (23″)

Length from centre back neck to hip   60cm (24″)

Sleeve seam   37cm (14½″)

TENSION (GAUGE)

26 sts and 36 rows to 10cm (4″) over st st on 3¼mm (US 3) needles or size needed to obtain this tension (gauge).

SPECIAL ABBREVIATIONS

C4F Sl 2 sts onto cable needle, hold at front, K2, then K2 from cable needle

M1   Make 1 st by picking up loop between sts from row below and knitting it TBL

LACE ABBREVIATIONS FOR COLLAR

YRN Make 1 st by winding yarn round needle between 2 purl sts

SL 1 SL 1 st from LH needle over to RH needle without knitting or purling it

MB   Make a bobble by K1, P1, K1 into next st without dropping loop of original st, turn, P4 sts just made, turn, (K2tog) twice, sl first st over second st

PSSO Pass slipped st over

BACK

Using 2¾mm (US 2) circular needles as straight and Twilleys 'Bubbly' cotton cast on 152 sts. Set patt for Welt as folls:

Row 1: (P2, K4), rep 25 times, P2.
Row 2: (K2, P4), rep 25 times, K2.

Rows 3 & 4: As *Rows 1 & 2*.
Row 5: (P2, C4F), rep 25 times, P2.
Row 6: As *Row 2*.
Rep **Rows 1–6** until Welt measures 14cm (5¾″).
Change to 3¼mm (US 3) needles, then work in st st until Back measures 36cm (14¼″) from beg of Welt.

SHAPE ARMHOLES

Cast (bind) off 10 sts at beg of next 2 rows, 4 sts at beg of foll 2 rows, then 2 sts at beg of foll 8 rows (108 sts).** Cont in st st until work measures 59cm (23½″).

DIVIDE FOR NECK

RS facing, K41 sts, then transfer these to spare needle. Cast (bind) off 26 sts, then K41 sts.

SHAPE SHOULDERS

Turn and P41 sts. Cont in st st, dec 1 st at beg of each alt (every other) row at inside neck edge until 37 sts remain. Cast (bind) off.
Working from the 41 sts on spare needle, shape other shoulder similarly.

FRONT

Work as for Back until**. (108 sts). Cont in st st until work measures 50cm (20″).

DIVIDE FOR NECK

RS facing, K48 sts, transfer these to spare needle. Cast (bind) off 12 sts, knit across rem 48 sts.

SHAPE SHOULDERS

Turn and purl across 48 sts. Cont in st st, dec 2 sts at beg of next 5 alt (every other) rows at inside neck edge. (38 sts). Purl next row, then dec 1 st at inside neck edge. Cont in st st with no further dec until Front measures 60cm (24″). Cast (bind) off. Complete other shoulder similarly.

SLEEVES

Using 2¾mm (US 2) circular needles as straight, and Twilleys 'Bubbly' cotton, cast on 68 sts. Work as for Back Welt, rep the 6 basic sts 11 times instead of 25, over the row rep. Cont until Cuff measures 14cm (5¾″).

INCREASE ROW

Change to 3¼mm (US 3) straight needles and inc sts as folls:
K1 (M1, K3) rep to last st, end in M1, K1. (91 sts).

Work in st st, but in 1 st at beg and end of every 3rd row until 135 sts exist, and Sleeve measures 34cm (13½″). Work 3cm (1½″) more in st st, with no further inc.

SHAPE SLEEVE HEAD

Dec 1 st at beg and end of every 3rd row, working in st st until Sleeve measures 44cm (17½″) and 119 sts rem. Cast (bind) off loosely.

NECKBAND

Using backstitch, join shoulder seams.
Using 2¾mm (US 2) circular needles and white Anchor Pearl Cotton No 5 pick up evenly and K144 sts from around neck opening. Work 1 round in purl, next round in knit, then cast (bind) off knitwise. This draws the neckline in and provides a base to attach collar to later.

COLLAR

Using 2mm (US 0) straight needles and white Anchor Pearl Cotton No 5, cast on 7 sts. Work lace as folls:

Row 1: SL 1, P3, YRN, P2tog, P1.
Row 2: P1, YRN, P2tog, P4.
Row 3: SL 1, P3, YRN, P2tog, YRN, (P1, K1) into last st.
Row 4: P1, YRN, P2, YRN, P2tog, P4.
Row 5: SL 1, P3, YRN, P2tog, YRN, P3, (P1, K1) into last st.
Row 6: P1, YRN, P2, YRN, P2tog, turn, P2tog, YRN, P3, YRN, (P1, K1) into last st.
Row 7: Cast (bind) off 5 sts, YRN, P2tog, P1, YRN, P2tog, P4.
Row 8: SL 1, P3, YRN, P2tog, (P1, K1) into next st, YRN, P2tog, YRN, (P1, K1) into last st.
Row 9: P3, YRN, P2tog, turn, YRN, P2tog, YRN, P2, YRN, (P1, K1) into last st.
Row 10: Cast (bind) off 5 sts, YRN, P2tog, YRN, P2, YRN, P2tog, P4.
Row 11: SL 1, P3, YRN, P2tog, P2, (P1, K1) into next st, YRN, P2tog, YRN (P1, K1) into last st.
Row 12: P3, YRN, P2tog, turn, YRN, P2tog, YRN, P2, YRN, (P1, K1) into last st.
Row 13: Cast (bind) off 5 sts, YRN, P2tog, YRN, P4, YRN, P2tog, P4.
Row 14: SL 1, P3, YRN, P2tog, P4, (P1, K1) into next st, YRN, P2tog, YRN (P1, K1) into last st.
Row 15: P3, YRN, P2tog, turn, YRN, P2tog, YRN, P2, YRN, (P1, K1) into last st.
Row 16: Cast (bind) off 5 sts, YRN, P2tog, YRN, P6, YRN, P2tog, P4.
Row 17: SL 1, P3, YRN, P2tog, P6, (P1, K1) into next st, YRN, P2tog, YRN, (P1, K1) into last st.
Row 18: P3, YRN, P2tog, turn, YRN, P2tog, YRN, P2, YRN, (P1, K1) into last st.
Row 19: Cast (bind) off 5 sts, YRN, P2tog, YRN, P3, MB, P4, YRN, P2tog, P4.
Row 20: SL 1, P3, YRN, P2tog, P8, (P1, K1) into next st, YRN, P2tog, YRN, (P1, K1) into last st.
Row 21: P3, YRN, P2tog, turn, YRN, P2tog, YRN, P2, YRN, (P1, K1) into last st.
Row 22: Cast (bind) off 5 sts, YRN, P2tog, YRN, SL 1, P2tog, PSSO, P1, MB, P1, MB, P3, YRN, P2tog, P4.
Row 23: SL 1, P3, YRN, P2tog, P6, P2tog, P1, YRN, P2tog, YRN, (P1, K1) into last st.
Row 24: P3, YRN, P2tog, turn, YRN, P2tog, YRN, P2, YRN, (P1, K1) into last st.
Row 25: Cast (bind) off 5 sts, YRN, P2tog, YRN, SL 1, P2tog, PSSO, MB, P4, YRN, P2tog, P4.

Row 26: SL 1, P3, YRN, P2tog, P4, P2tog, P1, YRN, P2tog, YRN, (P1, K1) into last st.

Row 27: P3, YRN, P2tog, turn, YRN, P2tog, YRN, P2, YRN, (P1, K1) into last st.

Row 28: Cast (bind) off 5 sts, YRN, P2tog, YRN, Sl 1, P2tog, PSSO, P3, YRN, P2tog, P4.

Row 29: SL 1, P3, YRN, P2tog, P2, P2tog, P1, YRN, P2tog, YRN, (P1, K1) into last st.

Row 30: P3, YRN, P2tog, turn, YRN, P2tog, YRN, P2, YRN, (P1, K1) into last st.

Row 31: Cast (bind) off 5 sts, YRN, P2tog, YRN, SL 1, P2tog, PSSO, P1, YRN, P2tog, P4.

Row 32: SL 1, P3, YRN, P2tog, P2tog, P1, YRN, P2tog, YRN (P1, K1) into last st.

Row 33: P3, YRN, P2tog, turn, YRN, P2tog, YRN, P2, YRN, (P1, K1) into last st.

Row 34: Cast (bind) off 5 sts, YRN, P2tog, P2tog, YRN, P2tog, P4.

Row 35: SL 1, P3, YRN, P2tog, P3tog, P1.

Row 36: P2tog, YRN, P2tog, P4.

Row 37–48: Rep *Rows 1 & 2* alt.

Rep *Rows 3–48* six more times, then cast (bind) off.

MAKING UP AND FINISHING

Using backstitch for st st and invisible seaming for ribbing, join side seams. Matching Sleeve and armhole shapings carefully, ease Sleeves into armholes, arranging gathers evenly at top of shoulders. Pin and tack (catch down) into place, then using backstitch, join securely. Remove pins and tacking (catching down) thread, then press seams on WS with warm iron over damp cloth. Using backstitch for st st and invisible seaming for ribbing, join Sleeve seams and press similarly.

Block lace collar, then using backstitch, and beg at RH shoulder corner, attach evenly around neckline, positioning 3rd lace scallop at centre front of neck.

Press sweater on RS with warm iron over damp cloth, omitting ribbing and lace collar.

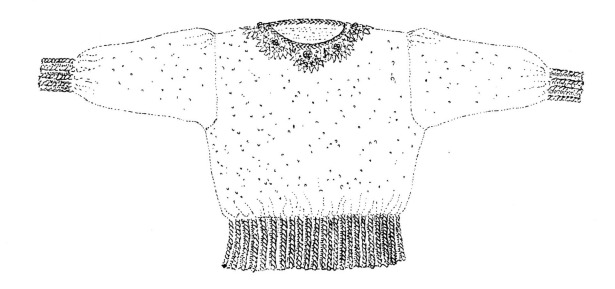

SHAMROCK LACE LAYETTE

(1820–1900)

Inspired by the delicacy of the lace made by the nuns at Carrickmacross, I designed this set of baby clothes using the finest spun wool available and traditional Shamrock stitch edgings and insertions.

Lace knitting of this type came to Ireland from the Scottish islands during the late nineteenth century and eventually influenced Aran knitting.

The layette, which consists of dress, bonnet, dainty bootees and matching shawl, could create a new family heirloom in the tradition of treasured Irish crafts.

The requirements and instructions for each item in the layette are given separately, in case you only want to make part of the set. The Special Abbreviations are given collectively for you to refer to as necessary.

SPECIAL ABBREVIATIONS

SL 1	Sl 1 st from LH needle over to RH needle without knitting or purling it.
YO	Yarn over needle to make a new st between 2 knit sts
YO2	Yarn over needle twice to make 2 new sts between 2 knit sts
YRN	Wind yarn round needle to make a new st between 2 purl sts
YFRN	Yarn forward and round needle to make a new st between a knit and a purl st
M1	Make 1 st by picking up loop from row below and knitting it TBL

SPECIAL PATTERN INSTRUCTIONS

The foll lace patts are used in the set and should be referred to as required.

PATTERN A   SHAMROCK EDGING

Cast on 14 sts using needle size and yarn as specified for each item.

Row 1: SL 1, (K1, YFRN, P2tog) twice, K2, YO2, K5.
Row 2: K6, P1, K2, YFRN, P2tog, K1, YFRN, P2tog, K2.
Row 3: SL 1, (K1, YFRN, P2tog) twice, K4, YO2, K5.
Row 4: K6, P1, K4, YFRN, P2tog, K1, YFRN, P2tog, K2.
Row 5: SL 1, (K1, YFRN, P2tog) twice, K3, YO2, K8.
Row 6: K9, P1, K3, YFRN, P2tog, K1, YFRN, P2tog, K2.
Row 7: SL 1, (K1, YFRN, P2tog) twice, K13.
Row 8: K13, YFRN, P2tog, K1, YFRN, P2tog, K2.
Row 9: As *Row 7*.
Row 10: Cast (bind) off 6 sts, K6, YFRN, P2tog, K1, YFRN, P2tog, K2.

PATTERN B   SHAMROCK INSERTION

Cast on 14 sts using needle size and yarn as specified for each item.

Row 1: SL 1, K1, YFRN, P2tog, K2, YO2, K4, YFRN, P2tog, K2.
Row 2: SL 1, K1, YFRN, P2tog, K2, K2tog, K1, P1, K2, YFRN, P2tog, K2.
Row 3: SL 1, K1, YFRN, P2tog, K4, YO2, K2tog, K1, YFRN, P2tog, K2.
Row 4: SL 1, K1, YFRN, P2tog, K3, P1, K2tog, K2, YFRN, P2tog, K2.
Row 5: SL 1, K1, YFRN, P2tog, K3, YO2, K2, K2tog, YFRN, P2tog, K2.
Row 6: SL 1, K1, YFRN, P2tog, K4, P1, K2tog, K1, YFRN, P2tog, K2.
Row 7: SL 1, K1, YFRN, P2tog, K4, K2tog, K1, YFRN, P2tog, K2.
Row 8: SL 1, K1, YFRN, P2tog, K6, YFRN, P2tog, K2.

DRESS

MATERIALS

YARN

Jamieson & Smith 1 Ply Cobweb Wool (White only)
1 × 100g/8 × ½oz hanks for both sizes.

NEEDLES

1 pair 2¼mm: 3¼mm (US 1:3) 80cm (31½″) circular needles
1 pair 2¼mm: 3¼mm (US 1:3) 30cm (12″) straight needles
1 set of double pointed 2¼mm: 3¼mm (US 1:3) spare needles
2 stitch holders

TRIMMINGS (NOTIONS)

4 tiny mother of pearl buttons
3 metres (10′) narrow satin ribbon

SIZES AND MEASUREMENTS

In 2 sizes to fit babies 0–5 months: 5–9 months

Actual width across back at underarm
22cm (9″): 25cm (10″)

Skirt length from waist   50cm (20″): 54cm (21½″)

Sleeve seam   16cm (6½″): 19cm (7½″)

TENSION (GAUGE)

40 sts and 48 rows to 10cm (4″) over st st on 2¼mm (US 1) needles: 34 sts and 42 rows to 10cm (4″) over st st on 3¼mm (US 3) needles or size needed to obtain this tension (gauge).

SKIRT FRILL

Beg with Shamrock edging lace for skirt hem frill. Using 2¼mm: 3¼mm (US 1:3) straight needles and Cobweb wool cast on 14 sts. Starting with **Row 1** of **Patt A**, rep **Rows 1–10** continuously 50 times, until 50 'points' have been made, and 500 rows have been worked. Cast (bind) off very loosely.

Using 2¼mm: 3¼mm (US 1:3) circular needles used as straight, pick up evenly and K500 sts from along the straight edge of the lace hem frill. (For even spacing of sts, pick up 10 sts over each 'point' and mark off every 100 sts with a coloured thread). Then make *TIER FRILL* as folls:

Row 1: (WS) K.
Rows 2 & 3: P.
Row 4: K.
Rows 5 & 6: Rep *Rows 3 & 4*.
Rows 7–12: Rep *Rows 1–6*.
Row 13: K.
Rows 14 & 15: P.
Row 16: K.

Cont in st st until tier frill, including lace border, measures 12cm (5″): 14cm (5½″). Next, dec for Skirt as folls:

SKIRT

Row 1: (WS facing) P2tog, rep along row to end. (250 sts).
Row 2: (RS) P.
Rows 3 & 4: K.
Row 5: P.
Rows 6 & 7: As *Rows 4 & 5*.
Rows 8–19: Rep *Rows 2–7* twice more.

Cont in st st until work measures 50cm (20″): 54cm (21½″) from edge of lace point, or lengthen or shorten as desired.

WAISTBAND

Cont to use 2¼mm: 3¼mm (US 1:3) circular needles as straight, work as folls:

Row 1: (RS) Reduce sts: (K1, K2tog) rep to last st, K1. (167 sts).
Row 2: Inc 1 st at beg of row, then K across row.
Row 3: Inc 1 st at beg of row, then P across row.
Row 4: P.
Row 5: (*Eyelet Row*): K1, (YO, K2tog) rep to end.
Rows 6 & 7: P.
Row 8: K.

Cont on same 2¼mm:3¼mm (US1:3) circular needles used as straight, RS facing, first make button band as follows: Cast on 3 sts. Then commence Bodice lace patt as folls: where Pattern B appears in instructions, foll row order as given for **Shamrock Insertion** patt.

Row 1: K3 button band sts, work *Row 1* of Patt B, K3, *Row 1* of Patt B, K21, (*Row 1* of Patt B, K3) 3 times, *Row 1* of Patt B, K21, *Row 1* of Patt B, K3, *Row 1* of Patt B.
Row 2: Cast on 3 sts for button band, K these sts, then commence lace patt: work *Row 2* of Patt B, P3, *Row 2* of Patt B, P21, (*Row 2* of Patt B, P3) 3 times, *Row 2* of Patt B, P21, *Row 2* of Patt B, P3, *Row 2* of Patt B, K3 button band sts.
Row 3: (K3, *Row 3* of Patt B) twice, K21, (*Row 3* of Patt B, K3) 3 times, *Row 3* of Patt B, K21, (*Row 3* of Patt B, K3) twice.
Row 4: K3, *Row 4* of Patt B, P3, *Row 4* of Patt B, P21, (*Row 4* of Patt B, P3) 3 times, *Row 4* of Patt B, P21, *Row 4* of Patt B, P3, *Row 4* of Patt B, K3.
Row 5: (K3, *Row 5* of Patt B) twice, K21, (*Row 5* of Patt B, K3) 3 times, *Row 5* of Patt B, K21, (*Row 5* of Patt B, K3) twice
Row 6: K3, *Row 6* of Patt B, P3, *Row 6* of Patt B, P21, (*Row 6* of Patt B, P3) 3 times, *Row 6* of Patt B, P21, *Row 6* of Patt B, P3, *Row 6* of Patt B, K3.
Row 7: (K3, *Row 7* of Patt B) twice, K21, (*Row 7* of Patt B, K3) 3 times, *Row 7* of Patt B, K21, (*Row 7* of Patt B, K3) twice.
Row 8: K3, *Row 8* of Patt B, P3, *Row 8* of Patt B, P21, (*Row 8* of Patt B, P3) 3 times, *Row 8* of Patt B, P21, *Row 8* of Patt B, P3, *Row 8* of Patt B, K3.

Rep *Rows 1–8* again (omitting inc once button bands have been established), and making a button hole on *Row 9* as folls: K1, YO, K2tog. Cont in patt as set, making second button hole on *Row 17* and work in patt until *Row 20* has been completed. Break off yarn. (183 sts)

DIVIDE FOR ARMHOLES

Sl 48 sts onto stitch holder.

BODICE FRONT

Join in yarn, then beg on *Row 5* of Bodice lace patt as given above, dec as folls:

Row 21: K2tog, K7, (*Row 5* of Patt B, K3) 3 times, *Row 5* of Patt B, K7, K2tog, then transfer rem 48 sts to second stitch holder.
Row 22: Do not dec at armhole edge but otherwise work *Row 6* of Bodice lace patt.

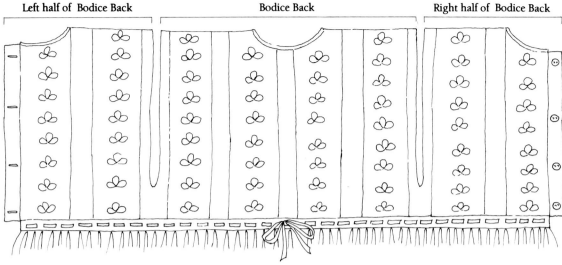

Left half of Bodice Back   Bodice Back   Right half of Bodice Back

Bodice diagram

Row 23: Dec 1 st at beg and end of row, work rest of row in *Row 7* patt as set.

Cont in patt, dec 1 st at beg and end of alt (every other) odd-numbered rows until 4th patt rep has been completed, *Row 32* has been worked and 5 sts have been dec at each edge. Cont in patt with no further dec until 8 reps of patt have been worked and *Row 64* completed.

DIVIDE FOR NECK

Work in patt for *Row 1* Bodice lace patt (i.e. for centre Front) until second lace pattern panel has been worked. Cast (bind) off next 4 sts, then work across in patt to end of row. Transfer 38 sts on RH needle onto a spare needle and leave.

LEFT SHOULDER

Cont in patt, dec 1 st at inside neck edge at beg of each alt (every other) row until *Row 72* (9th rep of Bodice lace patt) has been completed.

SHAPE SHOULDER

Dec 1 st at neck edge, work 1 row of patt.

Row 74: Cast (bind) off 9 sts, cont in patt to end.
Row 75: Dec 1 st at beg of row, cont in patt to end.
Row 76 & 77: As *Rows 74 & 75*.
Cast (bind) off very loosely.

RIGHT SHOULDER

Join in yarn, then reverse shapings to match left shoulder, working in patt as before until right shoulder is complete.

Cast (bind) off loosely.

RIGHT BACK

Transfer sts from stitch holder to 2¼mm: 3¼mm (US 1:3) straight needles, rejoin yarn at armhole edge, RS facing. Work right Back:

Row 21: Dec 1 st at beg of row, working in *Row 5* of Bodice lace patt and knitting the band sts, making no buttonholes.
Row 22: Work as *Row 6* of patt but make no dec.

Cont in this way, working in patt, dec 1 st at each alt (every other) row at armhole edge until only 6 sts exist in the st st panel at armhole edge. Cont to work in patt with no further dec until *Row 72* has been completed and 9 patt rep worked.

SHAPE SHOULDER

Row 73: Beg at *Row 1* of Bodice lace patt, cast (bind) off 9 sts at armhole edge, work across in patt to end.

Row 74: Work in *Row 2* of patt.
Row 75: Cast (bind) off 9 sts, cont in patt to end.
Row 76: Work in *Row 4* of patt.
Row 77: Cast (bind) off rem sts. Break off yarn.

LEFT BACK

RS facing, rejoin yarn at armhole edge. Shape to match right Back, but cont to make button holes at edge as already shown (i.e. K1, YO, K2tog) at *Rows 9, 31, 53 and 75*. Cast (bind) off loosely.

Using backstitch, join shoulder seams and Skirt back seam, then make Sleeves as folls:

SLEEVES

Using 2¼mm:3¼mm (US 1:3) circular needles as straight, beg at mid-point underarm, RS facing, pick up evenly and K100 sts.

It is most important the sts are picked up evenly otherwise Sleeve gathers will be irregularly spaced and will not hang well.

Row 1: WS facing, P34 (M1, P1) 32 times more, P34. (132 sts).
Dec 1 st at beg of next 32 rows, working in st st until 100 sts rem. Cont in st st until work measures 12cm (5"): 14cm (5¾"). (Or alter length to fit baby's arm).

DECREASE FOR WRIST

WS facing, P2tog, rep to end of row. (50 sts).

Next Row: P.
Next Row: K.
Eyelet Row: RS facing, K1*(K2tog, YO) rep from*to last st, K1.
Next 2 rows: P.
Cast (bind) off loosely knitwise.

WRIST FRILLS

Using 2¼mm: 3¼mm (US 1:3) straight needles, cast on 15 sts then K 1 row.
Work *Shamrock Lace Edging* Patt A, but attach Sleeve cuff as folls:

Row 1: Pick up 1 st from Sleeve cuff, K this st, and first st from lace edging row together. Cont in patt to end.
Row 2: Work in patt as set, but K the last st, do not join to Sleeve cuff. Cont lace frill in this way, attaching to Sleeve cuff each alt (every other) row until other edge of cuff is reached, and 10 lace points exist. Cast (bind) off. Repeat for second Sleeve.

MAKING UP AND FINISHING

Finish neckline as folls: Beg at button hole side edge, join in yarn, then RS facing, pick up evenly 70 sts across left Back,

Front and right Back.
Next Row: WS facing, K.
Next Row: P.
Cast (bind) off purlwise very loosely on a needle 2 sizes larger.

Using backstitch, join Sleeve seams. Darn in any loose ends, then sew on 4 tiny mother of pearl buttons. Wash garment in lukewarm water and soap flakes, rinse very gently then place carefully on towel to remove excess moisture. Place garment on blocking board and very gently arrange dress until desired measurements are achieved. Do not stretch as dress is very fragile. Using dressmaker's pins, pin garment to required shape, pinning each of the lace points out evenly. Allow to dry out of direct sunlight or white wool will yellow.

Finally, thread ribbons through cuffs and waist and tie in bows.

As the dress is so delicate and lacy, it should be worn over a white cotton underslip which can also be trimmed with lace.

BONNET

MATERIALS

YARN

Jamieson & Smith 1 Ply Cobweb Wool
1 × 25g/2 × ½oz hanks for both sizes

NEEDLES
1 pair 2¼mm:3¼mm (US 1:3) 30cm (12") straight needles

TRIMMINGS (NOTIONS)
1 metre (39") 2cm (1") wide satin ribbon

MEASUREMENTS

Around face   32cm (13"): 40cm (16")
Face to crown   17cm (7"): 20cm (8")

TENSION (GAUGE)

40 sts and 48 rows to 10cm (4") over st st on 2¼mm (US 1) needles:
34 sts and 42 rows to 10cm (4") over st st on 3¼mm (US 3) needles or size needed to obtain this tension (gauge).

BONNET LACE EDGING

Using 2¼mm:3¼mm (US 1:3) needles and Cobweb wool cast on 14 sts and work 20 reps of **Shamrock Edging** Patt A. Cast (bind) off.
Pick up evenly 135 sts knitwise along straight edge of lace, then work Crown as folls:

CROWN

Row 1: K.
Rows 2 & 3: P.
Row 4: K.

Rows 5 & 6: as *Rows 3 & 4.*
Rows 7–12: Rep *Rows 1–6.*
Row 13: K.
Rows 14 & 15: P.

SHAPE CROWN
Row 16: (K13, K2tog), rep to end. (126 sts).
Rows 17–23: St st.
Row 24: (K12, K2tog), rep to end. (117 sts).
Rows 25–31: St st.
Row 32: (K11, K2tog), rep to end. (108 sts).
Rows 33-39: St st.
Row 40: (K10, K2tog), rep to end. (99 sts).
Rows 41–47: St st.
Row 48: (K9, K2tog), rep to end. (90 sts).
Rows 49–53): St st.
Row 54: (K8, K2tog), rep to end. (81 sts).
Rows 55–59: St st.
Row 60: (K7, K2tog), rep to end. (72 sts).
Rows 61–65: St st.
Row 66: (K6, K2tog), rep to end. (63 sts).
Rows 67–71: St st.
Row 72: (K5, K2tog), rep to end. (54 sts).
Rows 73–75: St st.
Row 76: (K4, K2tog), rep to end. (45 sts).
Row 77: P.
Row 78: (K3, K2tog), rep to end. (36sts).
Row 79: P.
Row 80: K2tog all sts. (18 sts).
Cast (bind) off purlwise. Leave 50cm (20″) yarn at end.

MAKING UP AND FINISHING

Using this yarn, thread through the cast (bound) off sts with a darning needle, and draw together tightly. Using backstitch, join back seam.

Carefully wash and block, then sew on satin ribbons, half a metre (19½″) at each side.

(To adjust to babies' variable head sizes, the lace frill seam can be left unsewn at back of bonnet if required.)

BOOTEES

MATERIALS

YARN
Jamieson & Smith 1 Ply Cobweb Wool (White only)
1 × 25g/2 × ½oz hanks for both sizes

NEEDLES
1 pair 2¼mm:3¼mm (US 1:3) 30cm (12″) straight needles

TRIMMINGS (NOTIONS)
1 metre (39″) narrow satin ribbon

MEASUREMENTS
Length from heel to toe   9cm (3¾″): 11cm (4½″)

TENSION (GAUGE)

40 sts and 48 rows to 10cm (4″) over st st on 2¼mm (US 1) needles: 34 sts and 42 rows to 10cm (4″) over st st on 3¼mm (US 3) needles or size needed to obtain this tension.

SOLE OF FIRST BOOTEE

Using 2¼mm: 3¼mm (US 1:3) needles and Cobweb wool, cast on 26 sts.
Working in garter st, shape as folls:

Rows 1–8: Inc 1 st at beg of each row, K each row. (34 sts).
Rows 9–12: K.
Rows 13–20: Dec 1 st at beg of each row until 26 sts rem, K each row.
Row 21: Cast on 5 sts, K to end. (31 sts).
Change to st st and shape toe.

TOE SHAPING
Row 22: Inc 1 st at beg of row, P.
Rows 23–27: St st.
Cont in st st, inc 1 st at beg of *Rows 28, 30 & 32* with no inc on alt (every other) rows. (35 sts).
Row 33: Cast (bind) off 10 sts, K.
Row 34: P23, P2tog at end of row. (24 sts).
Row 35: K2tog, K22. (23 sts).
Row 36: P21, P2tog at end of row. (22 sts).
Row 37: K2tog, K20. (21 sts).
Rows 38–46: St st.
Row 47: Inc 1 st at beg of row, K.
Row 48: P22, inc 1 st at end of row.
Row 49: Inc 1 st at beg of row, K.
Row 50: P24, inc 1 st at end of row.
Row 51: Cast on 10 sts at beg of row, K.
Row 52: P2tog at beg of row, P.
Row 53: K.
Row 54: P2tog at beg of row, P.
Row 55: K.
Row 56: P2tog at beg of row, P.
Rows 57–61: St st.
Row 62: P2tog at beg of row, P. (31 sts).
Cast (bind) off.

BOOTEE CUFF

RS facing, pick up evenly 50 sts from around ankle front of Bootee.
Work eyelet patt as folls:

Row 1: (WS) P.
Row 2: P.
Row 3: K.
Row 4: K1, (YO, K2tog) rep to last st, K1.
Rows 5 & 6: K.

then cast on 14 more sts. K 1 row, then knitting together the first st of row with the first st from top of eyelet edge, turn and work **Shamrock Edging** Patt A to make a lace edging for top of Bootee. Cont to join in each alt (every other) row to Cuff edge as already described. After 5 reps have been worked, cast (bind) off. Work second Bootee as first, reversing shapings.

MAKING UP AND FINISHING

Using backstitch, join sole to sides of Bootees, then sew up back seam at heel. Wash and block. Later, thread in narrow ribbon and tie in bow, then turn down Cuff of Bootees.

SHAWL

MATERIALS

YARN

Jamieson & Smith 1 Ply Cobweb Wool (White only)
$1 \times 150g/11 \times \frac{1}{2}oz$ hanks

NEEDLES

1 pair $3\frac{1}{4}$mm (US 3) 40cm (12″) straight needles
1 pair $3\frac{1}{4}$mm (US 3) 25cm (10″) straight needles

MEASUREMENTS

Approximately 118cm ($46\frac{1}{2}$″) square

TENSION (GAUGE)

32 sts and 40 rows to 10cm (4″) over st st on $3\frac{1}{4}$mm (US 3) needles or size needed to obtain this tension (gauge)

CENTRE SQUARE

Using $3\frac{1}{4}$mm (US 3) 40cm (12″) needles and Cobweb wool cast on 122 sts. Work 1 row of eyelets: K1* (YO, K2tog), rep from* to last st, K1. Work 242 rows in garter st, starting each row with YO, K2tog, to make loops at edge. End centre square with another row of eyelets as already shown. P 1 row.

LACE BORDER

Make lace patt border along the first of the 4 edges as folls:

Row 1: Cast on 1 st, K this st, then set patt as folls by working *Row 1* of **Shamrock Lace Insertion** Patt B. K next st, rep Patt B as shown and cont in this way to end of row, end in K1.
Row 2: Cast on 1 st, K this st. P1, then work *Row 2* of Patt B as set, rep to end, P1. (Patt consists of lace panels divided by 1 st). Cont in Patt B as set, but inc 1 st at beg of every row, incorporating this st into patt as set so that diagonal shaping is formed on both edges. Cont to work in this way until 15 reps of Patt B have been worked and 16 lace panels exist. (241 sts). Then work Border edge as folls:
Cont with same needles and yarn and work *Rows 1–5*.

Row 1: RS facing, K.
Row 2: K.
Row 3: P.
Row 4: Work a row of eyelets: P1, (P2tog, YRN) rep to last st, P1.
Row 5: K.
Cast off very loosely, knitwise.

Work rem 3 sides in similar way, joining in sts at edges by knitting together and making a seam until lace borders are complete. Work **Shamrock Lace Edging** next.

EDGING LACE

Using $3\frac{1}{4}$mm (US 3) 25cm (10″) needles and Cobweb wool cast on 14 sts. Work Patt A continuously until a strip long enough to trim all 4 edges has been made, allowing extra reps to permit a smooth turn at the corners with no puckering. Using backstitch, sew in very carefully as the work proceeds to allow accurate estimation of how long to make the edging. Cast (bind) off, and using backstitch, sew in corner seam neatly.

MAKING UP AND FINISHING

Darn in any loose ends, then wash and block, pinning out every point of lace border as already described.

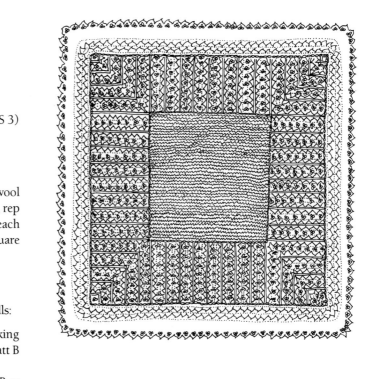

PRIMROSE PETALS

(1850–1900)

Crochet was another of the crafts established by the famine relief committees in the mid nineteenth century to assist the rural poor.

The contrasting white lace collar on this child's cotton dress is made using the picot lace technique which adapts Irish crochet designs to knitting. The traditional petal pattern is very like primrose petals when knitted in pale yellow.

Inspired by the wild primroses which flourish in the spring in Ireland's quiet countryside, this design celebrates the flowering of Irish crafts after the famine period.

MATERIALS

YARN
Twilleys Stalite Perlespun No 3 in Yellow (68)
4(4:5) × 50g/7¼oz (7¼:9)

Twilleys Lyscordet No 5 Mercerised Cotton in White (78)
1 (1:1) × 25g/1oz

NEEDLES
1 pair 2¾mm:3¼mm:3¾mm (US 2:3:5) 35cm (14″) straight needles
1 pair 2mm (US 0) 25cm (10″) straight needles
1 stitch holder

TRIMMINGS (NOTIONS)
5(6:6) tiny mother of pearl buttons
Shirring elastic

SIZES AND MEASUREMENTS

In 3 sizes to fit children 0–6 months: 6–12 months: 1–2 years.

Actual width across back at underarm
23cm (9″): 25cm (10″): 28cm (11″)

Length from centre back neck to hem
29cm (11½″): 36cm (14½″): 41cm (16½″)

Sleeve seam   14cm (6″): 17cm (7″): 20cm (8″)

TENSION (GAUGE)

28 sts and 36 rows to 10cm (4″) over st st on 2¾mm (US 2) needles:
26 sts and 34 rows to 10cm (4″) over st st on 3¼mm (US 3) needles:
24 sts and 32 rows to 10cm (4″) over st st on 3¾mm (US 5) needles: or size needed to obtain this tension (gauge).

SPECIAL ABBREVIATIONS

YRN-P2tog	Yarn round needle before purling 2 sts together
YO	Yarn over needle to make a new st between 2 knit sts
K4tog-BL	Knit 4 sts together through the back of the loops
M1	Make 1 st by picking up loop from row below and knitting it TBL

PETAL PATTERN

Cast on multiples of 9 sts + 3 sts.

Row 1: K2, (YO, K8, YO, K1), rep to last st, K1.
Row 2: K3, (P8, K3), rep to end.
Row 3: K3, (YO, K8, YO, K3), rep to end.
Row 4: K4,* (P8, K5), rep from*, but end last rep in K4, not K5.
Row 5: K4,* (YO, K8, YO, K5), rep from* but end last rep in K4, not K5.
Row 6: K5,* (P8, K7), rep from*, but end last rep in K5, not K7.
Row 7: K5,* (K4tog-BL, K4tog, K7) rep from* but end last rep in K5, not K7.
Row 8: K.
(These 8 rows form the patt rep).

FRONT

Using 2¾mm: 3¼mm: 3¾mm (US 2:3:5) needles, in yellow cotton cast on 102 sts. K 2 rows, then beg **Petal Pattern** as shown, working the 8 rows once. K 2 rows, then K2tog at beg and end of next row, knitting this row. (100 sts). Change to st st and cont until skirt measures 22cm (9″): 24cm (9½″): 27cm (10¾″), or adjust length to fit child. End after a purl row.

SHAPE FOR BODICE
RS facing, (K1, K2tog), rep to last st, K1. (67 sts). K 2 rows, then cast (bind) off 5 sts knitwise at beg of next row, K to last 4 sts, cast (bind) off these 4 sts knitwise. Break off yarn. (58 sts).**

WORK BODICE PATT AS FOLLS:
Rejoin yarn. RS facing:

Row 1: K18, P2, K1, YRN-P2tog, K2, YO, K8, YO, K2, YRN-P2tog, K1, P2, K18.
Row 2: P18, K2, P1, YRN-P2tog, P1, K2, P8, K2, P1, YRN-P2tog, P1, K2, P18.
Row 3: K18, P2, K1, YRN-P2tog, K3, YO, K8. YO, K3, YRN-P2tog, K1, P2, K18.

Row 4: P18, K2, P1, YRN-P2tog, P1, K3, P8, K3, P1, YRN-P2tog, P1, K2, P18.
Row 5: K18, P2, K1, YRN-P2tog, K4, YO, K8, YO, K4, YRN-P2tog, K1, P2, K18.
Row 6: P18, K2, P1, YRN-P2tog, P1, K4, P8, K4, P1, YRN-P2tog, P1, K2, P18.
Row 7: K18, P2, K1, YRN-P2tog, K5, K4tog-BL, K4tog, K5, YRN-P2tog, K1, P2, K18.
Row 8: P18, K2, P1, YRN-P2tog, P1, K10, P1, YRN-P2tog, P1, K2, P18.
Rep this 8 row patt 4 more times.

DIVIDE FOR NECK

K18, P2, K1, transfer these to stitch holder, cast (bind) off 16 sts, P2, K18.

SHAPE SHOULDERS

Cast (bind) off 1 st at neck edge at beg of next 2 alt (every other) rows of left shoulder. Work 2 more rows without dec, cast (bind) off. Complete other shoulder similarly.

BACK

Work as Front until**.
K29 sts, sl other 29 sts onto a stitch holder. Turn, cast on 2 sts to create a button-hole band for right Back. K4 sts, then purl across rem sts. Cont in st st, working 4 sts of button-hole band in garter st. Make button holes on 3rd st (YO, K2tog) of **Row 4** and every subsequent 8th row. Cont until Back measures 9cm(3½"):13cm(5"):16cm(6½") from waist ending on a RS row.

SHAPE NECK

Cast (bind) off 12 sts, work across row. Dec 1 st at beg of next 2 alt (every other) rows. Work 1 row with no dec, then cast (bind) off. Work left Back similarly, casting on 3 sts instead of 2 for button band, working this in garter st but omitting buttonholes and reversing shaping.

SLEEVES

Using 2¾mm:3¼mm:3¾mm (US 2:3:5) needles and yellow cotton, cast on 30 sts and K 2 rows. Work in **Petal Pattern** until *Row 8* is completed, then K 2 more rows.

INCREASE ROW

(K1, M1), rep to last st, end in K1, inc 1. (60 sts).
Change to st st and cont until Sleeve measures 8cm(3"):11cm(4¼"):14cm(5½"). Cast on 1 st at beg of next 6 (12:12) rows. (66:72:72) sts. Cast on 3 (5:5) sts at beg of next rows, then work 8 more rows without shaping. Cast (bind) off.

COLLAR (make 2 halves separately)

Using 2mm (US 0) needles and white cotton cast on 20 (24:28) sts.

Row 1: K.
Row 2: Beg by making a picot point as folls:

Insert needle into first st, cast on 2 sts. Cast (bind) off these 2 sts, then transfer rem st to LH needle.

Rep from * to * 3 more times, making 4 picot points which form 1 picot 'crown'. Knit and cast (bind) off next 3 sts, then transfer rem st to LH needle. Cont to rep until 6 (7:8) picot crowns have been made, then knit and cast (bind) off the last st from *Row 1*, leaving 1 st on needle.

Row 3: Make 6 picot points, then pick up and knit the st between the 2nd and 3rd picot point just made, to join the picot points into a 4-point crown. Cast (bind) off 1 st, leaving 1 st on RH needle. Transfer this st to LH needle, then make 2 more picot points.

Pick up and K1 st from 2nd and 3rd picot points of crown made on *Row 2* immediately above to join rows together, then cast (bind) off 1 st, leaving 1 st on needle. Transfer this to LH needle. Rep until 7 (8:9) crowns exist, ending with 2 picot points. Join in these 2 points to complete Collar by picking up and knitting the end st from *Row 1*, slipping it over the other to cast (bind) off. Make other half of Collar similarly.

MAKING UP AND FINISHING

Using backstitch, join shoulder seams at top of dress. Using backstitch, join Sleeve seams, then ease Sleeves into armholes so a slight puff is formed at shoulder when sewn in. Using backstitch, join base of Sleeve underarm to cast (bound) off edge at waist, making sure the purl ridges cont intact round the skirt. Using backstitch, join skirt seams.

Using invisible seaming and white thread, attach the 2 halves of the Collar to dress, beg at button band at Back and arranging it to end at outside edges of central Front decorative panel.

Sew on buttons and then thread shirring elastic through holes made on *Increase Row* at wrists, sewing in firmly to form comfortable gathers. If a more fitted bodice is desired, sew in shirring elastic on WS between 2 purl rows. Omit if a looser fit is preferred, depending on shape of child.

Press seams on WS with warm iron over damp cloth, then lightly press dress on RS similarly, omitting Collar.

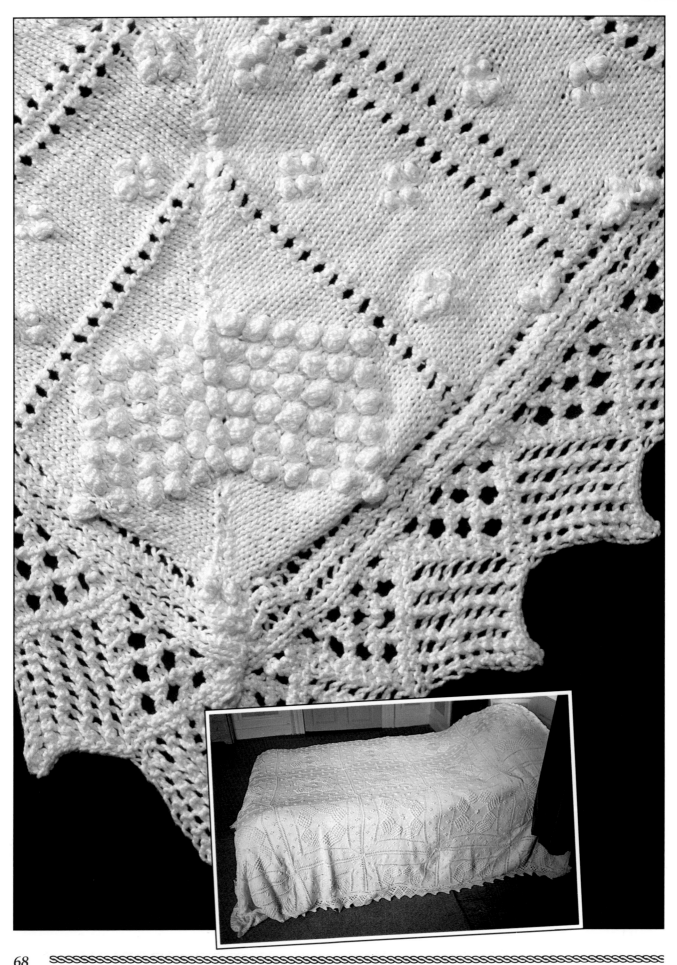

KERRY BEDSPREAD

(c1850)

Inspired by the beautiful collection of knitted and cro-cheted bedspreads at Muckross House, this design was adapted from a bedspread crocheted in cotton in the Lis-towel area of Co. Kerry in the mid nineteenth century.

These bedspreads are thought to have perhaps been made by older ladies for their daughters' or grand-daughters' trous-seau, or by domestic servants, over a long period as they man-aged to afford the cotton, for their own bottom drawers. At this time, the pattern books with knitting instructions would have been available for twenty years, and the bedspreads reveal the high degree of knitting expertise that already exis-ted in Ireland, on the mainland at least, during this period.

Carding and spinning fleece for the Donegal tweed cottage industry, late nineteenth century

This bedspread is less daunting to knit than you might suppose, as it is made in easily managed squares. When these are joined together later they create a richly textured pattern reminiscent of the elaborate plaster-work ceilings of the great country houses of the period. Yet the design would look equally well at home in the smaller scale of a modern room.

MATERIALS

YARN
Twilleys Stalite Mercerised Cotton in White
84 × 50g/148oz for double bed size

NEEDLES
1 pair 3¼mm (US 3) 35cm (14") straight needles

SIZE AND MEASUREMENTS

Instructions given for double bed size, measuring
236cm × 274cm (116" × 137")

Actual size of 1 square   28cm (11¼") on all 4 sides

Actual size of 1 triangle
28cm × 28cm × 38cm (11¼" × 11¼" × 15¼")

Actual size of 1 rep of lace border patt:

Length of triangle edge when attached to bedspread
6cm (2½")

Depth of lacy square from point of triangle edge   7cm (3")

To calculate quantities of yarn needed for bedspread of different size, the foll details are given:

1 square takes 68.75g (2.75oz) cotton

1 triangle takes 34.37g (1.37oz) cotton

16 reps of lace border patt take 50g (2oz) cotton

TENSION (GAUGE)

23 sts and 32 rows to 10cm (4") over st st on 3¼mm (US 3) needles or size needed to obtain this tension (gauge).

SPECIAL ABBREVIATIONS

MB3	Make a 3 st bobble by knitting into the front, the back and the front again of the next st, turn, K the 3 sts made from 1, turn, P these sts, then slip 2nd st over the 1st, then 3rd st over 1st so only 1 st remains.
MB4	(K1 into front and back of next st) twice, making 4 sts out of 1, (turn and K4 sts, turn, and P4 sts) twice, then using LH needle, lift 2nd, 3rd and 4th sts over 1 st st and off needle.
SL 1	Sl 1 st from LH needle over to RH needle without knitting or purling it.
PSSO	Pass the slipped st over.
YO, K2tog	Yarn over needle to make a new st, then K the next 2 sts together.
YO, K3tog	Yarn over needle to make a new st, then K the next 3 sts together.
YRN	Wrap yarn round needle to make a new st between 2 purl sts.
YO	Yarn over needle to make a new st between 2 knit sts.
YO2	Yarn over needle twice to make 2 new sts between 2 knit sts.
YON2	Yarn over needle twice to make 2 new sts between a purl and a knit st.

PRD   Purl reverse decrease. P1, sl next st on LH needle knitwise to RH needle, then transfer it back to LH needle. Return newly purled st to LH needle. Pull 2nd st on LH needle over first purled st and return first st to RH needle.

SQUARE

Using 3¼mm (US 3) needles and white mercerised cotton cast on 3 sts.

Row 1: K1, MB3, K1. (3 sts).
Row 2: Inc 1 st, P this st, P3, inc 1 st. (5 sts).
Rows 3–9: Inc 1 st at beg and end of each row, working in st st. (19 sts).
Row 10: Cast on 2 sts at beg only of row, P all sts. (21 sts).
Row 11: Cast on 2 sts at beg of row, K first st, MB4, K19, MB4, K1. (23 sts).
Row 12: As *Row 10*. (25 sts).
Row 13: Cast on 2 sts at beg of row, K first st, MB4, K3, MB4, K15, MB4, K3, MB4, K1. (27 sts).
Row 14: As *Row 10*. (29 sts).
Row 15: Cast on 2 sts at beg of row, K first st,* (MB4, K3) twice, MB4,* K11, rep from * to * once, K1. (31 sts).
Row 16: As *Row 10*. (33 sts).
Row 17: Cast on 2 sts at beg of row, K first st,* (MB4, K3) 3 times, MB4,* K7, rep from * to * once, K1. (35 sts).
Row 18: As *Row 10*. (37 sts).
Row 19: Cast on 2 sts at beg of row, K first st, (MB4, K3) 9 times, MB4, K1. (39 sts).
Row 20: As *Row 10*. (41 sts).
Row 21: Cast on 2 sts at beg of row, K first st, (MB4, K3) 10 times, MB4, K1. (43 sts).
Row 22: Inc 1 st at beg and end of row, P all sts. (45 sts).
Row 23: Inc 1 st at beg and end of row, K first inc st, K4, (MB4, K3) 9 times, MB4, K5, including end inc st. (47 sts).
Row 24: As *Row 22*. (49 sts).
Row 25: Inc 1 st at beg and end of row, K first inc st, K8,* (MB4,K3) 3 times, MB4,*K7. Rep from * to * once, end in K9 including last inc st. (51 sts).
Row 26: As *Row 22*. (53 sts).
Row 27: Inc 1 st at beg and end of row, K first inc st, K12,* (MB4, K3) twice, MB4,* K11, rep from * to * once, K13 including last inc st. (55 sts).
Row 28: As *Row 22*. (57 sts).
Row 29: Inc 1 st at beg and end of row, K first inc st, K16,* MB4, K3, MB4,* K15, rep from * to * once, K17 including last inc st. (59 sts).
Row 30: As *Row 22*. (61 sts).
Row 31: Inc 1 st at beg and end of row, K first inc st, K20, MB4, K19, MB4, K21 including last inc st. (63 sts).
Row 32: As *Row 22*. (65 sts).
Row 33: Inc 1 st at beg and end of row, K all sts. (67 sts).
Row 34: (Ridge Row) As *Row 33*. (69 sts).
Row 35: K1, (YO, K2tog), rep to end. (69 sts).
Row 36: (Ridge row) K all sts. (69 sts).
Rows 37–39: Inc 1 st at beg and end of each row, working in st st. (75 sts).

Row 40: Inc 1 st at beg only of row, P all sts. (76 sts).
Row 41: Inc 1 st at beg of row, K this st, K10, (MB3, K17) 3 times, MB3, K11. (77 sts).
Row 42: As *Row 40*. (78 sts).
Row 43: Inc 1 st at beg of row, K this st, K10, (MB3, K1, MB3, K15) 3 times, MB3, K1, MB3, K11. (79 sts).
Row 44: As *Row 40*. (80 sts).
Row 45: Inc 1 st at beg of row, K this st, K12, (MB3, K17) 3 times, MB3, K13. (81 sts).
Rows 46–48: Inc 1 st at beg of each row, working in st st. (84 sts).
Row 49: Inc 1 st at beg of row, K this st, K5, (MB3, K17) 4 times, MB3, K6. (85 sts).
Row 50: As *Row 40*. (86 sts).
Row 51: Inc 1 st at beg of row, K this st, K5, (MB3, K1, MB3, K15) 4 times, MB3, K1, MB3, K6. (87 sts).
Row 52: As *Row 40*. (88 sts).
Row 53: Inc 1 st at beg of row, K this st, K7, (MB3, K17) 4 times, MB3, K8. (89 sts).
Rows 54–56: As *Rows 46–48*. (92 sts).
Row 57: Inc 1 st at beg of row, K this st, (YO, K2tog), rep to end. (93 sts).
Row 58: (Ridge row) Inc 1 st at beg and end of row, K all sts. (95 sts).
Row 59: As *Row 58*. (97 sts).
Row 60: P1, turn so RS faces.* Transfer next st on RH needle to LH needle, MB3 on this st. When bobble is completed, turn so WS faces, transfer bobble st onto RH needle,* P93. Rep from * to * once, P1. (97 sts).
Row 61: K all sts. (97 sts).
Row 62: (Ridge row). K2tog, K all sts to last 2 sts, K2tog. (95 sts).
Row 63: SL 1, K1, PSSO, (YO, K2tog), rep to last 3 sts, YO, K3tog. (93 sts).
Row 64: P to last 2 sts, PRD. (92 sts).
Row 65: K to last 2 sts, K2tog. (91 sts).
Row 66: As *Row 64*. (90 sts).
Row 67: K8, (MB3, K17) 4 times, MB3, K7, K2tog. (89 sts).
Row 68: P to last 2 sts, PRD. (88 sts).
Row 69: K6, (MB3, K1, MB3, K15) 4 times, MB3, K1, MB3, K5, K2tog. (87 sts).
Row 70: As *Row 68*. (86 sts).
Row 71: K6, (MB3, K17) 4 times, MB3, K5, K2tog. (85 sts).
Rows 72–74: As *Rows 64–66*. (82 sts).
Row 75: K13, (MB3, K17) 3 times, MB3, K12, K2tog. (81 sts).
Row 76: As *Row 68*. (80 sts).
Row 77: K11, (MB3, K1, MB3, K15) 3 times, MB3, K1, MB3, K10, K2tog. (79 sts).
Row 78: As *Row 68*. (78 sts).
Row 79: K11, (MB3, K17) 3 times, MB3, K10, K2tog. (77 sts).
Row 80: As *Row 68*. (76 sts).
Row 81: K to last 2 sts, K2tog. (75 sts).
Row 82: P2tog, P to last 2 sts, PRD. (73 sts).
Row 83: SL 1, K1, PSSO, K to last 2 sts, K2tog. (71 sts).
Row 84: (Ridge row) K2tog, K to last 2 sts, K2tog. (69 sts).
Row 85: K1, (YO, K2tog), rep to end. (69 sts).
Row 86: (Ridge row) K all sts. (69 sts).

Row 87: As *Row 83*. (67 sts).
Row 88: As *Row 82*. (65 sts).
Row 89: SL 1, K1, PSSO, K20, MB4, K19, MB4, K20, K2tog. (63 sts).
Row 90: As *Row 82*. (61 sts).
Row 91: SL 1, K1, PSSO, K16, MB4, K3, MB4, K15, MB4, K3, MB4, K16, K2tog. (59 sts).
Row 92: As *Row 82*. (57 sts).
Row 93: SL 1, K1, PSSO, K12,* (MB4, K3) twice, MB4,* K11. Rep from * to * once, K12, K2tog. (55 sts).
Row 94: As *Row 82*. (53 sts).
Row 95: SL 1, K1, PSSO, K8,* (MB4, K3) 3 times, MB4,* K7, rep from * to * once, K8, K2tog. (51 sts).
Row 96: As *Row 82*. (49 sts).
Row 97: SL 1, K1, PSSO, K4, (MB4, K3) 9 times, MB4, K4, K2tog. (47 sts).
Row 98: As *Row 82*. (45 sts).
Row 99: SL 1, K1, PSSO, (MB4, K3) 10 times, MB4, K2tog. (43 sts).
Row 100: Cast (bind) off purlwise 2 sts at beg of row, P all sts. (41 sts).
Row 101: Cast (bind) off knitwise 2 sts at beg of row, (MB4, K3) 9 times, MB4, K1. (39 sts).
Row 102: As *Row 100*. (37 sts).
Row 103: Cast (bind) off knitwise 2 sts at beg of row,* (MB4, K3) 3 times, MB4,* K7, rep from * to * once, K1. (35 sts).
Row 104: As *Row 100*. (33 sts).
Row 105: Cast (bind) off knitwise 2 sts at beg of row,* (MB4, K3) twice, MB4,* K11, rep from * to * once, K1. (31 sts).
Row 106: As *Row 100*. (29 sts).
Row 107: Cast (bind) off knitwise 2 sts at beg of row, MB4, K3, MB4, K15, MB4, K3, MB4, K1. (27 sts).
Row 108: As *Row 100*. (25 sts).
Row 109: Cast (bind) off knitwise 2 sts at beg of row, MB4, K19, MB4, K1. (23 sts).
Row 110: As *Row 100*. (21 sts).
Row 111: Cast (bind) off knitwise 2 sts at beg of row, K all sts. (19 sts).
Row 112: P2tog, P to last 2 sts, PRD. (17 sts).
Row 113: SL 1, K1, PSSO, K to last 2 sts, K2tog. (15 sts).
Rows 114–117: Rep *Rows 112 & 113* twice. (7 sts).
Row 118: As *Row 112*. (5 sts).
Row 119: SL 1, K1, PSSO, MB3, K2tog. (3 sts).

This makes 1 square. For double bed size bedspread, make 48 more, then work 22 triangles as folls for edges:

TRIANGLE

Using 3¼mm (US 3) needles and white mercerised cotton, cast on 2 sts.

Row 1: MB3, K1. (2sts).
Row 2: Inc 1 st, P all sts. (3 sts).
Row 3–9: Inc 1 st at end of K rows and beg of P rows, working in st st. (10 sts).
Row 10: Cast on 2 sts, P all sts. (12 sts).

Row 11: K10, MB4, K1. (12 sts).
Row 12: As *Row 10*. (14 sts).
Row 13: K8, MB4, K3, MB4, K1. (14 sts).
Row 14: As *Row 10*. (16 sts).
Row 15: K6, (MB4, K3) twice, MB4, K1. (16 sts).
Row 16: As *Row 10*. (18 sts).
Row 17: K4, (MB4, K3) 3 times, MB4, K1. (18 sts).
Row 18: As *Row 10*. (20 sts).
Row 19: K2, (MB4, K3) 4 times, MB4, K1. (20 sts).
Row 20: As *Row 10*. (22 sts).
Row 21: (MB4, K3) 5 times, MB4, K1. (22 sts).
Row 22: Inc 1 st at beg of row, P all sts. (23 sts).
Row 23: K2, (MB4, K3) 4 times, MB4, K4, inc 1 st. (24 sts).
Row 24: As *Row 22*. (25 sts).
Row 25: K4, (MB4, K3) 3 times, MB4, K8, inc 1 st. (26 sts).
Row 26: As *Row 22*. (27 sts).
Row 27: K6, (MB4, K3) twice, MB4, K12, inc 1 st. (28 sts).
Row 28: As *Row 22*. (29 sts).
Row 29: K8, MB4, K3, MB4, K16, inc 1 st. (30 sts).
Row 30: As *Row 22*. (31 sts).
Row 31: K10, MB4, K20, inc 1 st. (32 sts).
Row 32: As *Row 22*. (33 sts).
Row 33: K all sts, inc 1 st. (34 sts).
Row 34: (Ridge row) Inc 1 st, K all sts. (35 sts).
Row 35: K1, (YO, K2tog) rep to end. (35 sts).
Row 36: (Ridge row) K all sts. (35 sts).
Row 37–40: Inc 1 st at end of K rows and beg of P rows, working in st st. (39 sts).
Row 41: K9, MB3, K17, MB3, K11. (39 sts).
Row 42: As *Row 22*. (40 sts).
Row 43: K8, MB3, K1, MB3, K15, MB3, K1, MB3, K11. (40 sts).
Row 44: as *Row 22*. (41 sts).
Row 45: K9, MB3, K17, MB3, K13. (41 sts).
Row 46: As *Row 22*. (42 sts).
Row 47: K all sts. (42 sts).
Row 48: As *Row 22*. (43 sts).
Row 49: (MB3, K17) twice, MB3, K6. (43 sts).
Row 50: As *Row 22*. (44 sts).
Row 51: (K1, MB3, K15, MB3) twice, K1, MB3, K6. (44 sts).
Row 52: As *Row 22*. (45 sts).
Row 53: (MB3, K17) twice, MB3, K8. (45 sts).
Row 54: As *Row 22*. (46 sts).
Row 55: As *Row 47*. (46 sts).
Row 56: As *Row 22*. (47 sts).
Row 57: K1, (YO, K2tog), rep to end. (47 sts).
Row 58: (Ridge row) Inc 1 st, K all sts. (48 sts).
Row 59: K all sts, inc 1 st. (49 sts).
Row 60: P1, turn so RS faces. Transfer next st on RH needle to LH needle, MB3 on this st. When bobble is completed, turn so WS faces, transfer bobble st onto RH needle, P37. (49 sts).
Row 61: K all sts. (49 sts).
Row 62: (Ridge row) K2tog, K all sts. (48 sts).
Row 63: K1, (YO, K2tog), rep to last 3 sts, YO, K3tog. (47 sts).
Row 64: P all sts. (47 sts).
Row 65: K to last 2 sts, K2tog. (46 sts).
Row 66: As *Row 64*. (46 sts).
Row 67: (MB3, K17) twice, MB3, K7, K2tog. (45 sts).

Row 68: As *Row 64*. (45 sts).

Row 69: (K1, MB3, K15, MB3) twice, K1, MB3, K5, K2tog. (44 sts).

Row 70: As *Row 64*. (44 sts).

Row 71: (MB3, K17) twice, MB3, K5, K2tog. (43 sts).

Row 72: As *Row 64*. (43 sts).

Row 73: K to last 2 sts, K2tog. (42 sts).

Row 74: As *Row 64*. (42 sts).

Row 75: K9, MB3, K17, MB3, K12, K2tog. (41 sts).

Row 76: As *Row 64*. (41 sts).

Row 77: K8, MB3, K1, MB3, K15, MB3, K1, MB3, K10, K2tog. (40 sts).

Row 78: As *Row 64*. (40 sts).

Row 79: K9, MB3, K17, MB3, K10, K2tog. (39 sts).

Row 80: As *Row 64*. (39 sts).

Rows 81–83: Dec 1 st at end of K rows and beg of P rows, working in st st. (36 sts).

Row 84: (Ridge row) K2tog, K all sts. (35 sts).

Row 85: K1, (YO, K2tog) rep to end. (35 sts).

Row 86: (Ridge row) K all sts. (35 sts).

Rows 87 & 88: Rep *Rows 81 & 82* once. (33 sts).

Row 89: K10, MB4, K20, K2tog. (32 sts).

Row 90: P2tog, P all sts. (31 sts).

Row 91: K8, MB4, K3, MB4, K16, K2tog. (30 sts).

Row 92: As *Row 90*. (29 sts).

Row 93: K6, (MB4, K3) twice, MB4, K12, K2tog. (28 sts).

Row 94: As *Row 90*. (27 sts).

Row 95: K4, (MB4, K3) 3 times, MB4, K8, K2tog. (26 sts).

Row 96: As *Row 90*: (25 sts).

Row 97: K2, (MB4, K3) 4 times, MB4, K4, K2tog. (24 sts).

Row 98: As *Row 90*. (23 sts).

Row 99: (MB4, K3) 5 times, MB4, K2tog. (22 sts).

Row 100: Cast (bind) off purlwise 2 sts at beg of row, P all sts. (20 sts).

Row 101: K2, (MB4, K3) 4 times, MB4, K1. (20 sts).

Row 102: As *Row 100*. (18 sts).

Row 103: K4, (MB4, K3) 3 times, MB4, K1. (18 sts).

Row 104: As *Row 100*. (16 sts).

Row 105: K6, (MB4, K3) twice, MB4, K1. (16 sts).

Row 106: As *Row 100*. (14 sts).

Row 107: K8, MB4, K3, MB4, K1. (14 sts).

Row 108: As *Row 100*. (12 sts).

Row 109: K10, MB4, K1. (12 sts).

Row 110: As *Row 100*. (10 sts).

Row 111: K all sts. (10 sts).

Rows 112–118: Dec 1 st at beg of P rows and end of K rows, working in st st. (3 sts).

Row 119: MB3, K2tog. (2 sts).

Cast (bind) off.

THE BORDER

The bedspread is trimmed with a lacy decorative border which is made as folls:

Using 3¼ (US 3) needles and white mercerised cotton, cast on 21 sts.

Row 1: (WS) (YRN, P2tog, P1) twice, YON2, K3tog, K2, (YO, K2tog) 4 times, YO, K2.

Row 2: YO, K2tog, K13, P1, K2, YO, K2tog, K2.

Row 3: (YRN, P2tog, P1) twice, K2, K2tog, K2, (YO, K2tog) 4 times, YO, K2.

Row 4: YO, K2tog, K16, YO, K2tog, K2.

Row 5: (YRN, P2tog, P1) twice, YON2, K2tog, YO2, K3tog, K1, (YO, K2tog) 4 times, YO, K2.

Row 6: YO, K2tog, K12, P1, K2, P1, K2, YO, K2tog, K2.

Row 7: (YRN, P2tog, P1) twice, K8, (YO, K2tog) 4 times, YO, K2.

Row 8: YO, K2tog, K19, YO, K2tog, K2.

Row 9: (YRN, P2tog, P1) twice, YON2, K2tog, (YO2, K3tog) twice, K1, (YO, K2tog) 4 times, YO, K2.

Row 10: YO, K2tog, K12, (P1, K2) 3 times, YO, K2tog, K2.

Row 11: (YRN, P2tog, P1) twice, K11, (YO, K2tog) 4 times, YO, K2.

Row 12: YO, K2tog, K22, YO, K2tog, K2.

Row 13: (YRN, P2tog, P1) twice, YON2, K2tog, (YO2, K3tog) 3 times, K1, (YO, K2tog) 4 times, YO, K2.

Row 14: YO, K2tog, K12, (P1, K2) 4 times, YO, K2tog, K2.

Row 15: (YRN, P2tog, P1) twice, K14, (YO, K2tog) 4 times, YO, K2.

Row 16: YO, K2tog, K25, YO, K2tog, K2.

Row 17: (YRN, P2tog, P1) twice, K25.

Row 18: Cast (bind) off 10, K16, YO, K2tog, K2.

For double bed size bedspread, rep this patt 149 times, then cast (bind) off.

MAKING UP AND FINISHING

Wash and block each square and triangle after completion, to prevent this becoming too huge a job when attempted in one session. Dry out of direct sunlight to prevent cotton yellowing, then store. Using backstitch, join the squares together when sufficient have been completed, to make this task easier by doing it in installments. Join together in groups of 4 in the arrangement shown in illustration, darning in all loose ends. Wrap in a white cloth or white tissue paper and store in a plastic bag in a safe place to keep clean, as this project will take a long time to complete.

After all the squares have been joined together, start filling in the gaps at the edges with the triangles, using backstitch. Check that all bobbles are sewn closely next to each other to form 'flowers' at each corner, and that there are no spaces between squares. Press lightly on WS with warm iron over damp cloth on seams and then on RS, avoiding bobbles, and airing before storing.

Finally, prepare the border. As this is too long to easily block, it is best to wash it and then press with a warm iron over damp cloth, pulling out the points carefully.

When ready, attach the border to the bedspread edges, using backstitch and pleating 1 repeat of border pattern into a box pleat at each corner.

When washing the bedspread in future use, it is best to hand wash it in the bath tub in warm water and soap flakes, finishing with a cold rinse. Drip dry on a clothes rack placed on towel inside the bath tub until ready for damp pressing, turning regularly. Do not dry outside in the sunlight to avoid yellowing, but a final airing on a washing line on a cloudy day will make it smell sweet and fresh.

SAMPLER

(1868)

During the nineteenth century, knitting and needle-work were compulsory subjects for girls in all Irish schools. Hoping to discover evidence that early Aran knitting may already have been known in this way in the rural Irish schools, I visited the centre for Kerry Folk-Life at Muckross House in Killarney.

Although sadly there were no examples of early Aran knitting here, the centre houses many other interesting textiles which I found most inspiring. Among these was a small hand embroidered sampler, depicting the Kilmoyly Female School near Tralee in 1868, where it was made.

I designed this sweater in soft traditional colours taken from the sampler, with Irish motifs including bands of sham-rock borders, the famous roses of Tralee and Kerry fuchsias. The central panel incorporates the Kilmoyly Schoolhouse, thatched cottages with haystacks and beautiful russet Irish waterhounds.

The sampler can be seen at Muckross House, where it has been on loan from Kerry Library since 1967.

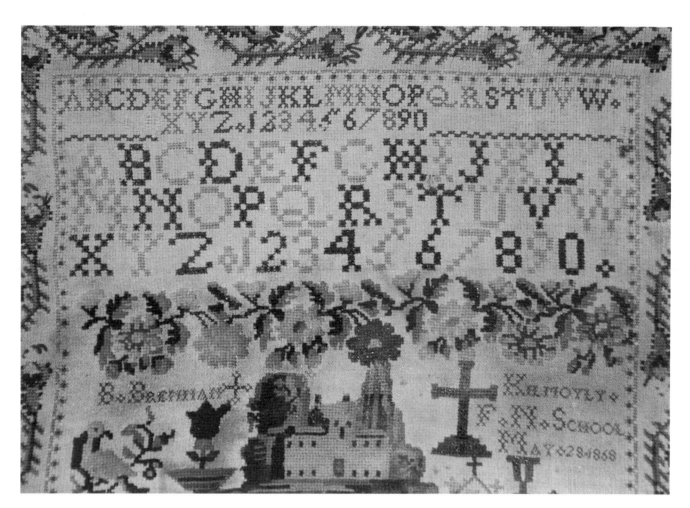

Hand embroidered sampler made at the Kilmoyly Female School

MATERIALS

YARN

Jamieson & Smith 2 Ply Jumper Weight Shetland Wool in the following colours and quantities

A	Cream (FC43)	400g/14½oz
B	Brown (143)	25g/1oz
C	Lemon (46)	25g/1oz
D	Emerald Green (FC11)	25g/1oz
E	Soft Cypress Green (29)	50g/2oz
F	Burnt Orange (FC8)	25g/1oz
G	Bright Yellow (91)	25g/1oz
H	Rose Pink (FC22)	50g/2oz
I	Light Brown (1281)	25g/1oz
J	Peach (FC7)	25g/1oz

NEEDLES

1 pair 2¾mm (US 2) 40cm (15½″) circular needles
1 pair 3¼mm (US 3) 40cm (15½″) circular needles
4 stitch holders
1 set of double pointed spare needles

SIZE AND MEASUREMENTS

One size only to fit up to 102cm (40″) bust

Actual width across back at underarm   56cm (22″)

Length from centre back neck to hip   66cm (26″)

Sleeve seam   54cm (21″)

TENSION (GAUGE)

28 sts and 32 rows to 10cm (4″) over st st on 3¼mm (US 3) needles or size needed to obtain this tension (gauge).

NOTES ON TECHNIQUE

This sweater uses fairisle to work its patterned borders, and intarsia for the multi-coloured motifs, over a plain st st ground. The required methods are specified in the chart.

When working the patterned areas in fairisle, carry colours not in use *very* loosely across the back of the work, weaving around the working yarn every third st to avoid long floats and puckering.

When working the intarsia motifs, use short lengths of wool around 60cm (24″) to avoid tangles, with separate lengths of yarn for each colour as shown on chart. Twist yarn together at each join to avoid holes, then leave in position to be worked in next row. Knit in the ends as you work by wrapping the ends around the new colour thread for two or three sts beyond where they were last used, to minimise later darning in.

BACK

Using 2¾mm (US 2) circular needles as straight and **J**, cast on 117 sts.
In **J**, work 2 rows in K1, P1 rib, then change to **A** and rib 2 more rows.

Change to **H** and rib 2 more rows, change back to **A** and rib until Welt measures 8cm (3″). Change to 3¼mm (US 3) circular needles used as straight and work increase row as folls:

Increase Row: (K3, M1), rep to end, then inc 1 st (157 sts). Beg to work patt in st st by referring to Charts 1 and 2, working from right to left for RS (K) rows and from left to right for WS (P) rows in sequence, joining in and breaking off different yarns as indicated.*

When the area of Alphabet Letters and Numbers is reached, work from small separate Charts on pages 79 and 80 showing letters *S – Z* and numbers *1–0* as shown, instead of letters *A – R* as shown on main chart for Front.

ARMHOLE SHAPING

Row 105: Transfer 8 sts onto stitch holders at beg and end of row cont in patt from charts 1 and 2. Work across rem 141 sts in patt until Alphabet section is reached, then work the *T – O* letters and numbers as shown on separate small Chart on pages 79 and 80.
Cont in patt as set until **Row 182** has been completed.

DIVIDE FOR NECK

RS facing, K54 sts across right Back, then leave rem 87 sts on a spare double pointed needle. Turn and P across the 54 sts, then cont in patt, K next row, dec 1 st at end of row. P next row, then cast (bind) off.

RS facing, transfer 33 sts for centre Back neck onto double pointed spare needle. K in patt across rem 54 sts, turn, then P across next row. Dec 1 st at beg of next row, K across rem sts. P next row, then cast (bind) off.

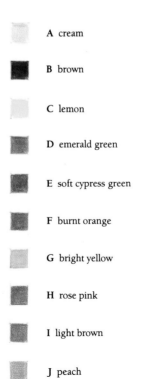

A cream

B brown

C lemon

D emerald green

E soft cypress green

F burnt orange

G bright yellow

H rose pink

I light brown

J peach

Chart 1 – Left Front, Right Back and Sleeve (lower half)

Chart 2 – Right Front, Left Back and Sleeve (lower half)

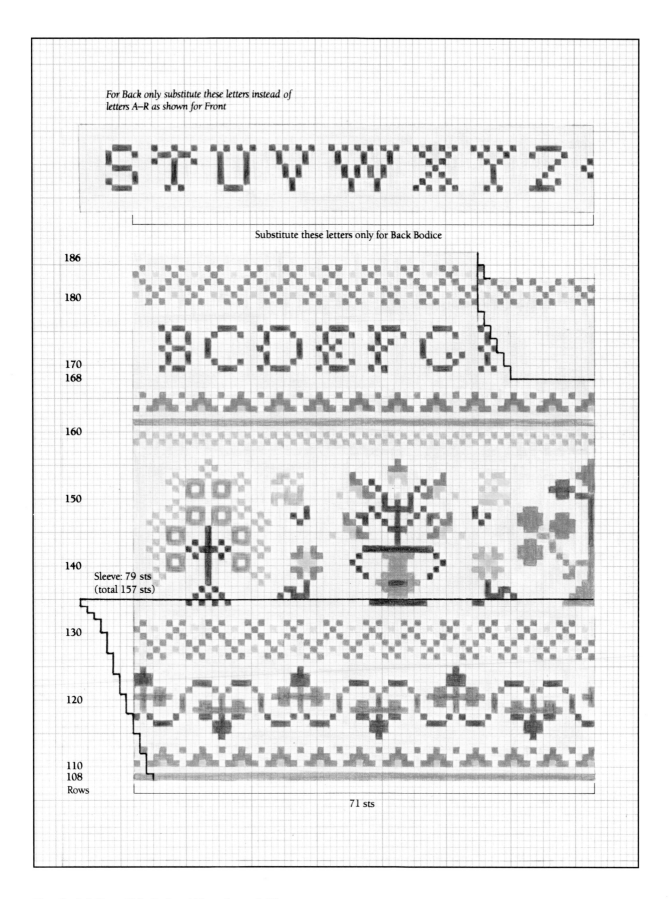

Chart 3 – Left Front, Right Back and Sleeve (upper half)

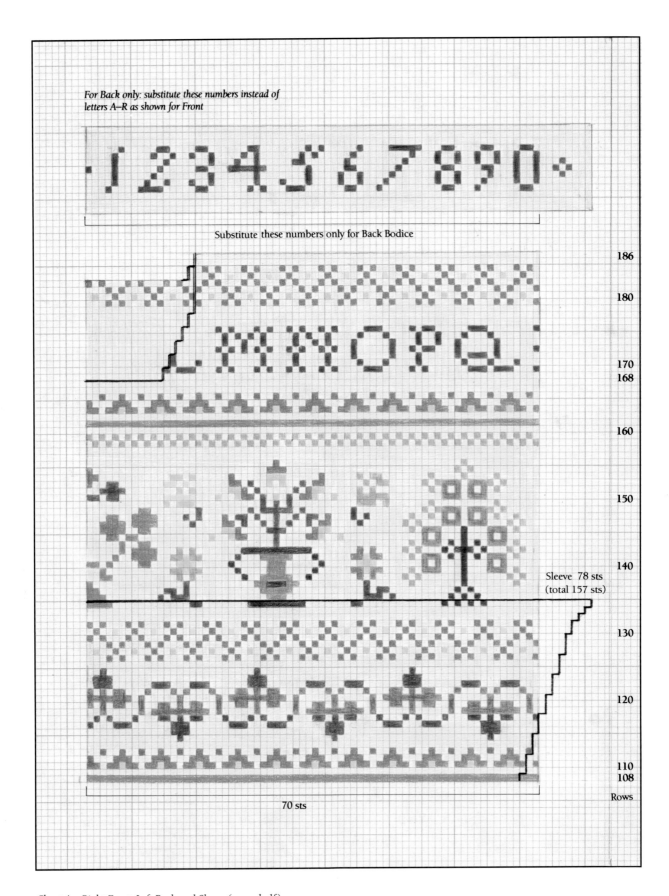

For Back only: substitute these numbers instead of letters A–R as shown for Front

Substitute these numbers only for Back Bodice

186
180
170
168
160
150
140

Sleeve 78 sts
(total 157 sts)

130
120
110
108
Rows

70 sts

Chart 4 – Right Front, Left Back and Sleeve (upper half)

FRONT

Work as for Back until * is reached. Work the Alphabet letters exactly as shown on Front Charts 1 and 2. Cont as for Back, dec at armholes and leaving sts on stitch holders as for Front. Cont in patt until **Row 168** is reached (Charts 3 and 4). Break off yarn.

DIVIDE FOR NECK

RS facing, rejoin in **A**, K across 58 sts, leave rem 83 sts on spare double pointed needle. P next row, foll Alphabet letters from chart, for right Front neck.

NECK SHAPING

K in patt as shown, dec 1 st at end of row. P next row.
Cont in this way, dec 1 st each alt (every other) row until 4 more sts have been dec at neck edge and 53 sts rem. Cont in patt until **Row 186** has been completed, then cast (bind) off in **A**. Transfer 25 sts to spare double pointed needle for centre Front neck and leave. Cont to shape left Front neck, reversing shapings to match right Front neck. Cast (bind) off in **A**.

NECKBAND

Using backstitch, join shoulder seams, then work Neckband in rounds as folls:

Round 1: RS facing, beg at RH seam at Back neck, using 2¼mm (US 2) circular needles and **H**, pick up evenly and K8 sts from right Back neck, 33 sts from spare needle at Back neck, 8 sts from left Back neck, 20 sts from right Front neck, 25 sts from spare needle at Front neck and 20 sts from left Front neck. (114 sts)
Round 2: In **H**, set K1, P1 rib.
Rounds 3 & 4: In **A**, rib.
Round 5: In **J**, rib.
Cast (bind) off ribwise in **J**.

SLEEVES

Using 3¼mm (US 3) circular needles as straight and in **A**, RS facing, pick up evenly and K157 sts from armhole edge. They must be exactly spaced with 78 sts each side of centre st, which is picked up from the shoulder seam, as the patt is then worked from the charts 3 and 4 as shown.

Working from charts, dec 1 st at beg and end of row for next 2 rows. Work next row with no dec, then dec 1 st at beg and end of next row.**

Work 2 rows with no dec, then dec 1 st at beg and end of next row.**

Rep from ** to **, dec every third row as before until end of patt is reached and 65 sts rem. Then work Cuffs as folls:

Change to 2¼mm (US 2) circular needles used as straight and **A**, set in K1, P1 rib. Cont in rib until 6.5cm (2½") has been completed. Change to **H**, rib 2 rows, then change back to **A** and rib 2 more rows. Change to **J**, rib 1 row, then cast (bind) off in **J** ribwise.

MAKING UP AND FINISHING

Darn in all loose ends, then using backstitch for st st and invisible seaming for ribbing, join side and Sleeve seams. Hand wash, drying out of direct sunlight, then lightly press seams on WS with warm iron over damp cloth. Press RS similarly, omitting ribbing.

FISHER GANSEY

(1902)

By now I had a much clearer picture of the progress that had been made in Irish hand knitting up to the end of the nineteenth century. I realized I needed to discover next how far these skills had been applied to fishermen's sweaters, the forerunners of Arans, and so I returned to the National Museum in Dublin.

Their collection of garments selected in 1937 by Muriel Gahan, of the co-operative movement Countryworkers Ltd she founded to help Irish crafts survive, contains a variety of Aran knitwear, stockings and fishermen's ganseys. One of these ganseys (Muriel said later that this term was always used to describe this type of knitwear in the west of Ireland) labelled as being 'of typical native design', is made of undyed cream coloured factory spun Donegal wool, and is decorated with simple bands of moss stitch. Constructed with a separate back and front and made in this natural undyed wool, it is clearly unlike the traditional fishermen's gansey of the English and Scottish coasts, made in the round in navy blue wool – descendants perhaps of seventeenth century damask knitting, and with patterns reminiscent of the embroidery on rural smocks.

Fishing fleet in Ardglass Harbour, Co. Down, late nineteenth century

Early photographs dating from the 1870s in the Lawrence collection in the Irish National Library in Dublin show fishermen from the west coast of Ireland wearing woven shirts, waistcoats and jackets. Those who appear to be wearing what could be fishermen's sweaters are in plain light coloured garments with no distinctive decoration. These may be the 'usual fisherman's jersey' J.M. Synge describes as being recently adopted by the younger men of Aran in his book *The Aran Islands*, where significantly no other intricately patterned types of Aran sweaters are mentioned during the period 1898 to 1902.

All my efforts to discover an elaborately patterned Donegal fisherman's sweater, perhaps deriving from the nineteenth century hand-knitting centres at Ardara and Glenties proved unsuccessful. Yet Muriel Gahan told me that the hand-weaving and hand-knitting industries at Donegal were encouraged and stimulated by her father, who in 1891 was given this responsibility by the Congested Districts Board. She said at this time, 'the typical Donegal gansey was in plain knit, blue and heavy'. She also told me that she had in her possession a child's knitted jersey, retained by her father from his young son who died in a fire in 1900. This jersey was 'like knitted jerseys from Scotland, with the same kind of coloured decoration round the neck'. She felt this type of design, handed down from Northern Irish with Scottish ancestry, was well known in Donegal at this period.

Returning to my search for fishermen's ganseys in the Aran Isles, I consulted a rather rare book that had been loaned to me by an Irish friend. This is a catalogue produced in 1907 entitled *Irish Rural Life and Industry*, issued in connection with the home industries section of the Irish National Exhibition in Dublin. It contains no reference to any home knitting industries anywhere in Ireland in that year other than knitted hosiery. No mention is made of any knitting at all being done for sale on the Aran Isles. For me, this was conclusive proof that before this date, elaborately patterned Aran sweaters were not being made for sale, as the catalogue is extremely detailed, even about the more obscure crafts being carried out at home during this period.

However, I felt my collection of designs would be incomplete without including a garment inspired by a fisherman's gansey. I adapted the moss stitch patterned Donegal sweater from the National Museum to make this version with a more comfortable neckline – the original has a heavy roll-over collar which looks rather constricting.

I knitted it in scarlet wool, as this was a favourite colour with the Aran islanders, who used madder to dye their own hand-spun wool. This was used to weave their belts – Crios – and also to weave into the cloth they used to make the distinctive red flannel skirts which are still worn by the older women as part of their traditional dress. Although to my knowledge, scarlet fishermen's ganseys were never made on the Aran Isles, the colour is so cheerful I couldn't resist including it.

MATERIALS

YARN

Jamieson & Smith 3 Ply (Knitting Worsted) Shetland Wool in Scarlet (H92)
9 (10:11:12) × 50g/16oz (17¾oz:19½oz:21¼oz)

NEEDLES

1 pair 3¼mm (US 3) 60cm (24″) circular needles
1 pair 4mm (US 6) 60cm (24″) circular needles
1 set of double pointed spare needles

SIZES AND MEASUREMENTS

In 4 sizes to fit chest size: 91cm (36″):
96cm(38″): 101cm(40″): 106cm(42″)

Actual width across back at underarm
47cm(18¾″): 49cm(19½″): 52cm(20¾″): 54cm(21½″)

Length from centre back neck to hip
59cm(23½″): 62cm(24½″): 65cm(26″): 68cm(27″)

Sleeve seam   49cm(19½″): 50cm(20″): 51cm(20½″): 52cm(20¾″)

TENSION (GAUGE)

20 sts and 27 rows to 10cm (4″) over st st on 4mm (US 6) needles or size needed to obtain this tension (gauge).

BACK

Using 3¼mm (US 3) circular needles as straight and scarlet wool, cast on 94 (98:102:106) sts and beg Welt as folls:

Set in K2, P2 rib and work 7½cm (3″) in this rib.
Change to 4mm (US 6) circular needles used as straight and K1 row.

This row is the foundation row before the st st area begins and on the RS of work appears as a ridged P row. Break off yarn and rejoin if on WS.

Beg st st area as folls

RS facing, K 1 row and P the next. Cont in st st until work measures 28cm (11″): 31cm(12¼″): 34cm(13½″): 37cm(14¾″) from beg of Welt, ending with a P row.

YOKE AND ARMHOLE SHAPING

Row 1: (RS) P across all sts.
Row 2: Cast (bind) off 8 sts purlwise, P across all rem sts until last 8, cast (bind) off these purlwise. Break off yarn.
Rows 3–12: Rejoin yarn at inside edge of armhole. Moss St for next 10 rows. Moss St: (K1, P1) to end of row on RS rows, beg (P1, K1) to end of row on WS rows.
Rows 13 & 14: K.
Row 15: K.
Row 16: P.
Rows 17–20: Rep *Rows 15 & 16* twice.
Row 21: P.

Row 22: P.
Row 23: K.
Rows 24–27: Rep *Rows 22 & 23* twice.
Row 28: K.
Row 29: K.
Rows 30–39: Moss St.
Row 40: P.
Row 41: P.
Row 42: P.
Row 43: K.
Rows 44–47: Rep *Rows 42 & 43* twice.
Row 48: K.
Row 49: K.
Row 50: P.
Row 51–54: Rep *Rows 49 & 50* twice.
This is the end of patt rep. Rep once more until *Row 33* (actual *Row 87*) has been worked again.

DIVIDE FOR NECK

Row 88: Moss St across as for *Row 34* of patt, but after 25 (27:29:31) sts have been worked, sl rem sts onto spare double pointed needle. Turn and cont shaping for right Back neck.

NECK SHAPING

Row 89: Dec 1 st at beg of row, Moss St to end.
Row 90: Moss St to last 2 sts, dec 1 st at end.
Row 91: As *Row 89*.
Rows 92 & 93: Moss St with no further dec 22 (24:26:28) sts.
Row 94: P, then leave these sts on spare needle for shoulder grafting later. Break off yarn. Transfer 53 (55:57:59) rem sts from first spare needle back onto the 4mm (US 6) needle and with rejoined yarn cast (bind) off 34 sts (all sizes) for Back neck. Work across in Moss St over rem 25 (27:29:31) sts and cont to work left Back neck, reversing shapings to match right Back neck, and leaving sts on spare needle for shoulder grafting later.

FRONT

Work as for Back until third Moss St band has been worked and *Row 15* of patt (actual *Row 69*) has been completed.

DIVIDE FOR NECK

Row 16 of patt (actual *Row 70*) P across 25 (27:29:31) sts, leave rem sts on spare double pointed needle. Turn and dec for right Front neck as folls:
Row 71: Dec 1 st at beg of row, K to end.
Row 72: P to last 2 sts, dec 1 st.
Rep last 2 rows once more. Cont in patt with no further dec until **Row 40** of patt (actual **Row 94**) has been completed. Leave rem sts on another spare needle for later shoulder grafting.

Complete left Front neck shaping similarly, casting (binding) off 28 sts (all sizes) at Front neck, and after shaping has been worked leaving rem sts on spare double pointed needle for shoulder grafting.

GRAFTING SHOULDERS TOGETHER

Place Front and Back together, WS facing each other. Cast (bind) off the sts from left Front shoulder with corresponding sts from right Back shoulder as folls: K each st together with matching st before casting (binding) st off, to form a ridged seam. Rep procedure for right Front shoulder and left Back shoulder sts.

NECKBAND

Change to 3¼mm (US 3) circular needles. Working in rounds, beg at RH Back neck shoulder seam, RS facing, pick up evenly and K4(6:8:10) sts from right Back neck, 30 sts from Back neck, 4(6:8:10) sts from left Back neck, 14(16:18:20) sts across right Front neck, 30 across Front neck, and 14(16:18:20) sts from left Front neck. (96:104:112:120) sts. Set patt as folls:

Round 1: (RS) P.
Round 2: K2, P2, rib to end.

Cont in this rib until 7 rounds have been completed. Cast (bind) off.

SLEEVES

Using 4mm (US 6) circular needles as straight, RS facing, pick up evenly and K80 (84:88:92) sts, working in rows, not rounds, as folls:
Row 1: RS facing, P.
Cont in patt as given for Yoke until *Row 14* has been completed. Commence dec, cont in patt until *Row 41* has been worked, but dec 1 st at beg and end of each 6th (6th:6th:7th) row. After *Row 41* has been worked, beg with *Row 42* as a purl row, cont in st st but cont decs as shown until 48 (52:56:60) sts rem. Cont with no further dec in st st until Sleeve measures 42cm (16¾"): 43cm (17¼"): 44cm (17½"): 45cm (18"). P 1 row, then change to 3¼mm (US 3) circular needles used as straight and work in K2, P2 rib for 7½cm (3"). Cast (bind) off.

MAKING UP AND FINISHING

Using backstitch for st st and invisible seaming for rib, join side seams, and Sleeve seams, attaching Moss St patterned band at top of Sleeve to the 8 st cast (bound) off sides at armhole shaping. Darn in any loose ends.

Press seams on WS with warm iron over damp cloth, then press RS similarly, omitting ribbing and Moss St areas.

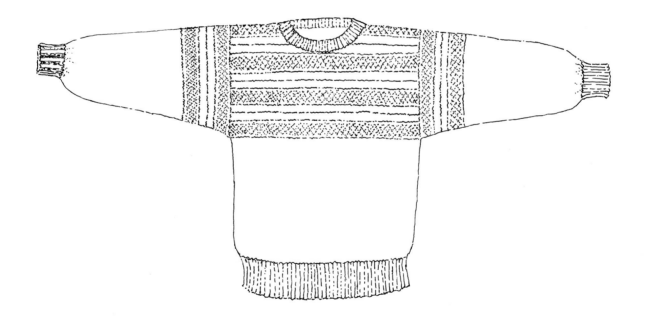

Arans

The American
Connection
(1906–1955)

I felt I was getting closer to the truth, but to learn more about how Aran knitting had really evolved I went back to Inishmore to talk to the elderly knitters. On a small island where the same families have lived for generations and everyone knows everyone else, I was soon directed to the person the islanders considered knew most about knitting in the early days.

Mary Dirrane (Direan in Irish) from Kilronan was a friendly old lady who welcomed me into her cottage, which could have been the original for a folk-museum replica. Scrutinising the sweater I was wearing, a navy blue flag-and-ladder knitted from an authentic Scottish fisherman's pattern, she said:

'Oh, we used to make those on Inishmore, in the old days.'

Inspecting the pattern carefully, which covered the whole garment, she added:

'But we only had pattern on the yoke, the rest plain.'

Remembering Muriel Gahan had told me that the earliest Aran hand-knits dating from 1930 in her Countryworkers collection had patterned decoration only on the yoke and sleeve tops, I was fascinated to hear more.

Mary told me the ganseys had been made in the round, using up to twelve double-pointed needles. I hadn't said a word about my sweater's origins, which would only be evident to someone with considerable knitting expertise, so I knew I should take her remarks seriously. When I asked her to recall all she could about the earliest days of Aran knitting, here is her surprising story.

She said that the first Aran knitting came to Inishmore in 1908 from the USA. Two years earlier, her mother Margaret (Mairead) Dirrane (Direan) and another islander Maggie O'Toole decided to visit America and went to stay 'on some islands just outside Boston, Massachusetts.' Here they were taught knitting stitches unknown to them before by an immigrant lady whose name and nationality unfortunately Mary couldn't remember.

After two years, they returned home to Inishmore, bringing their newly aquired knitting skills with them. At that time, immigrants from all over Europe, especially from Ireland, were pouring into the Boston area. The elaborate patterns in white yarn typical of knitting from the mountainous districts of Scandinavia and Central Europe are not unlike Aran knitting, and could perhaps have been taught to the two Irish ladies.

Before 1908, Mary said hoisery was the only knitting widely practised on Inishmore, and the variety of knitted socks in the Kilronan Folk Museum tends to corroborate this. Although in 1888 there had been a small cottage industry in children's 'jerseys, gloves and socks', reported by Dorothea Roberts in *The Woman's World*, the wages received by the knitters were very low. This had ceased entirely by 1907, when no handknitting industry at all is listed in the comprehensive *Irish Rural Life and Industry* catalogue. The 'usual fisherman's jersey', a simple undecorated garment mentioned by J. M. Synge in his book *The Aran Islands* was only beginning to appear in 1902, and it was from these that the ganseys described by Mary developed.

Inishmore fishermen, sometimes with their female relatives, continually visited the nearby port of Galway where Scottish, English and Channel Islands' fishing fleets regularly docked – there has been trade in wool between Galway and the Channel Islands since the sixteenth century. There would have been many opportunities for knitters to see and to wish to emulate the distinctive ganseys worn by seamen from all these places. However, it was only later that the heavier weight patterned sweaters began to evolve.

As Mairead and Maggie shared their new skills with neighbours and experimented with their own homespun undyed 'bainin' wool, they would have discovered how the intricate twisting patterns made the sweaters much warmer than the simple moss stitch and cable based designs of the ganseys. Mary said at first cable, diamonds and tree of life patterns were used, with honeycomb and trellis following later. The more elaborate their patterns became, the more the dark blue gansey wool would have disguised the clarity of the stitches and so lessened the beauty of their new creations. This reason as well as the superior water-repellant qualities of unscoured wool with its oils retained would have encouraged them to work with the wool in its natural state.

In 1934 Aran islander Robert Flaherty's documentary film *Man of Aran* had made the islands widely famous and topical, although none of the fishermen portraying themselves in the film wore patterned Aran sweaters. Yet only two years later the first highly patterned cream coloured Aran sweater was discovered by textile writer Heinz Edgar Kiewe in Muriel Gahan's Countryworkers Ltd shop in Dublin. Sometime therefore, between 1908 and 1936 the characteristic Aran sweater evolved.

Around the 1930s the hardy old caora ghlas breed of sheep, which produced the grey speckled fleece used in much of the west of Ireland's hoisery began to be replaced by newer breeds capable of producing a lighter creamier fleece able to take the dyes more easily for the region's tweed industry. It was from these new fleeces that the Aran sweater began to be produced.

Heinz Kiewe described the first Aran he saw as 'a peculiar whiskery-looking chunk of sweater in Biblical white ... which looked too odd for words.' He imported similar wool from the Scottish Outer Hebrides to make and sell Arans at his craft shop in Oxford, Art Needlework Industries, sadly closed since his death in 1986. He showed the original Aran to Mary Thomas, a fashion journalist who did much to publicise the garment by including a photograph and details of the discovery in her *Book of Knitting Patterns*, published in 1943. Knitting researcher Gladys Thompson's book *Patterns for Guernseys and Jerseys* (1955) which carefully analyses and notates the Arans in the Dublin Museum collection, continued this process. In this way, Aran sweaters began to be known world wide.

Muriel Gahan's first link with the Aran Isles began in the early thirties when she visited Inishmore and met many of the islanders. She was responsible for getting the first Aran made for Countryworkers Ltd into the Dublin shop for Heinz Kiewe to discover, but was not the only person to organise the production and sale of the early sweaters. According to Yvonne Mahood, in her *History and Organisation of the Aran Knitting Industy in Ireland*, several small family groups at that time began to set up businesses in different parts of the country, some of which still thrive today.

Mary Dirrane from Inishmore. Her explanation of the development of Aran knitting in America throws new light on its early history.

With the increasing commercial marketing of the garments, preference would have been for them to be knitted in separate pieces, rather than in the round, as the original blue ganseys Mary described had been made. A faster speed of production is obtained when knitting and finishing are carried out by different specialist groups of workers. Although even today, many elderly knitters in the industry still prefer to knit and seam the entire garment themselves, in their own homes.

At this stage, shapes became more sophisticated, less like the basic square of the fisherman's 'shirt' and fashioning with raglan shoulder styling began to replace the old saddle shoulder straps. Professional designers became involved and the garments began to turn into fashion products. Aran sweaters, pioneered by Mairead and Maggie who learned their skills in America, began to be produced in quantity and eventually came full circle when the Irish knitting companies started to export to the USA.

HOW ARAN PATTERNS DEVELOPED

(1906–today)

While the island women experimented with their new patterns, at first no instructions were written down. Although English knitting books showing written notation methods were available from the mainland during the 1910–1930 period, and many Gaelic-speaking islanders were also bilingual and literate, they seemed to prefer the time-honoured rural tradition of oral recording. The patterns themselves were the visual aids, and relatives watched the knitting in progress to learn how to make the new motifs.

As the craft developed, certain traditions grew up around the methods of design and the meanings of individual patterns. One tradition explains the variety and grouping of the panels on the sweaters as becoming heraldic-like emblems for the sons in a fishing family. It was said that a newly married island woman would commemorate the birth of her first son by making a plain sweater with one decorative panel knitted into the front of the garment. As subsequent sons were born, and became fishermen like their father, new panels with different designs were added on either side until the entire sweater was elaborately embellished. Should the boat be shipwrecked, these patterns would help to identify the body.

Other beliefs maintain that certain families guarded their own patterns, refusing to share them with other families, and only passed on the designs to the daughters of the same family. Only through marriage and the birth of sons would the patterns become disseminated around the island.

Traditions like these, and the romantic meanings attached to the actual motifs have become part of the mythology of Aran knitting. Their reality, and the truth behind them have become as difficult to disentangle as some of the more intricate interlace patterns that characterise the craft.

Nevertheless, examining the various patterns as they developed, gradually increasing in complexity as the knitters grew more adept, is fascinating, especially where they relate to earlier archetypal Irish art forms.

Cables

Variations of these were one of the earliest patterns used in Aran knitting. While obviously reflecting the ropes that are so much part of the lives of a fishing community, they have been part of the Irish artistic culture since the first torcs were made. Popularly said to be able to bring luck to the fisherman wearing them in his sweater.

Diamonds

These also occur in the earliest Arans in various forms. They are said to reflect the island's small fields that have been reclaimed from the barren rocks. Sometimes filled with Irish moss stitch which represents the seaweed that fertilizes the fields, bringing wealth. An ancient shape that occurs universally, they appear on the Newgrange passage graves. Popularly said to represent success and wealth for the wearer.

Tree of Life

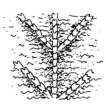

Another of the earliest stitches, this often appeared on the decorative welts of the first Arans. These textured welts are unique in knitting of this period. Trees of Life are a common symbol of growth in many cultures, and in Aran knitting have come to represent family unity, with long-lived parents and strong children.

Later, patterns appeared which are clearly variations of earlier basic forms.

Zig-Zag

This simple shape, half of the diamond, is often used, sometimes over a plain stocking(ette) stitch ground. It appears at Newgrange, and in early Irish metalwork. It popularly represents the twisting cliff paths along the shore.

Double Zig-Zag

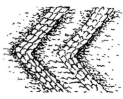

This is clearly an extension of the single zig-zag. It has popularly come to be called 'marriage lines', said to represent the ups and downs of married life.

Trellis and Interlace

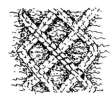

These trellis based patterns develop naturally from the diamonds and zig-zags. They are recurrent in Irish art, appearing on Celtic jewellery, early Christian manuscripts and the sculpted relief decoration of the High Crosses. Like the diamond, it has come to represent the stone walled fields of Aran, and the wealth they bring to the islands. They also are said to represent the fishing nets of the Aran seamen.

Plaits, Braids, Ribbon and The Link

  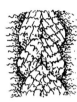

There are a huge variety of these intertwining patterns related to cables and trellis designs. Braiding has always been an ancient craft in Ireland, often worked using horsehair and surviving today in basketry and the St Brigid's crosses made from rushes. There are so many the meanings cannot all be given here, but The Link has come to symbolise the unbroken chain between the Irish who emigrate and those who remain at home.

Chevrons

These are related to the Tree of Life patterns, but vary in form, sometimes resembling half diamonds and sometimes looking more like anchors, or lucky wishbones.

In several early Aran garments, openwork stitch is used in conjunction with basic stitches such as zig-zags or diamonds. Occasionally, complete traditional Scottish lace patterns are incorporated to make a more Hebridean influenced garment. Scottish fishing fleets often visited the west coast of Ireland, and this has clearly had some impact on Aran knitting.

Ladder of Life

Sometimes called Jacob's Ladder, this is also related to the ladder stitches of Scottish guernseys. Popularly it has come to symbolize the human struggle to climb heavenwards.

The following group of stitches, having a very small stitch repeat, are useful as background patterns. They are often used to decorate the sides of a garment with a central group of patterned panels down the front or back. Where a range of sizes is required, the small repeat allows a varying number of stitches to be added or subtracted at the sides without disturbing the central patterns. Sometimes these stitches are used to fill in stitches such as diamonds or trellis designs.

Honeycomb

This stitch developed by grouping rows of cables next to each other and varying the way the stitches cross over. It is sometimes used as a single unit as a cable variation. The pattern has come to symbolize the hard work of the bee and the reward of honey this brings – diligence brings prosperity.

Irish Moss

This stitch is a very simple variation of ordinary moss stitch. It has become a symbol of Carrageen Moss, the seaweed collected by the islanders and used as fertilisers on their fields and for processing by the chemical and cosmetic industries for iodene.

Blackberry

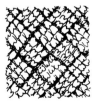

Also known as Holy Trinity stitch, as it is made in a simple make three from one stitch, then make one from three. It produces a knobbly all-over pattern not seen on the very early Arans.

Basket stitch

Another more recent introduction to Aran knitting, but one which works well with the traditional patterns. Already a folk-lore has developed linking it with the prosperity a full fisherman's basket brings. An ancient design motif, it often appeared on La Tène metalwork.

Bobbles

These were used from the very earliest times on Arans, and are sometimes used to infill diamonds or curving interlaced designs. They vary in construction but often add to the rich embossed quality of the garment. They recur in Irish Metalwork of the Bronze Age period.

RELIGIOUS SYMBOLISM

Since ancient times, the Aran islands have been a sanctuary for the religious, and this heritage seems to have left its mark on the knitting. Many of the islanders remain very religious, as the well tended Catholic shrines in their homes and around the islands show.

Several of the designs are taken to express Christian symbolism, although is some cases the actual art-forms they echo pre-date the Christian era. Cables, Trellis, Jacob's Ladder, Tree of Life and Holy Trinity stitch have all come to have spiritual meanings which interlace with their folk-loric traditions.

A detail from a High Cross showing interlace and cables

Bound up with this is the idea that when made by a knitter in the right spiritual state, using the appropriate stitches, the garment could become a protective talisman guarding the fisherman from hostile elements of a natural and supernatural nature. Belief in the fairies and elemental spirits was widespread on the Aran islands at this time.

CHANGES IN THE DESIGN
OF ARAN KNITTING

Originally, Aran stitch patterns were always arranged in vertical panels down the garment, unlike fisher gansey decoration which used both vertical and horizontal patterning.

Nowadays the patterns are arranged in any direction the designer chooses, and it is not only the shape and fashioning of the garment that has altered but the colour of yarns, the introduction of new stitch patterns, and even the use of the traditional early motifs. These are sometimes incorporated into bands of fairisle or intarsia, far from the original 'Biblical white' that had impressed Heinz Kiewe.

Ideas of design are continually altering in response to international fashion, commercial popularity, media interest and the technical aspects of knitting. These are the forces that shape all new design, and with which all crafts must continually contend. I had come to Ireland hoping to discover how Aran designs had evolved locally, perhaps being influenced by immigrant foreign cultures. Instead, it seemed it was the Irish who had gone abroad themselves, only to learn from foreign emigrants, before they brought their knowledge back to Ireland again. Such is the diversity and cross pollination of artistic ideas.

Aran knitting cannot remain static, and its eventual survival will depend on how it is able to adapt to the changing world. Already there is a shortage of younger people prepared to work for the rather low pay Aran knitters receive, not only on the Aran islands, but throughout Ireland. It will only be through capturing the imagination of these potential knitters through design that they will take sufficient interest in the craft to make their own contributions, and so ensure its survival.

Today, little handknitting for sale is carried out on the Aran islands. The insatiable demand for sweaters from visiting tourists from all over the world could not possibly be met by the islands' population. Even in the summer only around 2000 people live on Inishmore, Inishmaan and Inisheer.

Cottages on storm-bound Inishmore

Although there is a thriving co-operative on Inishmaan which supplies the visitors with sweaters, these are mostly handknitted on the mainland or machine made by the islanders. Several other craft shops on Inishmore sell similar products.

A plea from Mary Dirrane for me to settle in Inishmore and start a designer knitting business tempted me more than she knew. But probably a more useful project would be a handknitting skills workshop, made available to islanders and tourists, to help re-kindle the pleasures of Aran knitting.

DIAMOND AND CABLE ARAN

In this sweater, diamonds are teamed with cable and rib in a richly patterned yoke design, which according to Mary Dirrane, the elderly knitter from Inishmore, was how all the earliest Aran sweaters were decorated.

The sleeves and lower bodice are in plain stocking stitch, similar to the guernseys worn by fishermen from around the coasts of Britain during the early twentieth century, which influenced Aran designs.

Early Aran sweater showing diamond and cable patterns

Here the yokes have been extended with a central panel incorporating ribs which travel right down into the welt and around the V neck, echoing the diamond shapes.

The diamonds, infilled with moss stitch were also one of the earliest patterns to be used. It is said they symbolize material prosperity, representing the stony walled fields on the islands, fertilized with Carrageen moss seaweed.

MATERIALS

YARN

Rowan Fleck DK (Knitting Worsted) in Grey
14 × 50g/24¾oz

NEEDLES

1 pair 3¼mm (US 3) 60cm (24″) circular needles
1 pair 4mm (US 6) 60cm (24″) circular needles
2 cable needles
1 set of double pointed spare needles
2 stitch holders

SIZE AND MEASUREMENTS

One size only to fit up to 102cm (40″) chest.

Actual width across back at underarm   54cm (21½″)

Length from centre back neck to hip   71cm (28″)

Sleeve seam   53cm (21″)

TENSION (GAUGE)

22 sts and 30 rows to 10cm (4″) over st st on 4mm (US 6) needles or size needed to obtain this tension (gauge).

SPECIAL ABBREVIATIONS

C2F	Sl 1 st onto cable needle, hold at front, K1, then K1 from cable needle.
C2B	Sl 1 st onto cable needle, hold at back, K1, then K1 from cable needle.
C4F	Sl 2 sts onto cable needle, hold at front, K2, then K2 from cable needle.
C4B	Sl 2 sts onto cable needle, hold at back, K2, then K2 from cable needle.
FC	Sl 2 sts onto cable needle, hold at front, P1, then K2 from cable needle.
BC	Sl 1 st st onto cable needle, hold at back, K2, then P1 from cable needle.
FKC	Sl 2 sts onto cable needle, hold at front, K1, then K2 from cable needle.
BKC	Sl 1 st onto cable needle, hold at back, K2, then K1 from cable needle.
SFC	Sl 1 st onto cable needle, hold at front, P1, then K1 from cable needle.
SBC	Sl 1 st onto cable needle, hold at back, K1, then P1 from cable needle.
TC	Sl 2 sts onto cable needle, hold at front, sl next st onto 2nd cable needle, also hold at front. K next 2 sts from LH needle, then sl 1 st from 2nd cable needle in front of, and over, the 2 sts on 1st cable needle, then K the st from the 2nd cable needle, and lastly the 2 sts from cable needle.
K2togTBL	Knit 2 sts together through the back of loops.
P2togTBL	Purl 2 sts together through the back of loops.

PANEL A (LH SIDE) (40 sts)

Row 1: (WS) P37, K3.
Row 2: P3, K37.

(These 2 rows form patt rep)

PANEL B (RH SIDE) (40 sts)

Row 1: (WS) K3, P37.
Row 2: K37, P3.

(These 2 rows form patt rep)

PANEL C (LH CABLE PATTERN) (10 sts)

Row 1: (WS) P1, K2, P4, K2, P1.
Row 2: K1, P2, K4, P2, K1.
Rows 3 & 4: As *Rows 1 & 2*.
Row 5: As *Row 1*.
Row 6: K1, P2, C4F, P2, K1.

(These 6 rows form patt rep)

PANEL D (RH CABLE PATTERN) (10 sts)

Row 1: (WS) P1, K2, P4, K2, P1.
Row 2: K1, P2, K4, P2, K1.
Rows 3 & 4: As *Rows 1 & 2*.
Row 5: As *Row 1*.
Row 6: K1, P2, C4B, P2, K1.

(These 6 rows form patt rep)

PANEL E (CENTRAL DIAMOND PATTERN)

(29 sts)

Row 1: (WS) (K1, P1) 3 times, P1, K5, P5, K5, P1, (P1, K1) 3 times.
Row 2: (K1, P1) twice, K1, SBC, P4, BC, K1, FC, P4, SFC, (K1, P1) twice, K1.
Row 3: (K1, P1) 3 times, K5, P7, K5, (P1, K1) 3 times.
Row 4: (K1, P1) twice, SBC, P4, BC, P1, K1, P1, FKC, P4, SFC, (P1, K1) twice.
Row 5: (K1, P1) twice, P1, K5, P2, K1, P3, K1, P2, K5, P1, (P1, K1) twice.
Row 6: K1, P1, K1, SBC, P4, BC, (K1, P1) twice, K1, FC, P4, SFC, K1, P1, K1.
Row 7: (K1, P1) twice, K5, (P3, K1) twice, P3, K5, (P1, K1) twice.
Row 8: K1, P1, SBC, P4, BC, (K1, P1) 3 times, P1, FKC, P4, SFC, P1, K1.
Row 9: K1, P2, K5, P1, (P1, K1) twice, P2, (P1, K1) twice, P2, K5, P2, K1.
Row 10: K1, SBC, P4, BC, (K1, P1) 4 times, K1, FC, P4, SFC, K1.
Row 11: K1, P1, K5, P2, (P1, K1) twice, P3, (K1, P1) twice, P2, K5, P1, K1.
Row 12: SBC, P4, BKC, (P1, K1) 5 times, P1, FKC, P4, SFC.
Row 13: P1, K5, P2, (K1, P1) 3 times, P1, (P1, K1) 3 times, P2, K5, P1.
Row 14: SFC, P4, FC, (P1, K1) 5 times, P1, BC, P4, SBC.

Row 15: P2, K5, P2, (P1, K1) twice, P3, (K1, P1) twice, P2, K5, P2.
Row 16: P1, C2F, P4, FC, (K1, P1) 4 times, K1, BC, P4, C2B, P1.
Row 17: P1, K1, P1, K5, P1, (P1, K1) twice, P3, (K1, P1) twice, P1, K5, P1, K1, P1.
Row 18: P1, K1, SFC, P4, FC, (P1, K1) 3 times, P1, BC, P4, SBC, K1, P1.
Row 19: P1, K1, P2, K5, (P3, K1) twice, P3, K5, P2, K1, P1.
Row 20: P1, K1, P1, C2F, P4, FC, (K1, P1) twice, K1, BC, P4, C2B, P1, K1, P1.
Row 21: (P1, K1) twice, P1, K5, P2, K1, P3, K1, P2, K5, (P1,K1) twice, P1.
Row 22: (P1, K1) twice, SFC, P4, FC, P1, K1, P1, BC, P4, SBC, (K1, P1) twice.
Row 23: P1, (K1, P1) twice, P1, K5, P7, K5, P1, (P1, K1) twice, P1.
Row 24: P1, (K1, P1) twice, C2F, P4, FC, K1, BC, P4, C2B, (P1, K1) twice, P1.
Row 25: (P1, K1) 3 times, P1, K5, P5, K5, (P1, K1) 3 times, P1.
Row 26: (P1, K1) 3 times, K1, P5, TC, P5, K1, (K1, P1) 3 times.
Row 27: (P1, K1) 3 times, P1, K5, P5, K5, (P1, K1) 3 times, P1.
Row 28: (P1, K1) twice, P1, SBC, P4, BC, K1, FC, P4, SFC, (P1, K1) twice, P1.
Row 29: (P1, K1) twice, P2, K5, P7, K5, P2, (K1, P1) twice.
Row 30: (P1, K1) twice, SBC, P4, BC, P1, K1, P1, FKC, P4, SFC, (K1, P1) twice.
Row 31: (P1, K1) 3 times, K4, P2, K1, P3, K1, P2, K4, (K1, P1) 3 times.
Row 32: P1, K1, P1, SBC, P4, BC, (K1, P1) twice, K1, FC, P4, SFC, P1, K1, P1.
Row 33: P1, K1, P2, K5, (P3, K1) twice, P3, K5, P2, K1, P1.
Row 34: P1, K1, SBC, P4, BC, (P1, K1) 3 times, P1, FC, P4, SFC, K1, P1.
Row 35: P1, K1, P1, K5, P2, (K1, P1) twice, P1, (P1, K1) twice, P2, K5, P1, K1, P1.
Row 36: P1, SBC, P4, BC, (K1, P1) 4 times, K1, FC, P4, SFC, P1.
Row 37: P2, K5, P2, (P1, K1) twice, P3, (K1, P1) twice, P2, K5, P2.
Row 38: SBC, P4, BKC, (P1, K1) 5 times, P1, FKC, P4, SFC.
Row 39: P1, K5, P2, (K1, P1) 3 times, P1, (P1, K1) 3 times, P2, K5, P1.

(Rep over number of rows stated in instructions.)

BACK

Using 3¼mm (US 3) circular needles as straight and Rowan Fleck DK, cast on 129 sts and work Welt as folls:

Row 1: (K1, P1) 30 times, (K3, P1) twice, K1, (P1, K1) 30 times.
Row 2: (P1, K1) 30 times, (P1, K3) twice, P1, (K1, P1) 30 times.

Cont in rib patt as set until Welt measures 9cm (3½"). Break off yarn.

Change to 4mm (US 6) circular needles used as straight and rejoin yarn at beg of next WS row so that centre st will be continuous st st.

SET FOUNDATION ARAN PATT ROW AS FOLLS:

Row 1: (WS) *Panel A* over 40 sts; *Panel C* over 10 sts; *Panel E* over 29 sts; *Panel D* over 10 sts; *Panel B* over 40 sts.

Row 2: *Panel B* over 40 sts; *Panel D* over 10 sts; *Panel E* over 29 sts; *Panel C* over 10 sts; *Panel A* over 40 sts.

Cont in patt as set, working over the panels in sequence until **Row 39** of *Panel E* has been completed. Keeping patts of *Panels A, C, D & B* continuous, recommence *Panel E* at **Row 14**, and work **Rows 14–39** of *Panel E* continuously in future, omitting **Rows 1–13**, until 3rd diamond has been completed and **Row 76** has been worked.

INTRODUCE YOKE PATT

Row 77: (WS) *Edge st* K1; *Row 5* of *Panel C* over 10 sts; *Row 25* of *Panel E* over 29 sts; *Row 5* of *Panel C* over 10 sts; *Row 25* of *Panel E* over 29 sts; *Row 5* of *Panel D* over 10 sts; *Row 25* of *Panel E* over 29 sts; *Row 5* of *Panel D* over 10 sts; *Edge st* K1.

Row 78: *Edge st* P1; *Row 6* of *Panel D* over 10 sts; *Row 26* of *Panel E* over 29 sts; *Row 6* of *Panel D* over 10 sts; *Row 26* of *Panel E* over 29 sts; *Row 6* of *Panel C* over 10 sts; *Row 26* of *Panel E* over 29 sts; *Row 6* of *Panel C* over 10 sts; *Edge st* P1.

Cont in patt as set with Edge sts in reverse st st, until *Row 21* of the 7th rep of *Panel E* in centre of Back has been completed.

DIVIDE FOR NECK

RS facing, work in patt across 87 sts, but leave last 45 sts on stitch holder for Back neck later, then complete rem 42 sts. Transfer first 42 sts to spare needle and turn work.

NECK SHAPING

Keeping to patt as set, dec 1 st at neck edge, cont shaping this way dec 1 st each row at inside neck edge until **Row 28** of *Panel*

E has been completed and 35 sts rem. Cast (bind) off. Work other shoulder similarly.

FRONT

Using 3¼mm (US 3) circular needles as straight and Rowan Fleck DK, cast on 129 sts. Work as for Back until **Row 25** of 5th central diamond rep of *Panel E* has been completed.

SHAPE V NECK

Row 26 of *Panel E* Work in patt as set for 62 sts. Sl next 2 sts on cable needle, hold at front, then sl central st onto a stitch holder, leave at front until later. K2 from LH needle, then K2 from cable needle. Cont across in patt to end of row.

DIVIDE FOR NECK

Row 27 of *Panel E* Work in patt for 64 sts (last 2 sts are P2), then turn.

Leave rem sts on a spare needle and work left Front as folls: RS facing, at neck edge: FC, then cont to end of row in **Row 28** of *Panel E* patt.

Next Row: Patt as for *Row 29* of *Panel E*, end in P2, K1.

Next Row: Patt as for *Row 30* of *Panel E* but beg: sl 1 st onto cable needle, hold at front, sl next 2 sts onto 2nd cable needle, hold at front. Sl the st on the 1st cable needle back behind the 2 sts on the 2nd cable needle and onto the LH needle again, then P2tog. K the 2 sts from the 2nd cable needle, and cont to end of row in patt.

Next Row: Patt as for *Row 31* of *Panel E* with no dec, end in P2, K1.

Cont in patt as set, dec each alt (every other) neck edge row as shown until 4th diamond of yoke patt has been completed. Work 1 more row, then cast (bind) off.

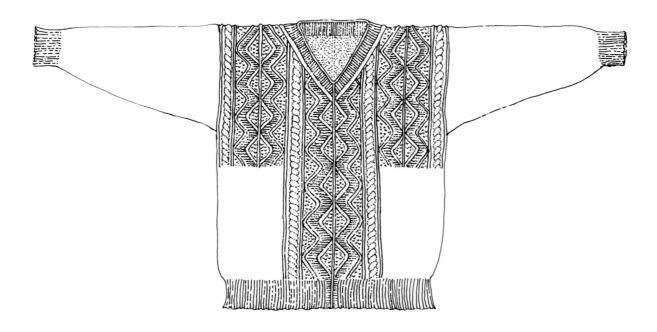

Turn and work right Front similarly, reversing shapings as folls:

Next Row: Patt as for *Row 28* of *Panel E* until last 4 sts. Sl next st onto cable needle, hold at back, K2, then transfer st on cable needle at back to LH needle and P tog with last st on LH needle.

Next row: Patt as for *Row 29* of *Panel E*, beg K1, P2. Cont to match other shoulder, dec similarly, then cast (bind) off.

Using backstitch, join cast (bound) off shoulders, WS facing, then work Neckband.

NECKBAND

Using 3¼mm (US 3) circular needles, RS facing, beg at RH corner of Back neck shoulder seam, pick up and K6 sts at right Back neck, 45 sts from Back neck, 6 sts from left Back neck, 32 sts from right side of V neck, the central st from the stitch holder and 32 sts from left side of V neck. (122 sts). Work in K1, P1 rib as folls:

Round 1: K1, P1 until within 2 sts of central front st, P2tog, K the central st, then P2togTBL, rib to end.
Round 2: Rib as set until within 2 sts of centre st, K2tog, K the central st then K2togTBL, rib to end.

Cont in this way, dec sts as shown but retaining central st as a K st on RS and a P st on WS until 7 rounds have been worked, then cast (bind) off knitwise.

SLEEVES

Using backstitch for st st and invisible seam for ribbing, join side seams until seam measures 43cm (17″) from hem to armhole, leaving 28cm (11″) at Yoke. Using 4 mm (US 6) circular needles as straight, pick up evenly and K110 sts from Edge st at armhole edges.

Row 1: (WS) P.
Row 2: Dec 1 st at beg and end of row, K.
Working in st st rep *Rows 1 & 2* twice more. (104 sts)
Row 7: Dec 1 st at beg and end of row. (102 sts)
Next 3 rows: No dec.
Row 11: Dec 1 st at beg and end of row. (100 sts)
Rep last 4 rows once more. (98 sts).
Cont in st st, dec 1 st at beg and end of each 6th row until 66 sts rem and Sleeve measures 46cm (18″).
Next K row: (K2tog, K9) rep to end. (60 sts).
Change to 3¼mm (US 3) circular needles used as straight. Set in K1, P1 single rib, rib for 9cm (3½″). Cast (bind) off.

MAKING UP AND FINISHING

Using backstitch for st st and invisible seam for ribbing join Sleeve seams. Darn in any loose ends, then press seams on WS with warm iron over a damp cloth. Press RS similarly, omitting ribbing and patterned areas.

CARRAGEEN

This crisp cotton sweater in Irish Moss stitch is decorated with an embossed cable pattern. Both stitches appeared very early in Aran knitting.

Irish moss stitch was said to be named after the Carrageen moss which is still harvested at low tide around the coasts of the Aran Isles. Mixed with sand, it forms a precious growing medium which augments the sparse soil on these rocky islands. Traditional seaweed rights were allocated to the island's householders in a centuries-old system – the 'moss' was a vital part of their subsistence economy.

MATERIALS

YARN

Rowan Handknit DK Cotton in White (263)
14 (15:16) × 50g/2¾oz (26½oz:28¼oz)

NEEDLES
1 pair 3¼mm (US 3) 60cm (24″) straight needles
1 pair 4mm (US 6) 80cm (31½″) circular needles
2 pairs 4mm (US 6) 80cm (31½″) spare circular needles
1 cable needle

SIZE AND MEASUREMENTS

In 3 sizes: Sizes 1 (2:3) to fit bust 91cm (36″):
96cm (38″): 101cm (40″)

Actual width across back at underarm
48cm (19″): 51cm (20″): 54cm (21½″)

Length from centre back neck to hip
58cm (23″): 60cm (24″): 63cm (25″)

Sleeve seam   45cm (18″)

TENSION (GAUGE)

17 sts and 28 rows to 10cm (4″) over Irish Moss st on 4mm (US 6) needles or size needed to obtain this tension.

NOTES ON TECHNIQUE

To achieve a graceful sleeve shape and to enhance the shoulder decoration by avoiding ugly seaming, the sweater is made in one piece. Begin with right Sleeve, work across Front and Back separately, and end with left Sleeve. The Welt and Cuffs are added later.

SPECIAL ABBREVIATIONS

IM	Irish Moss St (instructions given after Special Abbreviations).
LTC4	Left-twist Cable pattern (instructions given after Special Abbreviations)
RTC4	Right-twist Cable pattern (instructions given after Special Abbreviations).
CP	Centre Panel (patt given as part of main instructions as it repeats over 115 rows).
C4F	Sl 2 sts onto cable needle, hold at front, K2, then K2 from cable needle.
C4B	Sl 2 sts onto cable needle, hold at back, K2, then K2 from cable needle.
C4FM	Sl 2 sts onto cable needle, hold at front, K1, P1, then K2 from cable needle.
C4BM	Sl 2 sts onto cable needle, hold at back, K2, then K1, P1 from cable needle.
C4FP	Sl 2 sts onto cable needle, hold at front, P2, then K2 from cable needle.
C4BP	Sl 2 sts onto cable needle, hold at back, K2, then P2 from cable needle.
MB	Make a bobble as folls: K into front and back of next st twice, then K into front again making 5 sts from 1. Turn and K5 sts, turn and P5 sts, then lift 2nd, 3rd, 4th and 5th sts over 1st st and off needle.
MB2	Make 2 bobbles from next 2 sts, each bobble made as already shown for MB above.

PATTERNS

IRISH MOSS STITCH (IM)
(Irish Moss St over even number of sts)

Rows 1 & 2: (K1, P1) rep over even number of sts to end.
Rows 3 & 4: (P1, K1) rep over even number of sts to end.

(These 4 rows form patt rep).

IRISH MOSS STITCH (IM)

(Irish Moss St over uneven number of sts)

Row 1: (K1, P1) to last st, K1.
Row 2: (P1, K1) to last st, P1.
Row 3: As *Row 2*.
Row 4: As *Row 1*.

(These 4 rows form patt rep)

LEFT TWIST CABLE (LTC4) (4 sts)

Row 1: K.
Row 2: P.
Row 3: C4F.
Row 4: P.

(These 4 rows form patt rep)

RIGHT TWIST CABLE (RTC4) (4 sts)

Row 1: K.
Row 2: P.
Row 3: C4B.
Row 4: P.

(These 4 rows form patt rep).

CENTRE PANEL (CP) (12 sts)

Patt is worked over *Rows 1–115*, repeated from *Rows 2–115*, as given in main instructions.

BEGIN AT RIGHT SLEEVE EDGE

Using 4mm (US 6) circular needles as straight and Rowan Handknit Cotton, cast on 59 (67:75) sts. P 1 row, then set Foundation Rows as folls:

Row 1: IM 8 (12:16), P1, (LTC4, CP [P2, K3, P1, K1, P1, K2, P2], RTC4, P1) twice; IM 8 (12:16).
Row 2: IM 8 (12:16), K1, (RTC4, CP [K2, P3, K1, P1, K1, P2, K2], LTC4, K1) twice; IM 8 (12:16).
Row 3: As *Row 1*.

BEGIN SHAPING SLEEVE

Inc 1 st at beg of next 2 rows, then work foll 3 rows with no inc. Cont to shape in this way until *Row 101* is reached, incorporating the extra sts into the Moss st patt as already set.

Row 4: (Inc row) IM all Irish Moss sts, K1, (RTC4, CP [K2, P3, K1, P1, K1, P2, K2], LTC4, K1) twice, IM all Irish Moss sts.
Row 5: (Inc row) IM, P1, (LTC4, CP [P2, K3, P1, K1, P1, K2, P2], RTC4, P1) twice, IM.
Row 6: No inc, otherwise as *Row 4*.
Row 7: IM, P1, (LTC4, CP [P2, C4F, C4B, P2], RTC4, P1) twice, IM.
Row 8: IM, K1, (RTC4, CP [K2, P8, K2], LTC4, K1) twice, IM.
Row 9: (Inc row) IM, P1, (LTC4, CP [P2, K8, P2], RTC4, P1) twice, IM.
Row 10: (Inc row) As *Row 8*.
Row 11: IM, P1, (LTC4, CP [P2, C4B, C4F, P2] RTC4, P1) twice, IM.

Row 12: As *Row 8*.
Row 13: No inc, otherwise as *Row 9*.
Row 14: (Inc row) otherwise as *Row 8*.
Row 15: (Inc row) IM, P1, (LTC4, CP [P2, C4BM, C4FM, P2], RTC4, P1) twice, IM.
Row 16: No inc, otherwise as *Row 4*.
Row 17: No inc, otherwise as *Row 5*.
Row 18: No inc, otherwise as *Row 4*.
Row 19: (Inc row) As *Row 5*.
Row 20: (Inc row) As *Row 4*.
Row 21: IM, P1, (LTC4, CP [P2, C4FP, C4BP, P2], RTC4, P1) twice, IM.
Row 22: IM, K1, (RTC4, CP [K4, P4, K4], LTC4, K1) twice, IM.
Row 23: IM, P1, (LTC4, CP [P4, C4B, P4] RTC4, P1) twice, IM.
Row 24: (Inc row), otherwise as *Row 22*.
Row 25: (Inc row), IM, P1, (LTC4, CP [P4, K4, P4], RTC4, P1) twice, IM.
Row 26: As Row 22.
Row 27: IM, P1, (LTC4, CP [P2, MB, P1, C4B, P1, MB, P2], RTC4, P1) twice, IM.
Row 28: As Row 22.
Row 29: (Inc row) As *Row 25*.
Row 30: (Inc row), otherwise as *Row 22*.
Row 31: As Row 23.
Row 32: As Row 22.
Row 33: No inc, otherwise as *Row 15*.
Row 34: (Inc row) As *Row 4*.
Row 35: (Inc row) As *Row 5*.
Row 36: No inc, otherwise as *Row 4*.
Row 37: No inc, otherwise as *Row 5*.
Row 38: No inc, otherwise as *Row 4*.
Row 39: (Inc row), otherwise as *Row 7*.
Row 40: (Inc row), otherwise as *Row 8*.
Row 41: No inc, otherwise as *Row 9*.
Row 42: As *Row 8*.
Row 43: As *Row 11*.
Row 44: (Inc row), otherwise as *Row 8*.
Row 45: (Inc row), As *Row 9*.
Row 46: As *Row 8*.
Row 47: No inc, otherwise as *Row 15*.
Row 48: As *Row 16*.
Row 49: (Inc row) As *Row 5*.
Row 50: (Inc row) As *Row 4*.
Row 51: As *Row 17*.
Row 52: As *Row 16*.
Row 53: As *Row 21*.
Row 54: (Inc row) otherwise as *Row 22*.
Row 55: (Inc row) otherwise as *Row 27*.
Row 56: As *Row 22*.
Row 57: No inc, otherwise as *Row 15*.
Row 58: As *Row 16*.
Row 59: (Inc row) IM, P1, (LTC4, CP [C4BM, MB, P1, K1, MB, C4FM], RTC4, P1) twice, IM.
Row 60: (Inc row) IM, K1, (RTC4, CP [P3, K1, P1, K1, P1, K1, P1, K1, P2], LTC4, P1) twice, IM.
Row 61: IM, P1, (LTC4, CP [K3, P1, K1, MB2, P1, K1, P1, K2], RTC4, P1) twice, IM.

Row 62: No inc, otherwise as *Row 60*.

Row 63: IM, P1, (LTC4, CP [C4FP, MB, P1, K1, MB, C4BP], RTC4, P1) twice, IM.

Row 64: (Inc row) As *Row 4*.

Row 65: (Inc row) otherwise as *Row 21*.

Row 66: As *Row 22*.

Row 67: As *Row 27*.

Row 68: As *Row 22*.

Row 69: (Inc row) As *Row 15*.

Row 70: (Inc row) As *Row 4*.

Row 71: No inc, otherwise as *Row 5*.

Row 72: As *Row 6*.

Row 73: As *Row 71*.

Row 74: (Inc row) As *Row 4*.

Row 75: (Inc row) otherwise as *Row 7*.

Row 76: As *Row 8*.

Row 77: No inc, otherwise as *Row 9*.

Row 78: As *Row 8*:

Row 79: (Inc row) otherwise as *Row 7*.

Row 80: (Inc row) otherwise as *Row 8*.

Row 81: As *Row 77*.

Row 82: As *Row 8*.

Row 83: No inc, otherwise as *Row 15*.

Row 84: (Inc row) As *Row 4*.

Row 85: (Inc row) As *Row 5*.

Row 86: As *Row 6*.

Row 87: No inc, otherwise as *Row 5*.

Row 88: As *Row 6*.

Row 89: (Inc row) otherwise as *Row 21*.

Row 90: (Inc row) As *Row 24*.

Row 91: As *Row 23*.

Row 92: As *Row 22*.

Row 93: No inc, otherwise as *Row 25*.

Row 94: (Inc row) as *Row 24*.

Row 95: (Inc row) otherwise as *Row 27*.

Row 96: As *Row 22*.

Row 97: As *Row 93*.

Row 98: As *Row 22*.

Row 99: (Inc row) As *Row 23*.

Row 100: (Inc row) As *Row 24*.

Begin underarm shaping

Row 101: (Inc 1 st at beg of row) As *Row 15*.

Row 102: (Inc 1 st at beg of row) As *Row 4*.

Row 103: (Inc 1 st at beg of row) As *Row 5*.

Row 104: (Inc 1 st at beg of row) As *Row 4*.

Cont underarm shaping and shape for Back in separate sizes as folls:

(Size 1 only)

Row 105: (Inc 1 st at beg of row) *As Row 5*. (104 sts).

Row 106: (Inc 1 st at beg of row) As *Row 4*.

Row 107: (Inc 1 st at beg of row) then as *Row 7*.

Row 108: (Inc 1 st at beg of row) then as *Row 8*.

Row 109: (Inc 1 st at beg of row) As *Row 9*.

Row 110: (Inc 1 st at beg of row) then as *Row 8*.

Row 111: (Inc 1 st at beg of row) then as *Row 7*.

Row 112: (Inc 1 st at beg of row) then as *Row 8*.

Row 113: Cast on 38 sts, incorporating these into the IM pattern, then work as *Row 9*.

Row 114: Cast on 38 sts, incorporating these sts into the IM pattern, then as *Row 8*. (187 sts).

(Size 2 only)

Row 105: (Inc 1 st at beg of row) As *Row 5*. (112 sts).

Row 106: (Inc 1 st at beg of row) *As Row 4*.

Row 107: (Inc 1 st at beg of row) then as *Row 7*.

Row 108: (Inc 1 st at beg of row) then as *Row 8*.

Row 109: Cast on 40 sts, incorporating these sts into the IM pattern, no further inc, then as *Row 9*.

Row 110: Cast on 40 sts, incorporating these sts into the IM patterns, then as *Row 8*. (195 sts).

Row 111: As *Row 7*.

Row 112: *As Row 8*.

Row 113: No inc, otherwise as *Row 9*.

Row 114: As *Row 8*.

(Size 3 only)

Row 105: Cast on 42 sts, incorporate these into the IM pattern, no further inc, then work as *Row 5*. (161 sts).

Row 106: Cast on 42 sts, incorporate these into the IM pattern, no further inc, then work as *Row 6*.

Row 107: As *Row 7*.

Row 108: As *Row 8*.

Row 109: No inc, otherwise as *Row 9*.

Row 110: As *Row 8*.

Row 111: As *Row 7*.

Row 112: As *Row 8*.

Row 113: No Inc, otherwise as *Row 9*.

Row 114: As *Row 8*. (203 sts).

(All sizes)

Row 115: No inc, otherwise as *Row 15*.
This row marks the end of the pattern repeat.

Starting again at **Row 2** of Centre Panel, ignoring inc instructions, rep until **Row 139** is reached (i.e. on **Row 25** of 2nd patt rep).

DIVIDE FOR NECK

Work across in **Row 25** patt along 93 (97:101) sts. Transfer rem sts onto spare needle and leave – do not work **Row 25** on these sts. Turn work, and begin on WS of the 93 (97:101) sts to work across in **Row 26** of patt to end of row. Cont with no inc following patt as set until **Row 92** has been completed, as *Row 22*.

Leave these sts on spare needle, then return to sts previously left on spare needle. Join in new ball of yarn at inside neck edge, K2tog to remove centre P st, then work across the sts in **Row 25** of patt. Cont to work across this half of garment to match other half already worked, to make Front, ending after completing **Row 92**. Break off yarn.

Return to the sts on the spare needle, work across these 93 (97:101) sts in patt **Row 93**. Inc 1 st at beg of row of sts on other needle to replace centre st. P this st, then work across rem sts in patt **Row 93** so that all sts are now on 1 needle again. (187:195:203) sts. Cont to work in patt as set, beg 3rd rep again at **Row 2**. Complete **Row 3**.

DECREASE FOR SLEEVE

Work underarm shaping in separate sizes as folls:

(Size 1 only)

Patt Row 4: Cast (bind) off 38 sts. No inc, otherwise as *Row 4*.

Patt Row 5: Cast (bind) off 38 sts. No inc, otherwise as *Row 5*.

Patt Row 6: Dec 1 st at beg of row, otherwise as *Row 6*.

Patt Row 7: Dec 1 st at beg of row, otherwise as *Row 7*.

Patt Row 8: Dec 1 st at beg of row, otherwise as *Row 8*.

Patt Row 9: Dec 1 st at beg of row. No inc, otherwise as *Row 9*.

Patt Row 10: Dec 1 st beg of row. No inc, otherwise as *Row 10*.

Patt Row 11: Dec 1 st at beg of row, otherwise as *Row 11*.

Patt Row 12: Dec 1 st at beg of row, otherwise as *Row 12*.

Patt Row 13: Dec 1 st at beg of row, otherwise as *Row 13*.

(Size 2 only)

Patt Row 4: No inc, otherwise as *Row 4*.

Patt Row 5: No inc, otherwise as *Row 5*.

Patt Row 6: As *Row 6*.

Patt Row 7: As *Row 7*.

Patt Row 8: Cast (bind) off 40 sts at beg of row, otherwise as *Row 8*.

Patt Row 9: Cast (Bind) off 40 sts at beg of row. No inc. otherwise as *Row 9*.

Patt Row 10: Dec 1 st at beg of row. No inc, otherwise as *Row 10*.

Patt Row 11: Dec 1 st at beg of row, otherwise as *Row 11*.

Patt Row 12: Dec 1 st at beg of row, otherwise as *Row 12*.

Patt Row 13: Dec 1 st at beg of row, otherwise as *Row 13*.

(Size 3 only)

Patt Row 4: No inc, otherwise as *Row 4*.

Patt Row 5: No inc, otherwise as *Row 5*.

Patt Row 6: As *Row 6*.

Patt Row 7: As *Row 7*.

Patt Row 8: As *Row 8*.

Patt Row 9: No inc, otherwise, as *Row 9*.

Patt Row 10: No inc, otherwise as *Row 10*.

Patt Row 11: As *Row 11*.

Patt Row 12: Cast (bind) off 42 sts at beg of row, otherwise as *Row 12*.

Patt Row 13: Cast (bind) off 42 sts at beg of row, otherwise as *Row 13*.

(All 3 sizes)

Patt Row 14: Dec 1 st at beg of row, otherwise as *Row 14*.

Patt Rows 15–19: Dec 1 st at beg of row, work in patt as set.

Patt Rows 20–22: No dec, work in patt as set.

Patt Rows 23 & 24: Dec 1 st at beg of row, work in patt as set.

Patt Rows 25–27: No dec, work in patt as set.

Cont to shape Sleeve in this way, by dec 1 st at beg of next 2 rows, then working foll 3 rows with no dec, until **Row 115** of patt has been completed.

Work next row as **Row 2**, then end in 1 K row.

Cast (Bind) off 59 (67:75) sts.

CUFFS

Using 3¼mm (US 3) needles, RS facing, pick up evenly and K50 (58:66) sts along wrist edge of each Sleeve, then work 23 rows in single K1, P1, rib. Cast (bind) off.

WELTS

Using 3¼mm (US 3) needles, RS facing, pick up evenly and K78 (86:94) sts along the lower edges of Back and Front in turn. Work the same K1, P1 rib to match cuffs. for 23 rows. Cast (bind) off.

MAKING UP AND FINISHING

Using backstitch, join side and Sleeve seams. Darn in any loose ends neatly.

Press seams lightly on WS with warm iron over a damp cloth. Do not press RS of garment.

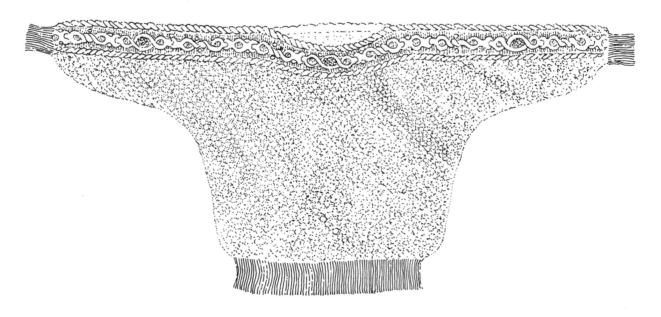

HONEYCOMB CABLE ARAN

This Aran features a central column of Honeycomb cable, decorated on either side with the upward reaching travelling rib branches taken from the Tree of Life pattern. Tree of Life is one of the oldest of the Aran patterns representing family unity and strong children from long-lived parents, and spiritual growth, as humans reach heavenwards.

Early Aran sweater showing the Tree of Life and Honeycomb cable patterns

The highly decorated welts, cuffs and neck edge incorporate cables and twisted ribs, a design element particular to Aran knitting.

The sweater is knitted in the authentic 'bainin' – pronounced 'bawneen' – a natural cream coloured wool.

MATERIALS

YARN

Rowan Aran Wool in Natural
18 (19:20) × 50g/3$\frac{3}{4}$oz (33$\frac{3}{4}$:35$\frac{1}{2}$)

NEEDLES

1 pair 3$\frac{3}{4}$mm (US 5) 60cm (24") circular needles
1 pair 4$\frac{1}{2}$mm (US 7) 36cm (14") straight needles
Stitch holder
Cable needle

SIZES AND MEASUREMENTS

In 3 sizes: Sizes 1 (2:3) to fit chest 91cm (36"):
96cm (38"): 101cm (40")

Actual width across back at underarm
48cm (19"):51cm (20$\frac{1}{4}$"):54cm (21$\frac{1}{2}$")
Length from centre back neck to hip   69cm (27$\frac{1}{4}$") all sizes
Sleeve seam from armhole inset
44cm (17$\frac{1}{2}$"): 45cm (17$\frac{3}{4}$"): 46cm (18$\frac{1}{4}$")

TENSION (GAUGE)

20 sts and 25 rows to 10cm (4") over st st on 4$\frac{1}{2}$mm (US 7) needles or size needed to obtain this tension.

SPECIAL ABBREVIATIONS

C4F   Sl 2 sts onto cable needle, hold at front, K2, then K2 from cable needle.

C6F   Sl 3 sts onto cable needle, hold at front, K3, then K3 from cable needle.

C6B   Sl 3 sts onto cable needle, hold at back, K3, then K3 from cable needle.

SFC   Sl 1 st onto cable needle, hold at front, P1, then K1 from cable needle.

SBC   Sl 1 st onto cable needle, hold at back, K1, then P1 from cable needle.

P1TBL   Purl 1 st through the back of loop.
K1TBL   Knit 1 st through the back of loop.

PATTERNS

PANEL A (CABLE PATTERN) (4 sts)

Row 1 K4.
Row 2: P4.
Row 3: C4F.
Row 4: P4.

(These 4 rows form patt rep)

PANEL B (HONEYCOMB CABLE PATTERN) (12 sts)

Row 1 K12.
Row 2 and all subsequent even rows: P the K sts of previous row.
Rows 3 & 4: As *Rows 1 & 2*.
Row 5: C6B, C6F.
Row 6 & 7: K12.
Rows 8 & 9: As *Rows 6 & 7*.
Row 11: C6F, C6B.
Row 12: As *Row 2*.
(These 12 rows form patt rep)

PANEL C (LEFT TRAVELLING RIB PANEL FROM TREE OF LIFE PATTERN) (9 sts)

Row 1 SFC, P2, SFC, P3.
Row 2 and all subsequent even rows: K the P sts of previous row and P the K sts.
Row 3: P1, SFC, P2, SFC, P2.
Row 5: P2, SFC, P2, SFC, P1.
Row 7: P3, SFC, P2, SFC.
Row 8: P1, K3, P1, K4.

(These 8 rows form patt rep)

PANEL D (RIGHT TRAVELLING RIB PANEL FROM TREE OF LIFE PATTERN) (9 sts)

Row 1: P3, SBC, P2, SBC.
Row 2 and all subsequent even rows: K the P sts of previous row and P the K sts.
Row 3: P2, SBC, P2, SBC, P1.
Row 5: P1, SBC, P2, SBC, P2.
Row 7: SBC, P2, SBC, P3.
Row 8: K4, P1, K3, P1.

(These 8 rows form patt rep)

BACK

Using 3¾mm (US 5) circular needles as straight and Rowan Aran wool, cast on 118 (125:132) sts. Work Cable and Rib Welt as folls:

Row 1 : *Edge st* K1, (K4, P1TBL, K1TBL, P1TBL) rep until 5 sts rem, K4, *Edge st* K1.
Row 2: *Edge st* K1, (P4, K1TBL, P1TBL, K1TBL) rep until 5 sts rem, P4, *Edge st* K1.
Rows 3 & 4: As *Rows 1 & 2*.
Row 5: *Edge st* K1, (C4F, P1TBL, K1TBL, P1TBL) rep until 5 sts rem, C4F, *Edge st* K1.
Row 6 As *Row 2*.
Rep *Rows 1–6* four more times.
Change to 4½mm (US 7) needles.
(*Sizes 1 & 3*): K1, P across all sts until 1 remains, K this st.
(*Size 2*): K2tog, P across all sts until 1 remains, K this st.
Rep row instructions just given for *Sizes 1 & 3* once more for all sizes.
(118:124:132) sts.

SET FOUNDATION ROW OF ARAN PATT AS FOLLOWS:

Row 1 : *Edge st* K1, P5 (8:12), (*Panel A* over 4 sts, P13) twice, *Panel A* over 4 sts, *Panel D* over 9 sts, *Panel B* over 12 sts, *Panel C* over 9 sts, (*Panel A* over 4 sts, P13) twice, *Panel A* over 4 sts, P5 (8:12), *Edge st* K1.
Row 2: *Edge st* K1, K5 (8:12), (*Panel A* over 4 sts, K13) twice, *Panel A* over 4 sts, *Panel C* over 9 sts, *Panel B* over 12 sts, *Panel D* over 9 sts, (*Panel A* over 4 sts, K13) twice, *Panel A* over 4 sts, K5 (8:12), *Edge st* K1.
These 2 rows establish the patt. Cont working appropriate rows of patt panels, and working areas between 4-st Cables on either side of Central Honeycomb and Tree of Life panel in reverse st st. Cont in this way until **Row 12** of 8th patt rep of Honeycomb Cable and appropriate sequence of Tree of Life ribs, and 4-st Cables have been completed.

YOKE PATT AND ARMHOLE SHAPING

Next Row: (RS) Cast (bind) off 5 (8:12) sts, K end st as new *Edge St*, then cont 4-St Cables but introduce extended Tree of Life Travelling Rib and Honeycomb Cable patts, starting with the foll sequences:
(*All sizes*): **Row 1** of *Panel D*, **Row 1** of *Panel B*, **Row 1** of *Panel C*. Rep this sequence twice more across all sts, cont to work 4-st Cables in between as set until 6 (9:13) sts rem. Cast (bind) off last 5 (8:12) sts leaving 1 Edge st. Break off yarn.
Next row: Rejoin yarn at armhole edge of Yoke, then beg with K1 *Edge St*, work across in patt as set, ending in K1 *Edge St*. Cont in patt until 11 reps of *Panel B* down Centre Back have been completed. Work should now measure 61cm (24½″) from Welt edge.

STRAP SHOULDER SHAPING

RS facing, cast (bind) off in patt 34 sts. Working across in patt, establishing K1 *Edge St* and cont *Panels A, D, B, C and A* ending in K1 *Edge St*, cast (bind) off rem sts. Break off yarn.*
Rejoin yarn at inner edge (WS) and patt across rem 40 sts until 2 more reps of *Panel B* and appropriate rows of other panels have been completed. Cast (bind) off.

FRONT

Work as for Back until *.

DIVIDE FOR NECK

RS facing, Edge St K1, patt across *Panel A*, *Panel D* then cast (bind) off next 12 sts over *Panel B*, then cont in patt to end.
Next Row: (WS) Work in patt across 14 sts, then transfer rem 14 sts onto stitch holder and leave.
Next Row: Cast (bind) off 4 sts at inside neck edge, complete row in patt.
Next Row: Patt across all sts.
Next Row: Dec 1 st at beg of row, patt to end.
Next Row: Patt to last 2 sts, K2tog.
Rep last 2 rows once more.
Work across last 6 sts, working K1 *Edge St* at either side of *Panel A*, cont cable patt until Front length matches Back. Cast (bind) off. Rejoin yarn and work other side similarly.

SLEEVES

Using 3¼mm (US 5) circular needles as straight cast on 55 (62:62) sts. Establish Cable and Rib patt used in Welt and cont until Cuff measures 9cm (3½").

Change to 4½mm (US 7) needles and P 2 rows, knitting *Edge St* at each end of row.

SET FOUNDATION ROW OF ARAN PATT AS FOLLS:

(Size 1): Inc 1 st at beg of row, P this st, P next 8 sts, work **Row 1** of *Panel A*, **Row 1** of *Panel D*, **Row 1** of *Panel B*, **Row 1** of *Panel C*, **Row 1** of *Panel A*, then P9 sts. (56 sts)

(Sizes 2 & 3): P12, **Row 1** of *Panel A*, **Row 1** of *Panel D*, **Row 1** of *Panel B*, **Row 1** of *Panel C*, **Row 1** of *Panel A*, then P12. (62 sts).

(Size 3 only): Inc 1 st at beg and end of next 4 rows, incorporating these sts into the 13 st reverse st st panel and into the new *Panel A*. (70 sts).

(All sizes): Cont in patt as set but inc 1 st at beg and end of every 5th row, incorporating sts into the 13 st reverse st st panels and 4-st Cables until 98 (104:106) sts exist, and 8 patt reps of *Panel B* have been completed.

STRAP SHOULDER SHAPING

Cast (bind) off 26 (29:33) sts, patt across next 40 sts, cast (bind) off last 26 (29:33) sts. Break off yarn.

Rejoin yarn at inner edge, and cont in patt as set across 40 sts, working K1 at *Edge Sts*. Cont until 11 patt reps of *Panel B* have been completed. Cast (bind) off.

NECKBAND

Using backstitch, join Front to Back, WS together, matching 6-st Cable sections of Front neck edges to corresponding Back neck Cables.

Using backstitch, attach Sleeve head so that centre Honeycomb Cable matches shoulder seam, then ease in Sleeves, carefully matching patts before sewing in place. Then make Neckband as folls:

Using 3¾mm (US 5) circular needles, beg at LH corner of Back neck, RS facing, pick up evenly and K23 (25:25) sts from right Front neck, 12 sts from *Panel B*, 23 (25:25) sts from left Front neck, and 33 (36:36) sts across Back neck. (58:65:65) sts.

Working in Rounds, beg with K4, P1TBL, K1TBL, P1TBL etc each round, cont until 6 rounds have been completed, crossing cable (C4F) at **Round 3** of patt, to produce patt similar to Welt and Cuffs but with shallow Neckband for comfort. Cast (bind) off.

If a deeper Neckband is preferred, work 10 rounds in patt with cable cross-over (C4F) on **Rounds 3 & 7**. Cast (bind) off.

MAKING UP AND FINISHING

Using backstitch for reverse st st and invisible seaming for ribbing, join Sleeve and side seams. Darn in all loose ends, then press seams on WS with warm iron over a damp cloth, but do not press on RS.

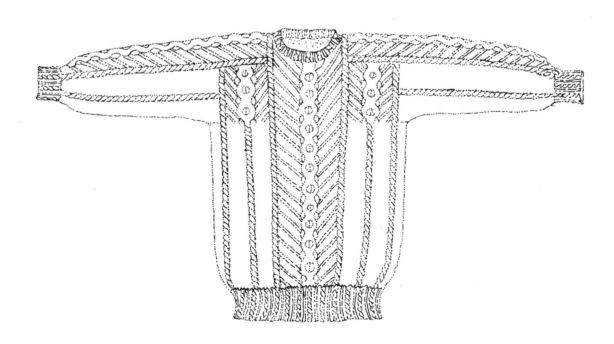

Betrothal Aran

This sweater incorporates a variety of traditional Aran stitches, each conveying a different meaning particularly appropriate for those about to marry. It would make a lovely engagement gift knitted by a mother for her daughter or daughter-in-law.

The central panel is decorated with Wishbone pattern, said to bestow the wearer with luck and wishes fulfilled. It is edged with wavy bands of Ribbon cable, representing the bounty of the sea which brings prosperity to the islands.

Panels of Double Zig-Zag alternating with areas of smooth stocking stitch and the bumpier moss stitch indicate the ups and downs that may be expected of married life. However, the lacy openwork that accompanies the 'marriage lines' zig-zags should ensure lighter moments among the difficulties that may await the newly-wed.

Securely twisted cables climb up the sweater and decorate the welts and cuffs. These represent the steadfastness and strength of the fishermen's ropes, and are symbolic of the hope of the enduring intertwining of the two lives.

Finally, the sweater is edged in Trinity stitch to bring a heavenly blessing to the future marriage. Trinity stitch is also named Blackberry stitch after the blackberries that grow abundantly on the islands, and these could also mean fruitfulness for the couple.

Materials

YARN
Rowanspun Tweed (Aran Weight) Iris (757)
9 × 100g/31¾oz

NEEDLES
1 pair 3¼mm (US 3) 60cm (24") circular needles
1 pair 4mm (US 6) 35cm (14") straight needles
1 cable needle
1 set of double pointed spare needles

Size and Measurements

One size only to fit up to 106cm (42") chest

Actual width across back at underarm   60cm (24")
Length from centre back neck to hip   72cm (28½")
Sleeve seam   47cm (18½")

Tension (Gauge)

20 sts and 30 rows to 10cm (4") over Zig-Zag pattern on 4mm (US 6) needles or size needed to obtain this tension (gauge).

Special Abbreviations

C4F	Sl 2 sts onto cable needle, hold at front, K2, then K2 from cable needle.
C4B	Sl 2 sts onto cable needle, hold at back, K2, then K2 from cable needle.
C4FP	Sl 2 sts onto cable needle, hold at front, P2, then K2 from cable needle.
C4BP	Sl 2 sts onto cable needle, hold at back, K2, then P2 from cable needle.
SFC	Sl 1 st onto cable needle, hold at front, P1, then K1 from cable needle.
SBC	Sl 1 st onto cable needle, hold at back, K1, then P1 from cable needle.
YO, Sl 1, K1, PSSO	Yarn over needle to make a new st between 2 knit sts, then slip next st on LH needle without knitting or purling it, K1, then pass the slipped st over this knit st.
K2tog, YO	Knit 2 together, then yarn over needle to make a new st between 2 knit sts.
M1	Make 1 st by picking up loop from row below and knitting it TBL.

Pattern Panels

PANEL A (TRINITY STITCH)
(LEFT AND RIGHT PANELS THE SAME) (12 sts)

Row 1: P.
Row 2: (K1, P1, K1 into next st, K3tog) 3 times.
Row 3: P.
Row 4: (K3tog, K1, P1, K1 into next st) 3 times.
(These 4 rows form patt rep)

PANEL B (CABLE PANEL)
(LEFT AND RIGHT PANELS THE SAME) (12 sts)

Row 1: P2, K2, P4, K2, P2.
Row 2 and all subsequent even rows: K the P sts of previous row and P the K sts.
Row 3: P2, C4FP, C4BP, P2.
Row 5: P4, C4F, P4.
Row 7: P2, C4BP, C4FP, P2.
Rows 9–14: As *Rows 3–8*.
Rows 15–20: Rep *Rows 1 & 2* three times.
(These 20 rows form patt rep.)

PANEL C (LEFT-SLOPE LACY DOUBLE ZIG-ZAG WITH MOSS STITCH) (23 sts)

Row 1: K5, (YO, SL1, K1, PSSO) twice, (P1, K1) 7 times.
Row 2: (K1, P1) 7 times, P9.
Row 3: K6, (YO, SL1, K1, PSSO) twice, (K1, P1) 6 times, K1.
Row 4: As *Row 2*.
Row 5: K7, (YO, SL1, K1, PSSO) twice, (P1, K1) 6 times.
Row 6: (K1, P1) 6 times, P11.
Row 7: K8, (YO, SL1, K1, PSSO) twice, (K1, P1) 5 times, K1.
Row 8: As *Row 6*.
Row 9: K9, (YO, SL1, K1, PSSO) twice, (P1, K1) 5 times.
Row 10: (K1, P1) 5 times, P13.
Row 11: K10, (YO, SL1, K1, PSSO) twice, (K1, P1) 4 times, K1.
Row 12: As *Row 10*.
Row 13: K11, (YO, SL1, K1, PSSO) twice, (P1, K1) 4 times.
Row 14: (K1, P1) 4 times, P15.
Row 15: K12, (YO, SL1, K1, PSSO) twice, (P1, K1) 3 times, K1.
Row 16: As *Row 14*.
Row 17: K13, (YO, SL1, K1, PSSO) twice, (P1, K1) 3 times.
Row 18: (K1, P1) 3 times, P17.
Row 19: K14, (YO, SL1, K1, PSSO) twice, (P1, K1) twice, K1.
Row 20: As *Row 18*.

(These 20 rows form the patt rep)

PANEL D (RIGHT-SLOPE LACY DOUBLE ZIG-ZAG WITH MOSS STITCH) (23 sts)

Row 1: (K1, P1) 7 times, (K2tog, YO), twice, K5.
Row 2: P10, (K1, P1) 6 times, K1.
Row 3: (K1, P1) 6 times, K1, (K2tog, YO) twice, K6.
Row 4: As *Row 2*.
Row 5: (K1, P1) 6 times, (K2tog, YO) twice, K7.
Row 6: P12, (K1, P1) 5 times, K1.
Row 7: (K1, P1) 5 times, K1, (K2tog, YO) twice, K8.
Row 8: As *Row 6*.
Row 9: (K1, P1) 5 times, (K2tog, YO) twice, K9.
Row 10: P14, (K1, P1) 4 times, K1.
Row 11: (K1, P1) 4 times, K1, (K2tog, YO) twice, K10.
Row 12: As *Row 10*.
Row 13: (K1, P1) 4 times, (K2tog, YO) twice, K11.
Row 14: P16, (K1, P1) 3 times, K1.
Row 15: (K1, P1) 3 times, K1, (K2tog, YO) twice, K12.
Row 16: As *Row 14*.
Row 17: (K1, P1) 3 times, (K2tog, YO) twice, K13.
Row 18: P18, (K1, P1) twice, K1.
Row 19: (K1, P1) twice, K1, (K2tog, YO) twice, K14.
Row 20: As *Row 18*.

(These 20 rows form the patt rep)

PANEL E (RIBBON CABLE, LEFT TWIST) (8 sts)

Row 1: P2, K4, P2.
Row 2: K2, P4, K2.
Rows 3 & 4: As *Rows 1 & 2*.
Row 5: P2, C4F, P2.
Row 6: As *Row 2*.

Rows 7–10: As *Rows 1–4*.
Row 11: P2, C4B, P2.
Row 12: As *Row 2*.
(These 12 rows form the patt rep.)

PANEL F (RIBBON CABLE, RIGHT-TWIST) (8 sts)

Row 1: P2, K4, P2.
Row 2: K2, P4, K2.
Rows 3 & 4: As *Rows 1 & 2*.
Row 5: P2, C4B, P2.
Row 6: As *Row 2*.
Rows 7–10: As *Rows 1–4*.
Row 11: P2, C4F, P2.
Row 12: As *Row 2*.

(These 12 rows form the patt rep).

PANEL G (WISHBONE PATTERN) (28 sts)

Row 1: P28.
Row 2: K4, P2, K16, P2, K4.
Row 3: P4, K2, P16, K2, P4.
Row 4: As *Row 2*.
Row 5: P3, SBC, SFC, P14, SBC, SFC, P3.
Row 6 and all subsequent even rows until Row 18: K all P sts of previous row and P all K sts.
Row 7: P3, SFC, SBC, P14, SFC, SBC, P3.
Row 9: P4, C4FP, P12, C4BP, P4.
Row 11: P6, C4FP, P8, C4BP, P6.
Row 13: P8, C4FP, P4, C4BP, P8.
Row 15: P10, C4FP, C4BP, P10.
Row 17: P12, C4F, P12.
Row 18: K4, P2, K6, P4, K6, P2, K4.
Row 19: P4, K2, P4, C4BP, C4FP, P4, K2, P4.
Row 20 and all subsequent even rows until Row 56: K all P sts of previous row and P all K sts.
Row 21: P3, SBC, SFC, P1, C4BP, P4, C4FP, P1, SBC, SFC, P3.
Row 23: P3, SFC, SBC, P1, C4FP, P4, C4BP, P1, SFC, SBC, P3.
Row 25: P4, C4FP, P2, C4FP, C4BP, P2, C4BP, P4.
Row 27–33: As *Rows 11–17*.
Row 35: P10, C4BP, C4FP, P10.
Row 37: P8, C4BP, P4, C4FP, P8.
Rows 39–41: As *Rows 13–15*.
Rows 43: P28.
Row 45: P12, K4, P12.
Rows 47–49: As *Rows 35–37*.
Rows 51–55: As *Rows 13–17*.
Row 56: K12, P4, K12.
Row 57: As *Row 35*.
Row 58 and all subsequent even rows until Row 70: K all P sts of previous row and P all K sts.
Row 59: As *Row 37*.
Row 61: P6, C4BP, P2, K4, P2, C4FP, P6.
Row 63: P4, C4BP, P2, C4BP, C4FP, P2, C4FP, P4.
Rows 65–67: As *Rows 21–23*.
Row 69: P4, K2, P4, C4FP, C4BP, P4, K2, P4.
Row 70: K12, P4, K12.

Row 71: As *Row 17*.
Row 72: As *Row 70*.
Row 73–76: As *Rows 35–38*.
Row 77: P6, C4BP, P8, C4FP, P6.
Row 78 and all subsequent even rows until Row 86: K all P sts of previous row and P all K sts.
Row 79: P4, C4BP, P12, C4FP, P4.
Rows 81–84: As *Rows 5–8*.
Row 85: As *Row 3*.
Row 86: K28.

(These 86 rows form the patt rep).

BACK

Using 3¼mm (US 3) circular needles as straight and Rowanspun Tweed, cast on 122 sts. Work Welt as folls:

Row 1: (P2, K2, P4, K2) 12 times, P2.
Row 2: K2, (P2, K4, P2, K2) 12 times.
Row 3: (P2, C4FP, C4BP) 12 times, P2.
Row 4: K2, (K2, P4, K4) 12 times.
Row 5: (P4, C4F, P2) 12 times, P2.
Row 6: As *Row 4*.
Row 7: (P2, C4BP, C4FP) 12 times, P2.
Row 8–14: As *Rows 2–8*.
Rows 15–20: (As *Rows 1 & 2*) 3 times.
Rows 21–34: As *Rows 1–14*.
Change to 4mm (US 6) needles and with RS facing work as folls:

INCREASE ROW

K7, (M1, K6) 18 times, K7. (140 sts).
Next Row: K.

SET FOUNDATION ARAN PATT ROW AS FOLLS:

Row 1: *Edge St* K1, *Panel A* over 12 sts, *Panel B*, over 12 sts, *Panel C* over 23 sts, *Panel E* over 8 sts, *Panel G* over 28 sts, *Panel F* over 8 sts, *Panel D* over 23 sts, *Panel B* over 12 sts, *Panel A* over 12 sts, *Edge St* K1.
Row 2: *Edge St* K1, *Panel A* over 12 sts, *Panel B* over 12 sts, *Panel D* over 23 sts, *Panel F* over 8 sts, *Panel G* over 28 sts, *Panel E* over 8 sts, *Panel C* over 23 sts, *Panel B* over 12 sts, *Panel A* over 12 sts, *Edge St* K1.

These 2 rows establish the patt. Cont working in patt as set until **Row 100** has been completed. (i.e. **Row 14** of 2nd patt rep of *Panel G*).

ARMHOLE SHAPING

Cast (bind) off 13 sts at beg of next 2 rows. Cont to work in patt as set until **Row 172** has been completed. (i.e. **Row 86** of 2nd patt rep of *Panel G*).

SHAPE BACK NECK

Row 173: Work 37 sts in patt, then cast (bind) off next 40 sts, then work last 37 sts in patt.
Row 174: Work 37 sts in patt.

Row 175: Cast (bind) off.
Complete shaping on opposite side similarly.

FRONT

Work as for Back but beg Front neck shaping as folls:
Complete **Row 140** in patt as set i.e. **Row 54** of 2nd patt rep of *Panel G*, then:

DIVIDE FOR NECK

Row 141: Work 45 sts in patt, then cast (bind) off next 24 sts. Leave on spare needle, then work rem 45 sts in patt. Working in patt, dec 2 sts at inside neck edge on *Rows 143, 145, 153 and 159*. Cont in patt with no further dec until *Row 174* has been completed. Cast (bind) off.
Work opposite shoulder similarly.

SLEEVES

Using 3¼mm (US 3) circular needles as straight, cast on 62 sts. Work Cuffs as folls:

Row 1: (P2, K2, P4, K2) 6 times, P2.
Row 2: K2, (P2, K4, P2, K2) 6 times.
Row 3: (P2, C4FP, C4BP) 6 times, P2.
Row 4: K2, (K2, P4, K4) 6 times.
Row 5: (P4, C4F, P2) 6 times, P2.
Row 6: As *Row 4*.
Row 7: (P2, C4BP, C4FP) 6 times, P2.
Rows 8–14: As *Rows 2–8*.
Rows 15–20: (As *Rows 1 & 2*) 3 times.
Rows 21–34: As *Rows 1–14*.
Change to 4mm (US 6) needles and work as folls:

INCREASE ROW

K7, (M1, K6) 8 times, K7. (70 sts).
Next Row: K.

SET FOUNDATION ARAN PATT ROW AS FOLLS:

Row 1: (K1, P1) 6 times, K1 from *Panel C* over 13 sts; *Panel E* over 8 sts; *Panel G* over 28 sts; *Panel F* over 8 sts; (K1, P1) 6 times, K1 from *Panel D* over 13 sts.
Row 2: (K1, P1) 6 times, K1 from *Panel D* over 13 sts; *Panel F* over 8 sts; *Panel G* over 28 sts; *Panel E* over 8 sts; (K1, P1) 6 times, K1 over 13 sts.

These 2 rows establish the patt. Cont working in patt as set, but inc 1 st at beg and end of each 6th row, incorporating new sts into patt to match Front and Back patts, until 112 sts exist, and **Row 107** has been completed. Cast (bind) off.

NECKBAND

Using backstitch, WS facing, join shoulders then work Neckband as folls: Using 3¼mm (US 3) circular needles, RS facing, beg at RH corner of Back neck shoulder seam, pick up evenly and K29 sts from left Front neck edge, 24 sts across Front neck, 29 sts from right Front neck edge, and 40 sts from Back neck (122 sts).

Work in rounds as folls:

Rounds 1 & 2: (P2, K2, P4, K2) 12 times, P2.
Round 3: (P2, C4FP, C4BP) 12 times, P2.
Round 4: P2 (P2, K4, P4) 12 times.
Round 5: (P4, C4F, P2) 12 times, P2.
Round 6: As *Round 4*.
Round 7: (P2, C4BP, C4FP) 12 times, P2.
Rounds 8–14: As *Rounds 2–8*.
Cast (bind) off loosely.

MAKING UP AND FINISHING

Using backstitch, set in Sleeves, matching centre points of shoulder seams to the Sleeve mid-points. Using backstitch for Aran patt seams and invisible seams for rib, join side seams and Sleeve seams. Darn in all loose ends, then press seams lightly on WS with warm iron over a damp cloth.

ROPE PLAIT ARAN

This bulky sweater is guaranteed to keep you warm even in the fiercest Aran storms.

Featuring an elaborate cable and rope plait design in the central panel, and interlacing borders, it celebrates the courage of the island's seamen, upon whom the isolated communities depend.

The sides are decorated with Honeycomb panels, which help to windproof the sweater by trapping tiny pockets of warmth in its cellular structure. The Honeycomb stitch is said to represent the sweet rewards hard work brings, like the honey and the bee.

MATERIALS

YARN
Rowan Aran 100% Wool in Natural
$11 \times 100g/39\frac{1}{4}oz$

NEEDLES
1 pair $3\frac{3}{4}$mm (US 5) 60cm (24") circular needles
1 pair $4\frac{1}{2}$mm (US 7) 40 cm ($15\frac{1}{2}$") straight needles
1 cable needle
1 set of double pointed spare needles

SIZE AND MEASUREMENTS

One size only to fit up to 109cm (43") chest

Actual width across back at underarm   57cm ($22\frac{1}{2}$")

Length from centre back neck to hip   68cm (27")

Sleeve seam   53cm (21")

TENSION (GAUGE)

27 sts and 28 rows to 10cm (4") over st st on $4\frac{1}{2}$mm (US 7) needles or size needed to obtain this tension (gauge).

SPECIAL ABBREVIATIONS

M1	Make 1 st by picking up loop between sts from row below and knit it TBL.
C2F	Sl 1 st onto cable needle, hold at front, K1, then K1 from cable needle.
C2B	Sl 1 st onto cable needle, hold at back, K1, then K1 from cable needle.
C4F	Sl 2 sts onto cable needle, hold at front, K2, then K2 from cable needle.
C4B	Sl 2 sts onto cable needle, hold at back, K2, then K2 from cable needle.
C8F	Sl 4 sts onto cable needle, hold at front, K4, then K4 from cable needle.
C8B	Sl 4 sts onto cable needle, hold at back, K4, then K4 from cable needle.
FC	Sl 2 sts onto cable needle, hold at front, P1, then K2 from cable needle.
BC	Sl 1 st onto cable needle, hold at back, K2, then P1 from cable needle.
DFC	Sl 4 sts onto cable needle, hold at front, P2, then K4 from cable needle.
DBC	Sl 2 sts onto cable needle, hold at back, K4, then P2 from cable needle.
DFKC	Sl 4 sts onto cable needle, hold at front, K2, then K4 from cable needle.
DBKC	Sl 2 sts onto cable needle, hold at back, K4, then K2 from cable needle.
K2TBL	Knit 2 sts through the back of loops.
P2TBL	Purl 2 sts through the back of loops.

PATTERN PANELS

PANEL A (HONEYCOMB STITCH) (24 sts)
(The same on both panels)
Row 1: (C2F, C2B) 6 times.
Row 2: P24.
Row 3: (C2B, C2F) 6 times.
Row 4: P24.

(These 4 rows form patt rep)

PANEL B (RIGHT TWIST CABLE) (4 sts)
Row 1: K4.
Row 2: P4.
Row 3 & 4: As *Rows 1 & 2*.
Rows 5: C4F.
Row 6: P4.

(These 6 rows form patt rep)

PANEL C (LEFT TWIST CABLE) (4 sts)
Row 1: K4.
Row 2: P4.
Row 3 & 4: As *Row 1 & 2*.
Row 5: C4B.
Row 6: P4.

(These 6 rows form the patt rep)

PANEL D (TRELLIS PATTERN) (18 sts)

Row 1: (P2, K2) 4 times, P2.
Row 2 and all subsequent even rows: K the P sts of previous row and P the K sts.
Row 3: As *Row 1*.
Row 5: (P2, FC, BC) twice, P2.
Row 7: P3, C4B, P4, C4B, P3.
Row 9: (P2, BC, FC) twice, P2.
Row 11: P2, K2, P2, FC, BC, P2, K2, P2.
Row 13: P2, K2, P3, C4F, P3, K2, P2.
Row 15: P2, K2, P2, BC, FC, P2, K2, P2.
Rows 17–22: As *Rows 5–10*.

(Alter *Rows 3–22* continuously for the patt rep)

PANEL E (ROPE PLAIT PATTERN) (36 sts)

Row 1: P4, C4B, P4, C8B, K4, P4, C4F, P4.
Row 2 and all subsequent even rows: K the P sts of previous row and P the K sts.
Row 3: P2, DBC, P4, K12, P4, DFC, P2.
Row 5: P2, Ç4B, P6, K4, C8F, P6, C4F, P2.
Row 7: P2, K4, P6, K12, P6, K4, P2.
Row 9: P2, C4F, P6, C8B, K4, P6, C4B, P2.
Row 11: P2, DFC, P4, K12, P4, DBC, P2.
Row 13: P4, C4F, P4, K4, C8F, P4, C4B, P4.
Row 15: P4, DFC, DBC, K4, DFC, DBC, P4.
Row 17: P6, C4F, K4, P2, K4, P2, K4, C4B, P6.
Row 19: P6, C8B, P2, K4, P2, C8F, P6.
Row 21: P6, K4, C4F, P2, K4, P2, C4B, K4, P6.
Row 23: P4, DBC, DFC, K4, DBC, DFC, P4.
Row 25: P4, K4, P4, C4F, K4, C4B, P4, K4, P4.
Row 27: P2, DBC, P4, DFC, DBC, P4, DFC, P2.
Row 29: P2, K4, P8, C4F, C4B, P8, K4, P2.
Row 31: P2, K4, P8, C8F, P8, K4, P2.
Row 33: P2, K4, P8, C4B, C2F, P8, K4, P2.
Row 35: P2, DFC, P4, DBKC, DFKC, P4, DBC, P2.
Row 37: P4, K4, P4, C4B, K4, C4F, P4, K4, P4.
Row 39: P4, DFC, DBC, K4, DFC, DBC, P4.
Row 41: P6, K4, C4B, P2, K4, P2, C4F, K4, P6.
Row 43: P6, C8F, P2, K4, P2, C8B, P6.
Row 45: P6, C4B, (K4, P2) twice, K4, C4F, P6.
Row 47: P4, DBC, DFC, K4, DBC, DFC, P4.

(These 48 rows form the patt rep)

BACK

Using 3¾mm (US 5) circular needles as straight and Aran wool, cast on 122 sts. Work Cable and Rib Welt as folls:

Row 1: (P2, K2TBL, P2, K2TBL, P2, K4) 8 times, P2, K2TBL, P2, K2TBL, P2.
Row 2: (K2, P2TBL, K2, P2TBL, K2, P4) 8 times, K2, P2TBL, K2, P2TBL, K2.
Rows 3 & 4: As *Rows 1 & 2*.
Row 5: (P2, K2TBL, P2, K2TBL, P2, C4F) 8 times, P2, K2TBL, P2, K2TBL, P2.
Row 6: As *Row 2*.

Rep **Rows 1–6** 3 more times, then rep **Rows 1 & 2** once more. Change to 4½mm (US 7) needles and RS facing, work inc row as folls:

Increase Row: K1, (K5, M1) 24 times, end in K1. (146 sts).
Next Row: K.

SET FOUNDATION ROW OF ARAN PATT AS FOLLS:

Row 1: *Edge St* K1, P2, *Panel A* over 24 sts, P2, *Panel B* over 4 sts, *Panel D* over 18 sts, *Panel B* over 4 sts, *Panel E* over 36 sts, *Panel C* over 4 sts, *Panel D* over 18 sts, *Panel C* over 4 sts, P2, *Panel A* over 24 sts, P2, *Edge St* K1.
Row 2: *Edge St* K1, K2, *Panel A* over 24 sts, K2, *Panel C* over 4 sts, *Panel D* over 18 sts, *Panel C* over 4 sts, *Panel E* over 36 sts, *Panel B* over 4 sts, *Panel D* over 18 sts, *Panel B* over 4 sts, K2, *Panel A* over 24 sts, K2, *Edge St* K1.

These 2 rows establish the patt. Cont working appropriate rows of patt panels, and working divider sts between the Honeycomb panels and 4-st Cables in reverse st st. Cont in this way until **Row 78** (**Row 30** of *Panel E*) has been completed.

ARMHOLE SHAPING

Row 79: Cast (bind) off 4 sts from beg of row, then set new 4-st Cable patt as folls: *Edge St* K1, *Panel B* over 4 sts: K4, P2, *Panel A* across 16 sts, then cont in patt as already set across other sts until 2nd Honeycomb *Panel A* is reached. Work across 16 sts of *Panel A*, then K4, P2, for other new 4-st Cable patt, *Edge St* K1. Cast (bind) off rem sts.
Next Row: Rejoin yarn at inner armhole edge, then matching cable twists on new cable panels to other cable *Panels B & C*, cont in patt until **Row 144** (**Row 48** of 3rd rep of *Panel E*) has been completed.

DIVIDE FOR NECK

Next Row: Work across 51 sts in patt as set, cast (bind) off 36 sts, then work across rem 51 sts. Transfer first 51 sts to spare needle.
Next Row: (WS) work in patt with no dec.
Next Row: Dec 1 st at neck edge, patt across row.
Rep last 2 rows twice more, then cast (bind) off in patt.

Complete other shoulder similarly.

FRONT

Work as for Back until **Row 30** of 3rd patt rep of *Panel E* (actual **Row 126**) has been completed.

DIVIDE FOR NECK

Row 127: Work across 53 sts in patt, cast (bind) off next 32 sts, then complete rem 53 sts in patt. Transfer first 53 sts onto spare needle.

Work across next 3 rows on second group of 53 sts with no dec, then dec 1 st at inside neck edge. Rep these last 4 rows twice more, then cast (bind) off in patt.

Complete other shoulder similarly.

SLEEVES

Using 3¾mm (US 5) circular needles as straight, cast on 52 sts. Work Cuff patt as folls:

Rep cable patt as already shown for Welt, rep patt **Rows 1–6** 3 times, ending in **Rows 1 & 2** once more, then work inc row as folls:

INCREASE ROW

K1, (M1, K5) 10 times, K1. (62 sts).
K 1 row, then change to 4½mm (US 7) needles.

SET FOUNDATION ROW FOR ARAN PATT AS FOLLS:

Row 1: P1, (K2, P2) twice across *Panel D* over 9 sts, *Panel B* over 4 sts, *Panel E* over 36 sts, *Panel C* over 4 sts, (P2, K2) twice, P1, across *Panel D* over 9 sts.

Cont in patt as set, inc 1 st at beg and end of **Row 2**, work **Rows 3 & 4** with no dec then inc 1 st at beg and end of **Row 5**, i.e. inc 4 sts over 5 rows, incorporating each new st into patt as set for Back. Cont to inc in this way until **Row 8** of 3rd patt rep of *Panel E* has been completed (actual **Row 104**) and 144 sts exist. Cast (bind) off in patt.

NECKBAND

Using backstitch, join shoulder seams, then using 3¾mm (US 5) circular needles, RS facing, beg at RH Back neck shoulder seam pick up evenly and K3 sts from right Back neck, 36 sts from Back neck, 3 sts from left Back neck, 10 sts from right Front neck, 36 sts from Front neck and 10 sts from left Front neck. (98 sts).

SET FOUNDATION PATT ROUND AS FOLLS:

Round 1: (P2, K2TBL, P2, K2TBL, P2, K4) 7 times.
Rounds 2 & 3: As *Round 1*.
Round 4: (P2, K2TBL, P2, K2TBL, P2, C4F) 7 times.
Rep **Rounds 1–4** twice more. Cast (bind) off.

MAKING UP AND FINISHING

Ease Sleeves into position matching Rope Plait centre to shoulder seam, then using backstitch join to armhole. Using backstitch for Aran patt areas and invisible seam for Cuffs and Welts, join Sleeve and side seams. Turn Neckband down and using slip st join to inside neck edge. Darn in any loose ends, press all seams on WS with warm iron over damp cloth.

COUNTRY
LIFE

My journey to the Aran Islands completed, I travelled back to the National Museum in Dublin and lodged everything Mary Dirrane had told me safely with their Textile Department for their further investigation. They had no previous record of this explanation I had discovered. They have many queries from all over the world from people wanting to know more about the origins of Aran knitting and I felt it was important to record whatever information we can gather from the people actually involved in the early days of the craft before it is too late.

I spent the remaining days of my trip visiting the loveliest parts of the country, which later inspired several garments which follow. My quest had opened my eyes and helped me to understand something of Ireland's history and the effect this has had on its crafts. But so many impressions remain – the quiet way of life, the Irish love of children, the beautiful countryside and coast – that I have ended my collection with designs that try to capture these images.

SAILBOATS

Kinsale harbour, the elegant yachting centre in south-west Ireland inspired this sweater.

The bay is dotted with boats of all types, and the bright pattern of their sails against the surf and the sea-gull flecked sky is captured in this child's summer top.

Yachts at Kinsale harbour

With its wide neckline and in cool cotton, it is an ideal holiday garment that will be useful all year round.

MATERIALS

YARN

Rowan Sea Breeze Soft Cotton in the following colours and quantities

Basic colours

A	Rain Cloud (528)	5 × 50g/9oz
B	Bleached (521)	1 × 50g/2oz
C	Turkish Plum (529)	1 × 50g/2oz
D	Fiord (531)	1 × 50g/2oz
E	Polka (530)	1 × 50g/2oz
F	Bermuda (539)	1 × 50g/2oz

Contrast Colours (less than 25g (1oz) required)

G	Terracotta (525)	1 × 50g/2oz
H	Caramel (524)	1 × 50g/2oz
I	Wheat (523)	1 × 50g/2oz
J	Baize (540)	1 × 50g/2oz
K	Burnt Orange (550)	1 × 50g/2oz
L	Sienna (535)	1 × 50g/2oz

NOTES ON MATERIALS

Colours **G – L** are only used in small quantities, and as the yarn is available only in 50g (2oz) balls, there will be quite a bit over. Some of this can be used for other garments in this book (Seabirds, Galway Racer, Tara) while other balls can be kept to add to your collection of yarns for future projects. Or, if preferred, use oddments from earlier projects, but do not mix fibres for this sweater, keep only to cotton.

NEEDLES
1 pair 2¾mm (US 2) 40cm (15½") circular needles
1 pair 3¼mm (US 3) 40cm (15½") circular needles
2 stitch holders
1 set of double pointed spare needles

SIZES AND MEASUREMENTS

In 2 sizes: Size 1 To fit child's chest 77cm (30")
Size 2 To fit child's chest 81cm (32")

Actual width across back at underarm
43cm (17"):45cm (18")

Length from centre back neck to hip
51cm (20"):53cm (21")

Sleeve seam   40cm (16"): 45cm (18")

TENSION (GAUGE)

30 sts and 33 rows to 10cm (4") over st st on 3¼mm (US 3) needles or size needed to obtain this tension (gauge).

NOTES ON TECHNIQUE

This sweater is made using a variety of techniques, combining intarsia over a fairisle background, and a wavy lace pattern.

INTARSIA
Use this technique for the sailboats and the seagull motifs, working from the chart, and using fairisle for the background sea pattern. When working intarsia, use only short lengths of yarn to avoid tangling, with separate lengths (60cm, 40") for each colour shown in the chart. Twist yarns together at each join to avoid holes, then leave in position to be worked in next row. K the ends in as you work, by wrapping the ends around the new colour thread for 2 or 3 sts beyond where they were last used, to minimise later darning in.

FAIRISLE
Use this technique to work sea and sky areas. Carry colours not in use very loosely across back of work to avoid long floats and puckering. Break off yarns used for fairisle sections

between intarsia sailboats motifs, and rejoin again to work background sea areas in fairisle.

WAVY LACE PATTERN

This pattern is made with lace sts and K and P rows to create a ridged wavy texture for surf areas. (See instructions).

SPECIAL ABBREVIATIONS

YO   Yarn over needle to make a new st between 2 knit sts.

BACK

Beg with main patterned area first, the Welt is added later. Using 3¼mm (US 3) circular needles as straight and J, cast on 130 (140) sts.

Working from Chart 1, read from right to left for RS (K) rows and left to right for WS (P) rows, and work in st st unless specified otherwise. Join in and break off colours as indicated, working across the 56 st rep to end of row as shown on chart.

Rows 1–3: In D, work 3 rows in st st.
Row 4: In E, P 1 row.
Row 5: In B, work as folls from chart:
(Size 1): K1, K2tog,* K1, (YO, K1) 4 times, K1, (K2tog) 4 times.* Rep from *to* until last st, K1.
(Size 2): (K2tog) 4 times, K1, (YO, K1) 4 times, K1.* Rep from *to* to end.
Row 6: In B, K 1 row.
Row 7: In E, K 1 row.
Row 8: In E, P 1 row.
Rows 9 & 10: As Rows 5 & 6.
Cont in st st as shown in chart, working sailboats in intarsia against fairisle background patt. Cont rest of patt in fairisle except where seagull motifs appear; work these in intarsia. Cont in patt until Row 41 has been completed. Now begin working from Chart 2 in st st, reading from right to left for RS (K) rows and left to right for WS (P) rows. Work the 28 st rep across the 130 (140) sts as shown. Cont the 50 row rep until Row 80 (88) has been completed.

ARMHOLE SHAPING

Cast (bind) off 8 (8) sts at beg and end of next row. Rejoin yarn and cont working in patt as shown until Row 140 (150) has been completed. (114:124) sts.

DIVIDE FOR NECK

Work across 33 sts in patt, then leave these sts on a spare needle. Work next 48 (58) sts and leave on stitch holder, then work across rem 33 sts. Cont to work this shoulder in patt but dec 1 st at inside neck edge every row until 26 (26) sts rem. Cast (bind) off. Work other shoulder similarly.

FRONT

Work as for Back until neck shaping.

DIVIDE FOR NECK

Complete Row 130 (141). Work across 32 (35) sts in patt, then leave these sts on a spare needle. K next 50 (54) sts and leave on stitch holder, then K across rem 32(35) sts.
Cont in patt, dec 1 st at inside neck edge for next 6 (9) rows until 26 (26) sts rem. Work in patt with no further dec until Row 148 (159) has been completed. Cast (bind) off. Work other shoulder similarly.

SLEEVES

Using 3¼mm (US 3) circular needles as straight and J, cast on 70 sts and work in patt as shown in Chart 1, beg at 49th st, working across chart, then ending on 7th st. Inc 1 st at each side of Sleeves every 3rd row until Row 110 (Row 126) has been completed and 142 (152) sts rem.

NECKBAND

Using backstitch, join shoulder seams, then using 3¼mm (US 3) circular needles, starting as LH shoulder seams at left Back neck, and J, pick up and K17(21sts) from right Front neck, 50 (54) sts from Front neck sts from stitch holder, 17 (21) sts from left Front neck, 7 (8) sts from right Back neck, 48 (58) sts from Back neck, and 7 (8) from left Back neck. 146 (170) sts.
Working in rounds, reduce sts as folls:
In J, (K1, K2tog), rep to end of round, ending in K1. 97 (113) sts. Change to 2¾mm (US 2) circular needles and C, and K 1 round.
In C, work 7 rounds in K1, P1 rib, then cast (bind) off tightly, knitwise.

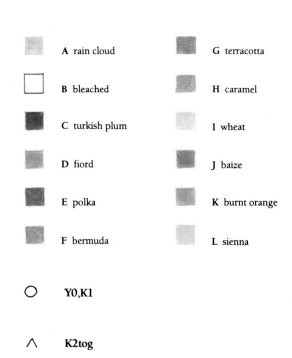

	A rain cloud		G terracotta
	B bleached		H caramel
	C turkish plum		I wheat
	D fiord		J baize
	E polka		K burnt orange
	F bermuda		L sienna

O   YO,K1

∧   K2tog

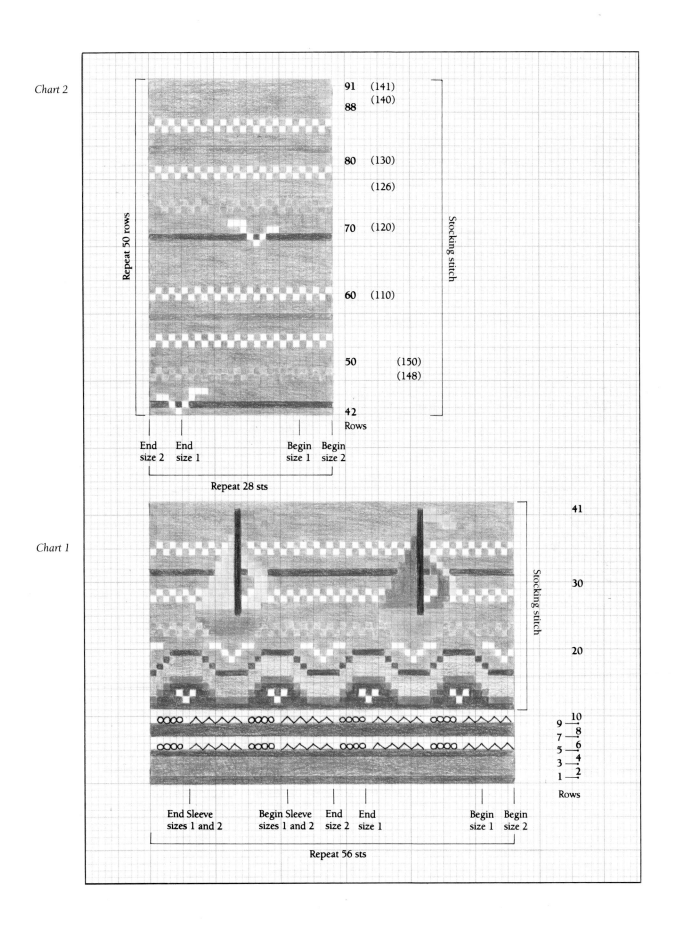

Chart 2

91 (141)
(140)
88

80 (130)
(126)

Repeat 50 rows

70 (120)

Stocking stitch

60 (110)

50 (150)
(148)

42
Rows

End   End   Begin   Begin
size 2 size 1   size 1   size 2

Repeat 28 sts

Chart 1

41

30

Stocking stitch

20

9 —— 10
7 —— 8
5 —— 6
3 —— 4
1 —— 2
Rows

End Sleeve   Begin Sleeve   End   End   Begin   Begin
sizes 1 and 2   sizes 1 and 2   size 2 size 1   size 1   size 2

Repeat 56 sts

WELTS

Using 2¼mm (US 2) circular needles as straight and C, RS facing, pick up evenly and K130 (140) sts from Back cast on row edge, which was worked in J. In C, work 6cm (2¼") in K1, P1 rib, then cast (bind) off. Work Front Welt similarly.

CUFFS

Using 2¾mm (US 2) circular needles as straight and C, RS facing, pick up evenly and K70 sts from cast on row of Sleeve at wrist edge. In C, work 6cm (2¼") in K1, P1 rib, then cast (bind) off.

MAKING UP AND FINISHING

Darn in all loose ends. Using backstitch, join Sleeve to arm-holes evenly, centring Sleeve at mid-point to shoulder seam. Join side seams and Sleeve seams, using backstitch for st st and invisible seaming for ribbing.

Press seams on WS with warm iron over damp cloth, then turn garment RS facing and press similarly on RS, omitting ribbing and raised wavy pattern.

GALWAY RACER

The Irish love of horses reaches a peak of excitement at the Galway Races. Nearby, I saw a child's pony grazing, and designed this sweater to capture the Galway atmosphere.

MATERIALS

YARN

Rowan Sea Breeze Soft Cotton in the following colours and quantities

A	Pine Forest (538)	6 × 50g/10¾oz
B	Terracotta (525)	2 × 50g/3¾oz
C	Burnt Orange (550)	1 × 50g/2oz
D	Sienna (535)	1 × 50g/2oz
E	Baize (540)	1 × 50g/2oz
F	Caramel (524)	1 × 50g/2oz
G	Bermuda (539)	2 × 50g/3¾oz
H	Ecru (522)	1 × 50g 2oz

NEEDLES

1 pair 2¾mm (US 2) 40cm (15½") circular needles
1 pair 3¼mm (US 3) 40cm (15½") circular needles
2 stitch holders
1 set of double pointed spare needles

SIZE AND MEASUREMENTS

One size only to fit child's chest size 81cm (32")

Actual width across back at underarm   45cm (18")

Length from centre back to hip   61cm (24")

Sleeve seam   46cm (18")

TENSION (GAUGE)

30 sts and 33 rows to 10cm (4") over st st on 3¼mm (US 3) needles or size needed to obtain this tension (gauge).

NOTE

This sweater is made using the intarsia technique. When working the motifs from the chart, use short lengths of yarn around 60cm (24") long to avoid tangles, with separate lengths of yarn for each colour as shown. Twist yarns together at each join to avoid holes, then leave in position to be worked in next row. Knit in the ends as you work by wrapping the ends round the new colour thread for two or three sts beyond where they were last used, to minimise darning in later.

BACK

Using 2¾mm (US 2) circular needles as straight and **F**, cast on 96 sts.
Work Welt as folls:

Row 1: In **F**, (K1TBL, P1) rep to end.
Rows 2 & 3: In **G**, (K1TBL, P1) rep to end. Cont to work rib by knitting into back of every K st to make a tight rib.
Rows 4–6: In **B**, rib.
Rows 7 & 8: In **F**, rib.
Rows 9–11: In **B**, rib.
Row 12: In **G**, rib.
Rows 13 & 14: In **E**, rib 2 rows.
Rows 15–17: In **B**, rib 3 rows.

Change to 3¼mm (US 3) circular needles used as straight and **F**, RS facing, work as folls:

INCREASE ROW

(K3, M1) rep to end. (128 sts).

Change to **G**, and work 4 rows in st st.
Change to **A**, and work 2 rows in st st.
Beg patt as shown in chart, working from right to left for RS (K) rows and from left to right for WS (P) rows in sequence, joining in and breaking off different coloured yarns as indicated. Use intarsia method and work in st st as folls:

In **A**, work 7 sts from chart of Side Panels; then work across the 38 st patt 3 times (over 114 sts); then work 7 sts from Side Panel. Cont in this way using **A** as main background colour until **Row 14** of 1st patt rep is reached. Work across Side Panels in **A** and **H** for fence patts, then across the main 38 st patt reps three times, ending with Side Panels in **A** and **H**. Cont in this way, working from charts, until 33rd row of 2nd 68-row patt rep has been completed, and fence patts have been incorporated into Side Panels.

ARMHOLE SHAPING

Cast (bind) off 7 sts at beg of next 2 rows, working across in patt as for **Rows 34 & 35** of 2nd patt rep. Cont in patt with no further shaping until **Row 33** of 3rd patt rep has been completed.

SHAPE NECK

In **A**, cast (bind) off 27 sts, K next 60 sts then leave on spare needle, and cast (bind) off last 27 sts.

FRONT

Work as for Back until 2 reps (i.e. 4 rows of horses) have been completed.

DIVIDE FOR NECK

RS facing, in patt work across **Row 1** of 3rd patt rep over 71 sts. Leave these on spare needle, then work across rem 43 sts.

Next Row: Work in patt as set.

Next Row: Dec 2 sts at inside neck edge, patt to end of row. Working in patt, dec 2 sts at inside neck edge of next 5 alt (every other) rows.

Work 4 more rows in patt with no dec, then dec 2 sts at next neck edge. Rep from *to* once more. Work in patt with no further dec to end of **Row 33** of patt. Cast (bind) off the 27 sts. Leave 28 sts for Front neck on spare needle, then shape other shoulder similarly.

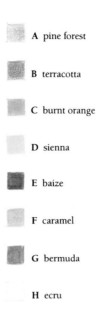

A pine forest

B terracotta

C burnt orange

D sienna

E baize

F caramel

G bermuda

H ecru

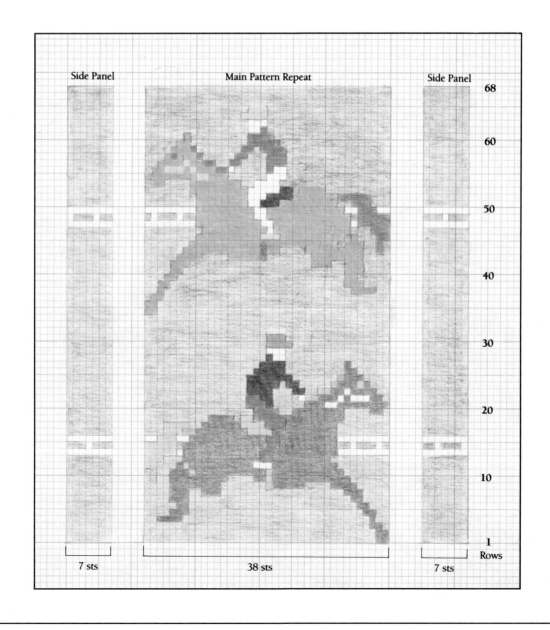

SHOULDER INSERTS (Make 2)

Using 3¼mm (US 3) circular needles as straight and **G**, cast on 4 sts. Work in st st until strip measures 10cm (4") and matches breadth of Front shoulder of 27 sts. Leave on a stitch holder.

Using backstitch, join Back shoulders to Front with Shoulder Insert between, keeping the cast on edge at neckline and edge with sts on stitch holder at armhole edge.

NECKBAND

Using 3¼mm (US 3) circular needles and **G**, RS facing, pick up evenly and K as folls:

Starting at Back neck, K60 sts from spare needle across Back neck, pick up evenly and K4 sts from Shoulder Insert edge, 36 sts along right Front neck, 28 sts from Front neck spare needle, 36 sts from left Front neck and 4 sts from other Shoulder insert. (168 sts)

In **G**, K 3 rounds, then change to F and work 1 round in (K1, K2tog) to end of round. (112 sts)

Change to 2¾mm (US 2) circular needles and in **B**, K 1 round, then in **B** set twisted rib patt as folls: (K1TBL, P1) to end of round. Cont with this rib, knitting into the back of the loop on all the K sts to form a tight rib. Rib 2 more rounds in **B**. Change to **E** and rib 2 rounds, then change to **G** and rib 1 round. Change to **B** and rib 2 rounds, change to **F** and rib 2 rounds, change to **G** and rib 1 round. In **G**, cast (bind) off tightly ribwise.

SLEEVES

Using 3¼mm (US 3) circular needles as straight and **G**, RS facing, beg at Front lower armhole edge and pick up evenly and K50 sts along front of armhole. K the 4 sts from stitch holder, then K50 sts across Back armhole (104 sts). Work Sleeve in st st.

In **G**, work 3 more rows, then change to **A** and work 3 rows.

Beg Sleeve dec as folls:
Dec 1 st at beg and end of every 7th row, changing colours as indicated.

In **G**, work 4 rows, then in **A**, work 4 rows, then in **G**, work 4 rows. In **A**, cont to work Sleeve until 66 sts rem, dec on every 7th row until Sleeve measures 38cm (15"). Change to **G** and work across 4 rows, change to **F** and work dec row as folls: (K2, K2tog) to end of row. Work Cuffs as folls:

Change to 2¾mm (US 2) needles used as straight and in **B**, RS facing, K 1 row.

Next Row: Set twisted rib patt as before: (K1TBL, P1) to end. Rib 1 more row in **B**, then change to **E** and rib 2 rows. Change to **G**, rib 1 row, change to **B**, rib 3 rows, change to **F**, rib 2 rows, change to **B**, rib 3 rows, change to **G**, rib 2 rows, change to **F**, rib 1 row then in **F** cast (bind) off ribwise.

MAKING UP AND FINISHING

Darn in all loose ends, then join side and Sleeve seams using backstitch for st st and invisible seaming for ribbing.

Press seams on WS with warm iron over a damp cloth, then turn RS out and press RS similarly, omitting ribbing.

SEABIRDS

Seabirds wheeling high above banks of billowing clouds, a sparkling blue sea and breakers crashing against the Cliffs of Moher all inspired this cotton sweater.

This pattern gives you an opportunity to work in as many different colours as you like. I used a mixture of textured slubbed cottons to contrast with smoother spun cottons and silks.

I chose a summery theme of blues with pale creamy gold-tinged clouds, but it would look good in deeper shades of indigos and violets with soft rose pink sunset colours. The yarns listed below are therefore suggested as a guide rather than as exact specifications.

MATERIALS

YARN
I chose from the following yarns:

Rowan Sea Breeze Soft Cotton in the following colours and quantities

A	Polka (530):	
	(For Welts and Cuffs)	2 × 50g/3¾oz
B	Ecru (522)	1 × 50g/2oz
C	Fiord (531)	1 × 50g/2oz
D	True Blue (541)	1 × 50g/2oz
E	Turkish Plum (529)	1 × 50g/2oz
F	Lilac (544)	1 × 50g/2oz
G	Bluebell (542)	1 × 50g/2oz
H	Wheat (523)	1 × 50g/2oz
I	Bermuda (539)	1 × 50g/2oz
J	Rain Cloud (528)	1 × 50g/2oz

Twilleys Bubbly Mercerised Cotton in the following colours and quantities

K	Cream (21)	3 × 50g/5½oz
L	Pale Blue (62)	2 × 50g/3¾oz
M	Dark Blue (36)	1 × 50g/2oz
N	Pale Pink (55)	1 × 50g/2oz

Twilleys Lyscordet Mercerised Cotton No 5

O	Mauve (2)	2 × 25g/2oz

Naturally Beautiful Aura 8/2 Silk

P	Silver (P72)	25g/1oz

NEEDLES
1 pair 2¾mm (US 2) 40cm (15½") circular needles
1 pair 3¼mm (US 3) 40cm (15½") circular needles
1 cable needle
1 double pointed spare needle

SIZE AND MEASUREMENTS
One size only to fit up to 117cm (46") bust.

Actual width across back to underarm   63cm (25")

Length from centre back neck to hip   62cm (24½")

Sleeve seam from armhole inset   40cm (15½")

TENSION (GAUGE)
25 sts and 34 rows to 10cm (4") over st st on 3¼mm (US 3) needles or size needed to obtain this tension (gauge).

NOTES ON TECHNIQUES
The sweater is made using a mixture of fairisle and intarsia methods, with Cuffs and Welt decorated in Ribbon cable and rib pattern.

Use the chart as a guide, working the wave motifs in **Rows 1–22** in fairisle, but using yarns of different lengths and shades to vary the colours across the rows.

As the design develops from **Row 22 to Row 183** cont working the motifs of cloud edges, wave crests and flocks of seabirds in intarsia technique, using colours which contrast with the background shades.

When working the fairisle sections, carry colours not in use very loosely across back of the work, weaving around the working yarn every 3rd st to avoid long floats and puckering.

When working in intarsia, use short lengths of yarn around 60cm (24") to avoid tangles, with separate lengths of yarn for each colour as required. Twist the yarns together at each join, then leave in position to be worked in next row. Knit in the ends as you work by wrapping the ends around the new colour thread for two or three sts beyond where they were used to minimise later darning in.

SPECIAL ABBREVIATIONS
C4F   Sl 2 sts onto cable needle, hold at front, K2, then K2 from cable needle.

C4B   Sl 2 sts onto cable needle, hold at back, K2, then K2 from cable needle.

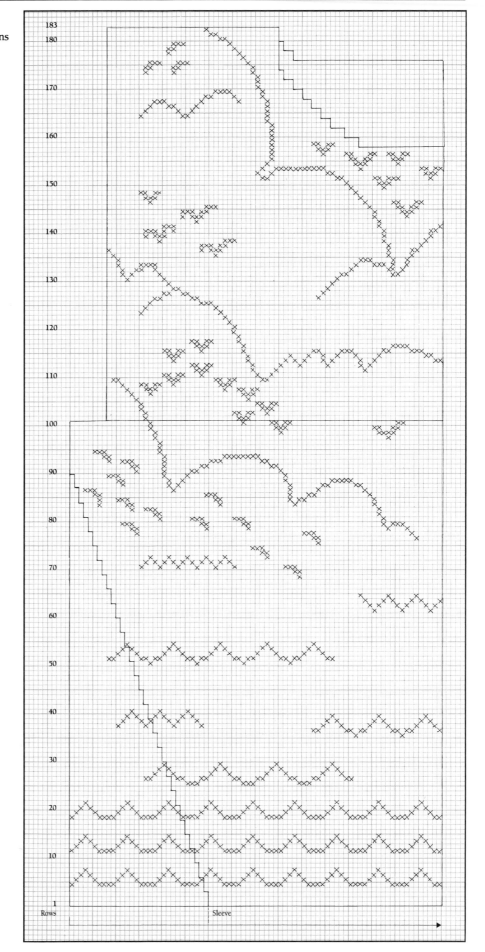

X outline of motifs work in yarns of your choice to contrast with background colours

Background colour for sea and sky

Left Front, Right Back and Sleeve

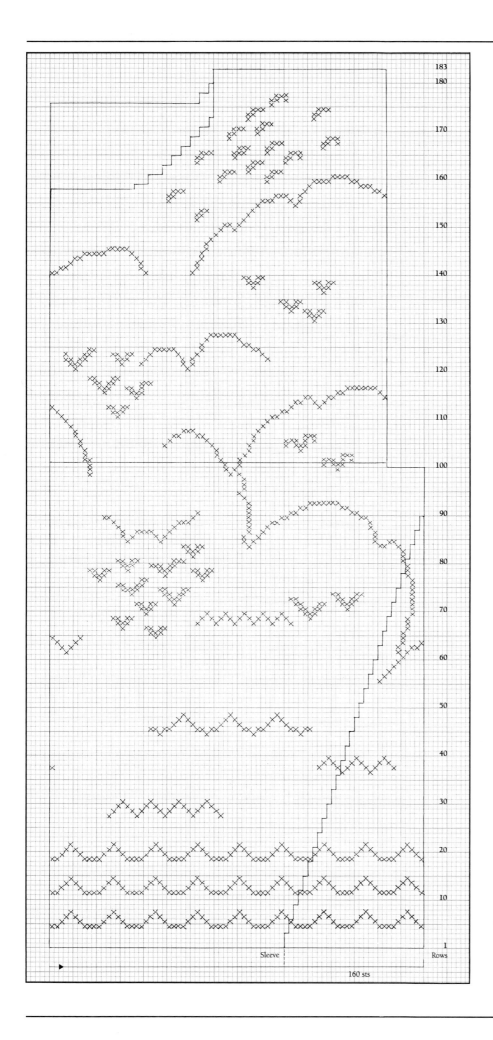

Right Front, Left Back and Sleeve

BACK

Beg with main patterned area first, the Welt and Cuffs are added later. Using 3¼mm (US 3) circular needles as straight and **C**, cast on 160 sts.

Work from the charts from right to left for RS (K) rows and from left to right for WS(P) rows in sequence, joining in and breaking off different coloured yarns as desired.

Work **Rows 1–22** in fairisle and cont afterwards in intarsia.

ARMHOLE SHAPING

Cast (bind) off 8 sts at beg of **Rows 101 & 102**. Cont working from charts until **Row 177**.

SHAPE NECK

Work across 40 sts in patt, cast (bind) off 64 sts, then work across rem 40 sts. Transfer first 40 sts to spare needle, then cont to shape rem 40 sts as folls:

Next Row: Work in patt with no dec.
Next Row: Dec 2 sts at neck edge, work to end of row.
Next Row: Work in patt with no dec.
Next Row: Dec 1 st at neck edge, work to end of row.
Work last 2 rows with no dec, cast (bind) off. Work other shoulder similarly.

FRONT

Work as for Back, but change the colours as desired, they do not need to be identical with Back. Work in patt until **Row 159**.

DIVIDE FOR NECK

Row 159: Work in patt across 54 sts, cast (bind) off 36 sts, then work in patt across rem 54 sts.
Transfer first 54 sts to spare needle, then work on rem sts as folls:

Work next row with no dec, then dec 3 sts at neck edge of foll 2 alt (every other) rows, work next row with no dec, then dec 2 st at neck edge for foll 5 alt (every other) rows. Work next row with no dec, then dec 1 st at neck edge of next row, then complete last 7 rows with no further dec.

Complete other shoulder similarly. Cast (bind) off.

SLEEVES

Using 3¼mm (US 3) needles and **C**, cast on 100 sts.

Work from chart similarly to Back, but inc 1 st at beg and end of every 3rd row until **Row 91** is completed. Cont to work in patt for a further 10 rows with no further inc, cast (bind) off.

NECKBAND

Using backstitch, join shoulder seams, then work Neckband as folls:

Using 2¾mm (US 2) circular needles and **F**, RS facing, beg at LH corner of Back neck shoulder seam, pick up evenly and K20 sts from right Front neck, 18 sts from Front neck, 20 sts from left Front neck, and 42 sts from Back neck (100 sts). Change to **G** and in K1, P1 single rib, work 2 rounds. Change to **P**, rib 1 round, change to **J**, rib 3 rounds, then cast (bind) off in **J** ribwise.

WELTS

Using 2¾mm (US 2) circular needles as straight and **A**, WS facing, from Back, and later from Front cast on edge, pick up evenly and P104 sts. Set Ribbon cable and rib patt as folls:

Row 1: (P2, K1, P2, K4) 11 times, P2, K1, P2.
Row 2: K2, P1, K2, (P4, K2, P1, K2) 11 times to end.
Rows 3 & 4: As *Rows 1 & 2*.
Row 5: (P2, K1, P2, C4F) 11 times, P2, K1, P2.

Row 6: As *Row 2*.
Rows 7–10: As *Rows 1–4*.
Row 11: (P2, K1, P2, C4B) 11 times, P2, K1, P2.
Row 12: As *Row 2*.
Rep *Rows 1–12* twice more, then work *Rows 1–8* once more. Cast (bind) off.

CUFFS

Using 2¾mm (US 2) circular needles as straight and **A**, WS facing, pick up evenly from cast-on Sleeve edge at wrist and P56 sts. Set Ribbon cable and rib patt as folls:

Row 1: (P2, K1, P2, K4) 6 times, end in P2.
Row 2: K2, (P4, K2, P1, K2) 6 times to end.
Rows 3 & 4: As *Rows 1 & 2*.

Row 5: (P2, K1, P2, C4F) 6 times, end in P2.
Rows 6: As *Row 2*.
Rows 7–10: As *Rows 1–4*.
Row 11: (P2, K1, P2, C4B) 6 times, end in P2.
Row 12: As *Row 2*.
Rep *Rows 1–12* twice more, then work *Rows 1–8* once. Cast (bind) off.

MAKING UP AND FINISHING

Darn in all loose ends, then using backstitch, join cast (bound) off 8 sts at armhole edges to Sleeve edges at under-arm, then set in Sleeves carefully. Join Sleeve seams and side seams using backstitch for st st and invisible seaming for rib.

Press seams tightly on WS with warm iron over damp cloth. Finally press RS similarly, omitting ribbing.

WILD FUCHSIAS

All along the west coast of Ireland, wild fuchsia hedges line the twisting country tracks leading down to the sea. Tumbling over the tops of austere stone walls, their bright delicate beauty epitomises the Irish spirit – irrepressibly outwitting the elements as they endure the fierce Atlantic gales.

I tried to capture their grace in this dark green mohair sweater patterned with silk and fine wool.

MATERIALS

YARN
Spunlaine Mohair
A Dark Green (867)   12 × 50g/21¼oz

Naturally Beautiful Aura 8/2 Silk
B Bronze (305)   25g/1oz
C Russett (804)   25g/1oz

Jamieson & Smith 2 ply Jumper Weight Shetland Wool in the following colours and quantities

D Mauve (FC9)   1 × 25g/1oz
E Fuchsia Pink (52)   1 × 25g/1oz
F Scarlet (93)   1 × 25g/1oz
G Bright Green (79)   3 × 50g/5½oz

NEEDLES
1 pair 4mm (US 6) 40cm (15½″) circular needles
1 pair 5mm (US 8) 40cm (15½″) straight needles
1 cable needle
1 spare needle

SIZES AND MEASUREMENTS
One size only to fit up to 96cm (38″) bust

Actual width across back at underarm   51cm (20″)
Length from centre back neck to hip   62cm (24½″)
Sleeve seam   46cm (18″)

TENSION (GAUGE)
16 sts and 22 rows to 10cm (4″) over patt on mohair on 5mm (US 8) needles or size needed to obtain this tension (gauge).

NOTES ON TECHNIQUES
This sweater is made in a simple all over pattern similar to moss stitch, but is decorated over the yoke and sleeves with intarsia and cabled fuchsia motifs and silk bobbles.

When working in intarsia from the chart, use only short lengths of yarn (60cm, 24″) to avoid tangling, with separate lengths for each colour as indicated. Twist yarns together at each join to avoid holes, then leave in position to be worked in next row. Knit the ends in as you work by wrapping the ends around the new colour thread for 2 or 3 sts beyond where they were last used to minimise later darning in.

Follow instructions for cabling fuchsia stems so they form a subtle diagonal pattern around the neckline.

SPECIAL ABBREVIATIONS

C2F	Sl 1 st onto cable needle, hold at front, K next st, using yarn in colour as shown in chart, then K st on cable needle in colour as shown. .
C2B	Sl 1 st onto cable needle, hold at back, K next st using yarn in colour as shown in chart, then K st on cable needle in colour as shown.
MB	Make a bobble as folls: on RS row, using **B**, make 3 sts from 1 by K1,P1,K1 into st where shown in chart.
CB	Complete bobble as folls: on WS row, using **B**, K3, bring yarn forward then slip these 3 sts back onto LH needle, pick up the loop into which the 3 from 1 was made, slip it onto LH needle then pass the 3 sts in **B** over this st, then in **B**, P this st.
M1	Make 1 st by picking up loop between sts from row below and knit it TBL.

BACK

Using 4mm (US 6) circular needles as straight and **A**, cast on 70 sts.
Set in K1, P1 single rib and rib for 22 rows, until Welt measures 8cm (3″).

Increase Row

(K10, M1) 6 times, to last 10 sts, K10. (76 sts)

Change to 5mm (US 8) circular needles used as straight, P 1 row.

RS facing, commence patt:

Row 1: (K2,P2) rep to end.
Row 2: P.
Row 3: (P2, K2) rep to end.
Row 4: P.
Rep **Rows 1–4** continuously until 19 reps have been worked and Back measures 44cm (17½") from beg of Welt.

ARMHOLE SHAPING

Row 77: Cont in patt as set, dec 2 sts at beg of next 2 rows then dec 1 st at beg of foll 6 rows. (66 sts)

Work from chart on page 133, reading from right to left for RS (K) rows and from left to right for WS (P) rows over intarsia fuchsia motifs, working these in wool and silk as specified, but cont with Moss St-like background patt in mohair as before. Work bobbles as instructed in contrast colours, in silk, leaving sufficiently long ends to easily darn in on completion.

SHOULDER SHAPING

Work as shown in chart, using **A** where indicated but casting (binding) off using **G**.

FRONT

Work as for Back until Yoke contrast colours are introduced. Foll Front chart on page 134 for these, then divide for neck as shown after 29 sts of **Row 111** have been worked, dec at inner neck edge as shown, in **G**. Leave rem 37 sts on spare needle while working right shoulder from chart. Work left shoulder similarly, casting (binding) off in yarns as shown in chart. (Or work both shoulders simultaneously using separate balls of yarn if preferred.)

SLEEVES

Using 4mm (US 6) circular needles as straight and **A** cast on 36 sts. Work 22 rows in K1, P1 single rib as in Welt.

INCREASE ROW

Cast on 1st, K this st. Then (K4, M1) rep to last 4 sts, end in K1, inc 1. (46 sts).

Change to 5mm (US 8) needles. P 1 row then work in patt as given for Back, inc 1 st at beg and end of 4th and every subsequent 9th row until 62 sts exist. Cont in patt until Sleeve measures 44cm (17½") from Cuff edge.

Work Sleeve head patt as shown in chart on page 133, then cast (bind) off in **A** at Sleeve head edge.

NECKBAND

Using backstitch, join Back and Front shoulder seams. Using 4mm (US 6) circular needles, beg at LH shoulder seam at Back neck, in **G**, RS facing, pick up evenly and P74 sts from Front neck edge and 46 sts from Back neck. (120 sts).
Next Round: Cast (bind) off purlwise.

MAKING UP AND FINISHING

Darn in all loose ends and neaten work, then using **A**, gather Sleeve head until it measures 12cm (5"). Ease Sleeve head into place in armhole, smoothing gathers until they are even, then centre at shoulder seam to form a puff sleeve. Using backstitch, stitch firmly into place. Using backstitch for Moss St areas and invisible seam for ribbing, join Sleeve and side seams. Do not press, but brush up mohair to finish.

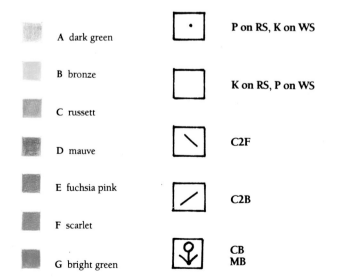

A dark green

B bronze

C russett

D mauve

E fuchsia pink

F scarlet

G bright green

· P on RS, K on WS

K on RS, P on WS

\ C2F

/ C2B

CB
MB

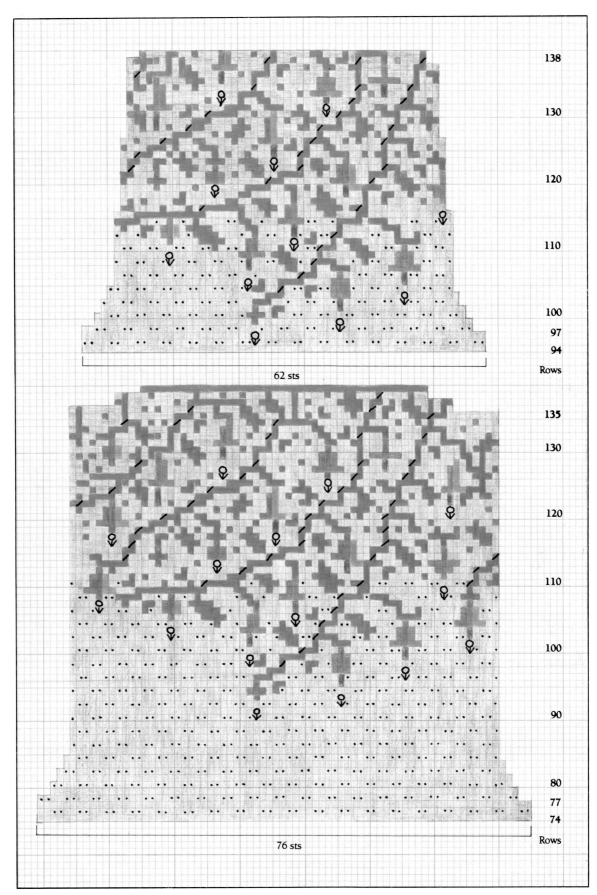

138
130
120
110
100
97
94
Rows

62 sts

135
130
120
110
100
90
80
77
74
Rows

76 sts

Back and Sleeve Head

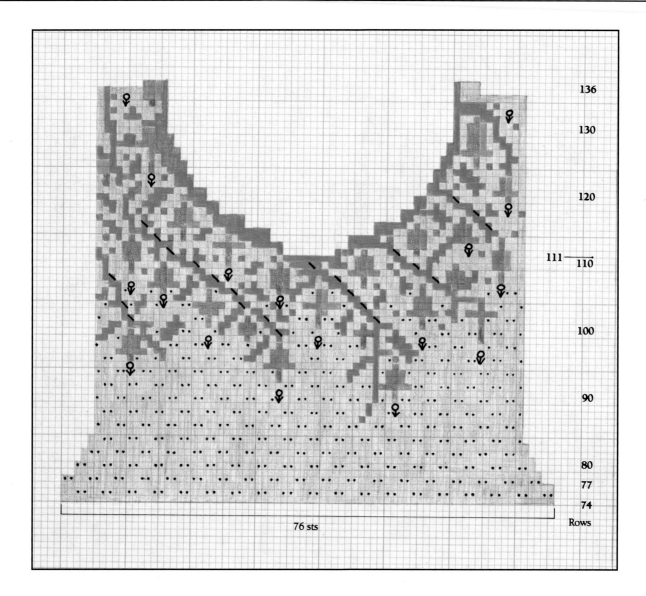

136

120

111 ─ 110

100

90

80
77
74
Rows

76 sts

Front

Technical Information

Abbreviations

alt	alternate (ly)
approx	approximately
beg	begin (ning)
cm	centimetres
cont	continu (e) (ing)
dec	decreas (e) (ing)
foll(s)	follow (s) (ing)
g	gram (s)
inc	increas (e) (ing)
K	knit
K2tog	knit 2 together
K3tog	knit 3 together
LH	left hand
M1	make 1 st by picking up loop from row below and knitting if through back of loop
mm	millimetre (s)
oz	ounce
patt	pattern
P	purl
P2tog	purl 2 together
PRD	purl reverse decrease
PSSO	pass the slipped st over
rem	remain (ing)
rep	repeat (s)
RH	right hand
RS	right side of work
sl	slip
SL 1	slip 1 st from LH needle over to RH needle without knitting or purling it
st (s)	stitch (es)
st st	stocking (stockinette) stitch (1 row K, 1 row P) or (K every round)
TBL	through the back of loop (s)
tog	together
WS	wrong side of work

Cable Abbreviations

C2F	Slip 1 st onto cable needle, hold at front, K1, then K1 from cable needle.
C2B	Slip 1 st onto cable needle, hold at back, K1, then K1 from cable needle.
C4F	Slip 2 sts onto cable needle, hold at front, K2, then K2 from cable needle.
C4B	Slip 2 sts onto cable needle, hold at back, K2, then K2 from cable needle.
C6F	Slip 3 sts onto cable needle, hold at front, K3, then K3 from cable needle.
C6B	Slip 3 sts onto cable needle, hold at back, K3, then K3 from cable needle.
C8F	Slip 4 sts onto cable needle, hold at front, K4, then K4 from cable needle.
C8B	Slip 4 sts onto cable needle, hold at back, K4, then K4 from cable needle.
C4FM (cable 2 to front & moss)	Slip 2 sts onto cable needle, hold at front, K1, P1, then K2 from cable needle.
C4BM (cable 2 to back & moss)	Slip 2 sts onto cable needle, hold at back, K2, then K1, P1 from cable needle.
C4FP (cable 2 to front & purl)	Slip 2 sts onto cable needle, hold at front, P2, then K2 from cable needle.
C4BP (cable 2 to back & purl)	Slip 2 sts onto cable needle, hold at back, K2, then P2 from cable needle.
SFC (single front cross)	Slip 1 st onto cable needle, hold at front, P1, then K1 from cable needle.
SBC (single back cross)	Slip 1 st onto cable needle, hold at back, K1, then P1 from cable needle.
FC (front cross)	Slip 2 sts onto cable needle, hold at front, P1, then K2 from cable needle.
BC (back cross)	Slip 1 st onto cable needle, hold at back, K2, then P1 from cable needle.
DFC (double front cross)	Slip 4 sts onto cable needle, hold at front, P2, then K4 from cable needle.
DBC (double back cross)	Slip 2 sts onto cable needle, hold at back, K4, then P2 from cable needle.

FKC (front knit cross)	Slip 2 sts onto cable needle, hold at front, K1, then K2 from cable needle.
BKC (back knit cross)	Slip 1 st onto cable needle, hold at back, K2, then K1 from cable needle.
DFKC (double front knit cross)	Slip 4 sts onto cable needle, hold at front, K2, then K4 from cable needle.
DBKC (double back knit cross)	Slip 2 sts onto cable needle, hold at back, K4, then K2 from cable needle.
TC (triple cross)	Slip 2 sts onto cable needle, hold at front, slip next st onto 2nd cable needle, also hold at front. K next 2 sts from LH needle then sl 1 st from 2nd cable needle in front of, and over, the 2 sts on 1st cable needle, then K the st from the 2nd cable needle, and lastly the 2 sts from 1st cable needle.

LACE ABBREVIATIONS

YO (between 2 K sts)	(Yarn over needle) to make a new st between 2 K sts.
YO2 (between 2 K sts)	(Yarn over needle) twice to make 2 new sts between 2 K sts).
YRN (between 2 P sts)	Wind yarn round needle to make a new st between 2 P sts.
YFRN (between a K and a P st)	Yarn forward and round needle to make a new st between a K and a P st.
YON2 (between a P and a K st)	(Yarn over needle) twice to make 2 new sts between a P and a K st.
YRN-P2tog	Yarn round needle before purling 2 sts together
K4tog-BL	Knit 4 sts together through the back of the loops.
YO, K2tog	(Yarn over needle) to make a new st, then K the next 2 sts together.
K2tog, YO	Knit 2 together, then yarn over needle to make a new st between 2 knit sts.

BOBBLE ABBREVIATIONS

MB (first type)	Make a bobble by K1, P1, K1 into next st without dropping loop of original st, turn, P4 sts just made, turn, (K2tog) twice, sl first st over second st.
MB (second type)	K into front and back of next st twice, then K into front again making 5 sts from 1. Turn and K5, turn and P5, then lift 2nd, 3rd, 4th and 5th sts over 1st st and off needle.
MB2	Make 2 bobbles from next 2 sts, each bobble in method shown for MB (second type) as shown immediately above.
MB3	Make separately, then sew into place later. Cast on 3 sts, K1, P1, K1, turn, P3, then P2, sl first st on RH needle over centre st on LH needle, P1, then sl first st on RH needle over rem st, sl yarn through last st to cast (bind) off.
MB4	(K into front and back of next st) twice, making 4 sts out of 1, (turn and K4 sts, turn and P4 sts) twice, then using LH needle, lift 2nd, 3rd, 4th sts over 1st st and off needle.
MB & CB	Make a bobble over 2 rows as folls: on RS row, make 3 sts from 1 by K1, P1, K1 into next st. Complete bobble on WS row by K3 on sts previously made, bring yarn forward, then sl these 3 sts back onto LH needle, pick up loop from which the 3 from 1 was made, sl it onto LH needle, then pass the 3 sts over this st, then P this st.
Bobble	With First colour, K2tog. With second colour, make 3 sts, by K1, P1, K1 into the same st. Turn, K3 in second colour, turn, K3 in second colour, sl st over next st, rep until 1 st remains. With first colour, make 1 new st by picking up loop between sts from row below and knitting it TBL.

KNITTING TERMS OCCASIONALLY USED IN THE PATTERNS

Sizes in brackets are listed in smallest sizes ranging up to largest size, and yarn quantities, stitches required and actual size are always listed in this order, e.g. 6 (7:8:9)

Where a number of stitches are given at the end of a row, this is the number you should have on your needle at this stage in the pattern, e.g. (5 sts).

Where instructions are given in brackets, immediately followed by a number, e.g. (P1, K1) twice, you must work the given instructions the stated number of times.

Where asterisks appear, repeat from the first asterisk until second asterisk. The reason asterisks are given rather than brackets is often the instructions would be too long to include in brackets, e.g. where it states Back and Front the same until... asterisk.*

Asterisks are also used in a line of knitting instructions where brackets already appear, for simplicity and to avoid confusion.

e.g. K2tog* (M1, P6) twice, P9.* Rep from *to* once more.

Turn. This simply means turn work as you would at the end of a row, only this instruction is often given in the middle of a row. It often appears at neck shaping instructions, or in lace instructions.

Right side (RS). This is usually **Row 1**. If **Row 1** begins on WS, this is stated as **Row 1 (WS)**. Otherwise **Row 1** appears as simply **Row 1** with no (RS) afterwards.

KNITTING AND FINISHING TECHNIQUES

Each pattern in this book clearly describes the knitting techniques required for the particular project, at the beginning of the instructions.

With the single coloured fabrics, the decoration is with the stitch construction such as cabling, lace or moss stitch for example, and the necessary methods are listed under the Special Abbreviations section at the start of the instructions.

With multi-coloured fabrics, the techniques used vary depending on the type of design specified. All over repeating patterns are usually knitted in the fairisle method, with the yarns not in use either stranded or woven into each other at the back of the work. Separate motifs on a plain or textured ground are usually worked in the intarsia method with short lengths of coloured yarns as specified, twisted together at each join to prevent holes forming, then left in position to be worked in the next row. The size of the area of colour shown on the chart also affects the method specified, as motifs over only one or two stitches can be worked in fairisle or intarsia.

Some patterns combine cabling with intarsia creating a textured surface in several different colours. Other patterns combine fairisle and intarsia in the same area of the fabric.

The important thing to remember when working in several colours and techniques simultaneously is to keep the yarns as loose as possible, as the fabric will pucker if the threads are pulled too tightly.

If all this sounds rather daunting, don't worry but practise on a small sample until you feel confident enough to have a go at the real thing.

Another point to note is that when working with many colours, the loose ends at the back of the fabric can take ages to darn in when neatening the garment. If you knit them in as you work by wrapping the ends around the main colour yarn for two or three stitches beyond where they were last used, you'll save yourself hours of work later on.

The following more detailed information about blocking the garments where necessary before sewing up, and seaming methods, may be helpful. It really does make all the difference to the end result to use the appropriate methods for finishing, as these will give your work a professional, hand-made rather than home-made look.

BLOCKING

All garments benefit from being blocked before being sewn up and for some of the items in this book this is absolutely essential.

Basically this means pinning out each garment piece (or in some cases the finished garment) onto a soft flat surface to the correct measurements. This is then dampened (a plant sprayer is useful here) and left to dry naturally. Fairisle and other multi-coloured flat fabrics also improve with pressing with a warm iron over a damp cloth at this stage, but don't press ribbing or textured fabrics, just leave them to dry.

I use a large board made of fibre board covered in a plain white table cloth to block on, but towels on a table, or foam covered in a cotton sheet will also work well. Dressmakers stainless steel pins should be used.

Blocking is particularly important with lace knitting, where each point is stretched out with a pin at the end of the point, and the openwork stitches are clearly visible.

SEAMING

The type of seaming specified in the patterns is either backstitch or invisible seaming.

Backstitch is suitable for most seams providing it is worked with a firm but not too tight tension and is sewn as close to the edge as possible to avoid a bulky ridge. It is worked on the inside of the garment, with RS facing each other. Check every four stitches to make sure both sides of the fabric match.

Invisible seaming, or edge to edge seam as it is sometimes called, is used where a more delicate ridgeless seam is necessary. This is also worked on the WS, and must be worked fairly firmly so the stitches of the sewing cannot be seen, but don't allow the seam to pucker. Again, check every four stitches or so to make sure patterns match.

COMPARATIVE TERMS

UK	US
Cast off	Bind off
Alternate rows	Every other row
Tension	Gauge
Stocking stitch	Stockinette stitch
Tack	Catch down

(Other terms are the same in both countries)

YARN EQUIVALENTS

The following table lists the equivalent UK and US yarns in terms of thickness. When substituting yarns, it is essential to check tension before buying enough for the whole garment.

UK	US
4 ply	Sport
Double knitting (DK)	Knitting worsted
Aran-weight	Fisherman
Chunky	Bulky

The 2 ply jumper weight (which knits as standard 4 ply (sport)), and 1 ply Cobweb, as supplied by Jamieson & Smith Ltd are known by these terms in both countries.

CONVERSION CHART FOR YARN WEIGHTS AND MEASUREMENTS

WEIGHT (Rounded up to nearest $\frac{1}{4}$oz)		*LENGTH* (to nearest $\frac{1}{4}$in)			
g	*oz*	*cm*	*in*	*cm*	*in*
25	1	1	$\frac{1}{2}$	55	$21\frac{3}{4}$
50	2	2	$\frac{3}{4}$	60	$23\frac{1}{2}$
100	$3\frac{3}{4}$	3	$1\frac{1}{4}$	65	$25\frac{1}{2}$
150	$5\frac{1}{2}$	4	$1\frac{1}{2}$	70	$27\frac{1}{2}$
200	$7\frac{1}{4}$	5	2	75	$29\frac{1}{2}$
250	9	6	$2\frac{1}{2}$	80	$31\frac{1}{2}$
300	$10\frac{3}{4}$	7	$2\frac{3}{4}$	85	$33\frac{1}{2}$
350	$12\frac{1}{2}$	8	3	90	$35\frac{1}{2}$
400	$14\frac{1}{4}$	9	$3\frac{1}{2}$	95	$37\frac{1}{2}$
450	16	10	4	100	$39\frac{1}{2}$
500	$17\frac{3}{4}$	11	$4\frac{1}{4}$	110	$43\frac{1}{2}$
550	$19\frac{1}{2}$	12	$4\frac{3}{4}$	120	47
600	$21\frac{1}{4}$	13	5	130	$51\frac{1}{4}$
650	23	14	$5\frac{1}{2}$	140	55
700	$24\frac{3}{4}$	15	6	150	59
750	$26\frac{1}{2}$	16	$6\frac{1}{4}$	160	63
800	$28\frac{1}{4}$	17	$6\frac{3}{4}$	170	67
850	30	18	7	180	$70\frac{3}{4}$
900	$31\frac{3}{4}$	19	$7\frac{1}{2}$	190	$74\frac{3}{4}$
950	$33\frac{3}{4}$	20	8	200	$78\frac{3}{4}$
1000	$35\frac{1}{2}$	25	$9\frac{3}{4}$	210	$82\frac{3}{4}$
1200	$42\frac{1}{4}$	30	$11\frac{3}{4}$	220	$86\frac{1}{2}$
1400	$49\frac{1}{4}$	35	$13\frac{3}{4}$	230	$90\frac{1}{2}$
1600	$56\frac{1}{2}$	40	$15\frac{3}{4}$	240	$94\frac{1}{2}$
1800	$63\frac{1}{2}$	45	$17\frac{3}{4}$	250	$98\frac{1}{2}$
2000	$70\frac{1}{2}$	50	$19\frac{3}{4}$	300	118

CONVERSION CHART FOR NEEDLE SIZES

Needle sizes given in the patterns are recommended as starting points for you to make your tension samples before you begin to knit the garment. If you can't obtain the given tension, try a different needle size until your sample matches the given one. It really is well worth going to the trouble of checking your tension. Care taken at this stage will prevent needless disappointment later from strangely sized garments.

METRIC	*US*	*OLD UK*
2mm	0	14
$2\frac{1}{4}$mm	1	13
$2\frac{1}{2}$mm		
$2\frac{3}{4}$	2	12
3mm		11
$3\frac{1}{4}$	3	10
$3\frac{1}{2}$	4	
$3\frac{3}{4}$	5	9
4mm	6	8
$4\frac{1}{2}$	7	7
5mm	8	6
$5\frac{1}{2}$mm	9	5
6mm	10	4
$6\frac{1}{2}$mm	$10\frac{1}{2}$	3
7mm		2
$7\frac{1}{2}$mm		1
8mm	11	0
9mm	13	00
10mm	15	000

YARN
SUPPLIERS

Rowan Yarns
Green Lane Mill
Washpit
Holmfirth
West Yorkshire HD7 1RW

Kilcarra Yarns Ltd
Kilcar
Co Donegal
Ireland

H G Twilley Ltd
Roman Mills
Stamford
Lincolnshire PE9 1BG

Colinette Yarns
Park Lane House
High Street
Welshpool
Powys

**Jamieson & Smith
(Shetland Wool
Brokers) Ltd**
90 North Road
Lerwick
Shetland ZE1 0PQ

Spunlaine Wools
Marley Street Mills
Keighley
West Yorkshire BD21 5JY

**Coats Domestic Marketing Division
(Anchor Cottons)**
39 Durham Street
Glasgow G41 1BS

Naturally Beautiful
Broadfield House
Dent
Cumbria LA10 5TG

Selected Bibliography

The Complete Book of Traditional Knitting Rae Compton, Batsford, 1983.

Irish Rural Life and Industry (Published in connection with the Home Industries Section of the Irish International Exhibition 1907) Hely's, 1907.

The Complete Book of Traditional Aran Knitting Shelagh Hollingworth, Batsford, 1982.

The Sacred History of Knitting Heinz Edgar Kiewe, Art Needlework Industries. Oxford, 1971.

History and Organisation of the Aran knitting industry in Ireland Yvonne Mahood, Irish Export Board, 1979.

A History of Hand Knitting Richard Rutt, Bishop of Leicester, Batsford, 1987.

The Aran Islands J M Synge, Oxford University Press, 1979.
Mary Thomas's Book of Knitting Patterns Mary Thomas, Hodder, 1943.

Patterns for Guernseys, Jerseys and Arans Gladys Thompson, Dover, 1979.

INDEX

American Connection, the 86
Anglo-Norman 47
Aran Isles 7, 13, 23, 29, 53, 83, 86, 87, 90, 97, 114

basket (st) 89
Betrothal Aran 105
blackberry (st) 89, 105
bobbles (st) 90, 136
Book of Kells 7, 35
Boston, Massachusetts 86
Brecan, Saint 29

cables (st) 87–91, 97, 101, 105, 111, 135
Carrageen 89, 91, 97
Carrickmacross 55, 59
chevron (st) 89
Congested Districts Board 53, 83
Countryworkers Ltd 83, 87
Crios 17, 83
crochet 53, 55, 65, 69

diamonds (st) 87–89, 91
Diamond and Cable Aran 91
Dirrane, Mairead 86
Dirrane, Mary 86
Donegal fisherman's sweater 83
double zig-zag (st) 88, 105
Dublin Silver 41

Enda, Saint 29

Fir Bolg 23
Fisher Gansey 83

Gahan, Muriel 83, 86, 87
Galway Racer 121

hallstatt 23
Herald 47
high crosses 7, 41, 89
holy trinity (st) 89, 90, 105
honeycomb (st) 89, 101, 111
Honeycomb Cable Aran 101

Inisheer 90
Inishmaan 90
Inishmore 13, 17, 86, 87, 90
irish moss (st) 88, 89, 97
Irish Rural Life and Industry (1907) 83, 86

jacob's ladder (st) 89, 90

Kells Mosaic 35
Kerry Bedspread 69
Kiewe, Hienz Edgar 87
Kilronan Folk Museum 17, 86
knitting pattern books 33, 55, 88
kniótail 29

lace-making 53, 55, 59
ladder of life (st) 89
La Tène 29, 35, 89
Lawrence Collection 83
link (st) 89
Loughnashade bronze trumpet 23

Moher, Cliffs of 125
Muckross House 69, 75

nalbinding 9, 13, 35
National Library, Dublin 83
National Museum, Dublin 21, 23, 29, 41, 83, 114
Newgrange 9, 88

O'Toole, Maggie 86, 87

Phoenicians 7, 13
picot lace 65
plait (st) 89
Primrose Petals 65

ribbon (st) 89, 105
Rope Plait Aran 111

Sailboats 115
Sampler 75
Seabirds 125
Shamrock Lace Layette 59
soleless stockings 53
stockings 47, 53, 83, 86, 87

Tara 29
Thomas, Mary 87
Thompson, Gladys 87
Torc 21, 88
tree of life (st) 87–90, 101
trellis (st) 29, 87, 89, 90

Wild Fuchsias 131
wishbone (st) 89, 105

zig-zag (st) 88, 105